GRAMMAR
EXPLORER 3B

Amy Cooper and Samuela Eckstut-Didier

Series Editors: Rob Jenkins and Staci Johnson

 NATIONAL GEOGRAPHIC LEARNING

 CENGAGE Learning

Australia • Brazil • Japan • Korea • Mexico • Singapore • Spain • United Kingdom • United States

Grammar Explorer 3B

Amy Cooper and Samuela Eckstut-Didier

Publisher: Sherrise Roehr

Executive Editor: Laura Le Dréan

Managing Editor: Eve Einselen Yu

Senior Development Editor: Kimberly Steiner

Associate Development Editor: Alayna Cohen

Assistant Editor: Vanessa Richards

Senior Technology Product Manager: Scott Rule

Director of Global Marketing: Ian Martin

Marketing Manager: Lindsey Miller

Sr. Director, ELT & World Languages:
Michael Burggren

Production Manager: Daisy Sosa

Content Project Manager: Andrea Bobotas

Print Buyer: Mary Beth Hennebury

Cover Designer: 3CD, Chicago

Cover Image: BRIAN J. SKERRY/National
Geographic Creative

Compositor: Cenveo Publisher Services

For product information and technology assistance, contact us at
Cengage Learning Customer & Sales Support,
1-800-354-9706

For permission to use material from this text or product,
submit all requests online at **www.cengage.com/permissions.**
Further permissions questions can be e-mailed to
permissionrequest@cengage.com.

Student Book 3B: 978-1-111-35136-6

National Geographic Learning
20 Channel Center Street
Boston, MA 02210
USA

Cengage Learning is a leading provider of customized learning solutions with office locations around the globe, including Singapore, the United Kingdom, Australia, Mexico, Brazil and Japan.

Cengage Learning products are represented in Canada by Nelson Education, Ltd.

Visit National Geographic Learning online at **ngl.cengage.com**

Visit our corporate website at **www.cengage.com**

Printed in China
Print Number: 05   Print Year: 2019

CONTENTS

UNIT 15 Learning   424
Combining Ideas

ACKNOWLEDGMENTS

The authors and publisher would like to thank the following reviewers and contributors:

Gokhan Alkanat, Auburn University at Montgomery, Alabama; **Dorothy S. Avondstondt**, Miami Dade College, Florida; **Heather Barikmo**, The English Language Center at LaGuardia Community College, New York; **Kimberly Becker**, Nashville State Community College, Tennessee; **Lukas Bidelspack**, Corvallis, Oregon; **Grace Bishop**, Houston Community College, Texas; **Mariusz Jacek Bojarczuk**, Bunker Hill Community College, Massachusetts; **Nancy Boyer**, Golden West College, California; **Patricia Brenner**, University of Washington, Washington; **Jessica Buchsbaum**, City College of San Francisco, California; **Gabriella Cambiasso**, Harold Washington College, Illinois; **Tony Carnerie**, English Language Institute, University of California San Diego Extension, California; **Whitney Clarq-Reis**, Framingham State University; **Julia A. Correia**, Henderson State University, Arkansas; **Katie Crowder**, UNT Department of Linguistics and Technical Communication, Texas; **Lin Cui**, William Rainey Harper College, Illinois; **Nora Dawkins**, Miami Dade College, Florida; **Rachel DeSanto**, English for Academic Purposes, Hillsborough Community College, Florida; **Aurea Diab**, Dillard University, Louisiana; **Marta Dmytrenko-Ahrabian**, English Language Institute, Wayne State University, Michigan; **Susan Dorrington**, Education and Language Acquisition Department, LaGuardia Community College, New York; **Ian Dreilinger**, Center for Multilingual Multicultural Studies, University of Central Florida, Florida; **Jennifer Dujat**, Education and Language Acquisition Department, LaGuardia Community College, New York; **Dr. Jane Duke**, Language & Literature Department, State College of Florida, Florida; **Anna Eddy**, University of Michigan-Flint, Michigan; **Jenifer Edens**, University of Houston, Texas; **Karen Einstein**, Santa Rosa Junior College, California; **Cynthia Etter**, International & English Language Programs, University of Washington, Washington; **Parvanak Fassihi**, SHOWA Boston Institute for Language and Culture, Massachusetts; **Katherine Fouche**, The University of Texas at Austin, Texas; **Richard Furlong**, Education and Language Acquisition Department, LaGuardia Community College, New York; **Glenn S. Gardner**, Glendale College, California; **Sally Gearhart**, Santa Rosa Junior College, California; **Alexis Giannopolulos**, SHOWA Boston Institute for Language and Culture, Massachusetts; **Nora Gold**, Baruch College, The City University of New York, New York; **Ekaterina V. Goussakova**, Seminole State College of Florida; **Lynn Grantz**, Valparaiso University, Indiana; **Tom Griffith**, SHOWA Boston Institute for Language and Culture, Massachusetts; **Christine Guro**, Hawaii English Language Program, University of Hawaii at Manoa, Hawaii; **Jessie Hayden**, Georgia Perimeter College, Georgia; **Barbara Inerfeld**, Program in American Language Studies, Rutgers University, New Jersey; **Gail Kellersberger**, University of Houston-Downtown, Texas; **David Kelley**, SHOWA Boston Institute for Language and Culture, Massachusetts; **Kathleen Kelly**, ESL Department, Passaic County Community College, New Jersey; **Dr. Hyun-Joo Kim**, Education and Language Acquisition Department, LaGuardia Community College, New York; **Linda Koffman**, College of Marin, California; **Lisa Kovacs-Morgan**, English Language Institute, University of California San Diego Extension, California; **Jerrad Langlois**, TESL Program and Office of International Programs, Northeastern Illinois University; **Janet Langon**, Glendale College, California; **Olivia Limbu**, The English Language Center at LaGuardia Community College, New York; **Devora Manier**, Nashville State Community College, Tennessee; **Susan McAlister**, Language and Culture Center, Department of English, University of Houston, Texas; **John McCarthy**, SHOWA Boston Institute for Language and Culture, Massachusetts; **Dr. Myra Medina**, Miami Dade College, Florida; **Dr. Suzanne Medina**, California State University, Dominguez Hills, California; **Nancy Megarity**, ESL & Developmental Writing, Collin College, Texas; **Joseph Montagna**, SHOWA Boston Institute for Language and Culture, Massachusetts; **Richard Moore**, University of Washington; **Monika Mulder**, Portland State University, Oregon; **Patricia Nation**, Miami Dade College, Florida; **Susan Niemeyer**, Los Angeles City College, California; **Charl Norloff**, International English Center, University of Colorado Boulder, Colorado; **Gabriella Nuttall**, Sacramento City College, California; **Dr. Karla Odenwald**, CELOP at Boston University, Massachusetts; **Ali Olson-Pacheco**, English Language Institute, University of California San Diego Extension, California; **Fernanda Ortiz**, Center for English as a Second Language, University of Arizona, Arizona; **Chuck Passentino**, Grossmont College, California; **Stephen Peridore**, College of Southern Nevada, Nevada; **Frank Quebbemann**, Miami Dade College, Florida; **Dr. Anouchka Rachelson**, Miami Dade College, Florida; **Dr. Agnieszka Rakowicz**, Education and Language Acquisition Department, LaGuardia Community College, New York; **Wendy Ramer**, Broward College, Florida; **Esther Robbins**, Prince George's Community College, Maryland; **Helen Roland**, Miami Dade College, Florida; **Debbie Sandstrom**, Tutorium in Intensive English, University of Illinois at Chicago, Illinois; **Maria Schirta**, Hudson County Community College, New Jersey; **Dr. Jennifer Scully**, Education and Language Acquisition Department, LaGuardia Community College, New York; **Jeremy Stubbs**, Tacoma, Washington; **Adrianne Thompson**, Miami Dade College, Florida; **Evelyn Trottier**, Basic and Transitional Studies Program, Seattle Central Community College, Washington; **Karen Vallejo**, University of California, Irvine, California; **Emily Young**, Auburn University at Montgomery, Alabama.

The publisher would also like to thank Heidi Fischer for her writing of Connect the Grammar to Writing in level 3 of this series.

From the Authors: We would like to thank Tom Jefferies for selecting us to work together on this project and Laura Le Dréan for steering it through to completion. We can't thank our editors, Eve Einselen Yu and Kim Steiner, enough for their expertise and perseverance through charts, drafts, and countless e-mails. We also wish to thank Heidi Fischer for her clear models and writing tasks in Connect the Grammar to Writing. In addition, we are grateful for the inspiration of our fellow authors Daphne Mackay and Paul Carne, as well as Daria Ruzicka in the early stages of the project. Their head start on Levels 1 and 2 set the high standards to which we knew we had to aspire.

Dedication: To Gary, for your patience, support, and invaluable native speaker intuitions.
    À Robert, pour tous les bons repas et toutes les belles journées.

National Geographic images introduce the unit theme—real world topics that students want to read, write, and talk about.

UNIT **2** Passions

Present and Past: Perfect and Perfect Progressive

Climbers BASE jump from Half Dome at Yosemite National Park, California.

Lesson **1**	Lesson **2**	Lesson **3**	Review the Grammar
page 32	page 41	page 48	page 58
Present Perfect	Present Perfect Progressive and Present Perfect	Past Perfect and Past Perfect Progressive	Connect the Grammar to Writing
			page 60

31

Units are organized in **manageable lessons**, which ensures students **explore, learn, practice,** and **apply** the grammar.

LESSON 1 **Present Perfect**

EXPLORE

🎧 CD1-09 **1** **READ** the book review of *Polar Obsession*. What is Paul Nicklen's passion?

Paul Nicklen's *Polar Obsession*

For most people, the Arctic and Antarctica are strange places that we know very little about. Paul Nicklen's collection of photographs and stories, *Polar Obsession*, offers an excellent introduction.

Nicklen grew up on an island in Northern Canada, where he learned all about the outdoors from his Inuit[1] neighbors. Ever since that time, he **has loved** animals, cold weather, and adventure.

As a photojournalist, Nicklen **has spent** a lot of time in icy polar waters. He **has followed** sea lions, **dived** with whales, and **studied** polar bears. One of the most exciting parts of the book covers Nicklen's unforgettable encounter with a leopard seal in Antarctica.

As the photographs clearly show, leopard seals are very large—up to 12 feet (4 meters) long and weighing over 1000 pounds (450 kilograms). They have huge, sharp teeth, and they move quickly through the water searching for food such as fish and penguins.

Leopard seals can be dangerous, but this didn't stop Nicklen from trying to photograph one. When a huge seal approached his boat, Nicklen got into the water. He was shaking with fear, but much to his surprise the seal treated him gently. She even tried to feed him! The seal brought him penguins to eat, and he photographed her. Nicklen says it was the most incredible experience that he has...

In *Polar Obsession*,... He also helps us to und...

[1] **Inuit**: indigenous people livin...

32 PRESENT AND PAST: PERFECT AND P...

Each lesson begins with the *Explore* section, featuring a captivating National Geographic article that introduces the target grammar and builds students' knowledge in a variety of academic disciplines.

Present Perfect Progressive and Present Perfect   **LESSON 2**

EXPLORE

🎧 CD1-13 **1** **READ** the magazine article about Helen Thayer. What advice does she have for other people?

Helen Thayer: A Lifelong Adventurer

Helen Thayer **has** never **let** age stop her. She and her husband, Bill, fulfilled a lifelong dream for their 40th wedding anniversary. They walked 1600 mile...

In recent years, Thayer **has been**... to travel and bring back stories to sh... people to follow... goals, plan for su...

[1] **nomads**: people who...
[2] **inspire**: to make som...
[3] **fulfill one's dream**:...

▶ The Gobi Desert covers parts of Mongolia and China.

LESSON 3   **Past Perfect and Past Perfect Progressive**

EXPLORE

🎧 CD1-15 **1** **READ** the article about Alex Honnold. What big risk did he take to fulfill his dream?

Daring. Defiant. Free.
A new generation of superclimbers is pushing the limits in Yosemite

Every rock climber who has come to Yosemite has a dream. Alex Honnold's dream was to free solo Half Dome, a 2130-foot (649-meter) wall of granite. Free soloing means climbing with only rock shoes and some chalk to help keep the hands dry. Honnold couldn't use a rope or anything else to help him stick to the slippery stone. The few people who **had climbed** Half Dome before **had used** ropes, and it **had taken** them more than a day to do the climb.

On a bright September morning, Honnold was clinging[2] to the face of Half Dome, less than 100 feet (30 meters) from the top. He **had been climbing** for two hours and forty-five minutes, but all of a sudden he stopped. Something potentially disastrous had occurred—he had lost some of his confidence. He **hadn't felt** that way two days before when **he'd been racing** up the same rock *with* a rope. That climb **had gone** well. Today though, Honnold hesitated. He knew that even the slightest doubt could cause a deadly fall, thousands of feet to the valley floor below. He knew he had to get moving, so he chalked his hands, adjusted his feet, and started climbing again. Within minutes, he was at the top.

Bloggers spread the news of Honnold's two-hour-and-fifty-minute free solo, and climbers were amazed. On this warm fall day, 23-year-old Alex Honnold **had** just **set** a new record in one of climbing's biggest challenges.

[1] **granite**: a kind of very hard rock
[2] **cling**: to hold something tightly

◀ Alex Honnold free soloing in Yosemite National Park, California

48 PRESENT AND PAST: PERFECT AND PERFECT PROGRESSIVE

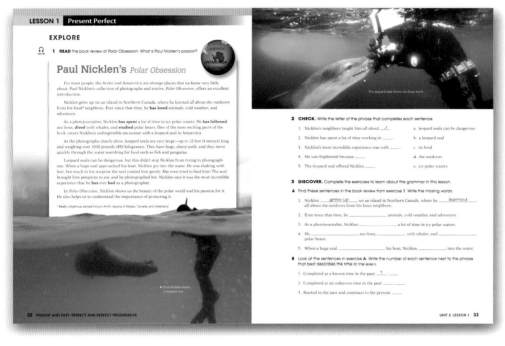

In the **Explore** section, students discover how the grammar structures are used in the readings and in real academic textbooks.

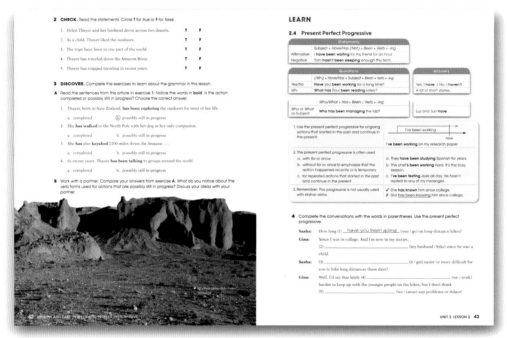

The **Learn** section features clear grammar charts and explanations followed by controlled practice of the grammar forms.

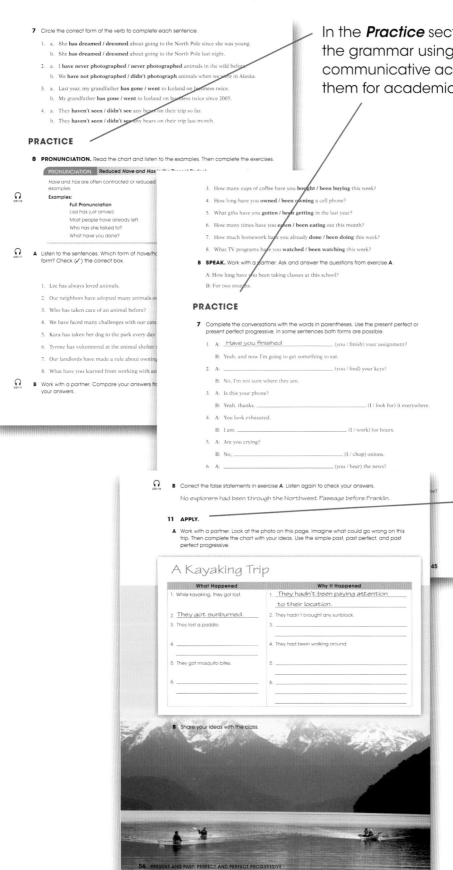

7 Circle the correct form of the verb to complete each sentence.

1. a. She **has dreamed / dreamed** about going to the North Pole since she was young.

   b. She **has dreamed / dreamed** about going to the North Pole last night.

2. a. I **have never photographed / never photographed** animals in the wild before.

   b. We **have not photographed / didn't photograph** animals when we were in Alaska.

3. a. Last year, my grandfather **has gone / went** to Iceland on business twice.

   b. My grandfather **has gone / went** to Iceland on business twice since 2005.

4. a. They **haven't seen / didn't see** any bears on their trip so far.

   b. They **haven't seen / didn't see** any bears on their trip last month.

PRACTICE

In the ***Practice*** section, students practice the grammar using all four skills through communicative activities that prepare them for academic work.

8 **PRONUNCIATION.** Read the chart and listen to the examples. Then complete the exercises.

PRONUNCIATION	Reduced *Have* and *Has* in the Present Perfect

Have and *has* are often contracted or reduced... examples.

Examples:

Full Pronunciation

Lisa has just arrived.

Most people have already left.

Who has she talked to?

What have you done?

A Listen to the sentences. Which form of *have/ha...* form? Check (✓) the correct box.

1. Lee has always loved animals.

2. Our neighbors have adopted many animals o...

3. Who has taken care of an animal before?

4. We have faced many challenges with our cats...

5. Kara has taken her dog to the park every day...

6. Tyrone has volunteered at the animal shelter...

7. Our landlords have made a rule about owning...

8. What have you learned from working with an...

B Work with a partner. Compare your answers fr... your answers.

3. How many cups of coffee have you **bought / been buying** this week?

4. How long have you **owned / been owning** a cell phone?

5. What gifts have you **gotten / been getting** in the last year?

6. How many times have you **eaten / been eating** out this month?

7. How much homework have you already **done / been doing** this week?

8. What TV programs have you **watched / been watching** this week?

B **SPEAK.** Work with a partner. Ask and answer the questions from exercise **A**.

A: How long have you been taking classes at this school?

B: For two months.

PRACTICE

7 Complete the conversations with the words in parentheses. Use the present perfect or present perfect progressive. In some sentences both forms are possible.

1. A: ___Have you finished___ (you / finish) your assignment?

   B: Yeah, and now I'm going to get something to eat.

2. A: _____ (you / find) your keys?

   B: No, I'm not sure where they are.

3. A: Is this your phone?

   B: Yeah, thanks. _____ (I / look for) it everywhere.

4. A: You look exhausted.

   B: I am. _____ (I / work) for hours.

5. A: Are you crying?

   B: No, _____ (I / chop) onions.

6. A: _____ (you / hear) the news?

B Correct the false statements in exercise **A**. Listen again to check your answers.

No explorers had been through the Northwest Passage before Franklin.

11 **APPLY.**

A Work with a partner. Look at the photo on this page. Imagine what could go wrong on this trip. Then complete the chart with your ideas. Use the simple past, past perfect, and past perfect progressive.

Students use their new language and critical thinking skills in the ***Apply*** section.

A Kayaking Trip

What Happened	Why It Happened
1. While kayaking, they got lost.	1. They hadn't been paying attention to their location.
2. They got sunburned.	2. They hadn't brought any sunblock.
3. They lost a paddle.	3.
4.	4. They had been walking around.
5. They got mosquito bites.	5.
6.	6.

B Share your ideas with the class.

56 PRESENT AND PAST: PERFECT AND PERFECT PROGRESSIVE

Review the Grammar **UNIT 2**

Charts
2.1–2.7

1 Complete the paragraph. Use the correct form of each verb in parentheses.

I (1) _____ had _____ (have) a terrible car accident when I was
sixteen. I (2) _____ (lose) a leg. As an athlete, this was
especially devastating. I (3) _____ (be) a gymnast from
the age of eight, and I (4) _____ (win) three national
competitions. It (5) _____ (take) me a lot of time to recover,
and I (6) _____ (not think) about competing again. Then, one
of my coaches (7) _____ (tell) me about the Paralympics and
(8) _____ (suggest) that I train for swimming. I could do that with
only one leg. I (9) _____ (always / want) to be in the Olympics. In
fact, I (10) _____ (train) for the Olympics at the time of my accident. So
I (11) _____ (listen) to my coach and (12) _____
(start) swimming. I (13) _____ (swim) ever since that day
and I love it. I (14) _____ (win) several competitions. Lately, I
(15) _____ (train) for the next Paralympics. I hope to win a medal!

Charts
2.1, 2.3–2.7

2 EDIT. Read the text by a traveler on safari. Find and correct eight more errors with the simple
past, present perfect, past perfect, or past perfect progressive.

Mason's Travels on Safari

It had always been our dream to travel to southern Africa, and we'd ~~make~~ made a lot
of plans for our trip. I wanted to take a lot of wildlife photographs, so my friend has
recommended that I bring two cameras. When I got to Namibia, I had panicked. One
camera had been missing. Luckily, I was finding it later.

The next day, we had started out on our safari with a tour. By the end of our tour, we
saw some amazing things. One time, when we stopped to take pictures, we were only a
few feet away from a cheetah. Amazing!

We had never bothered the animals at night. How[...]
and other noises outside our tent every night. At first,[...]
but not by the end of the trip. It was really the most i[...]

Cheetah running, ▶
Namibia

58

3 LISTEN & SPEAK.

Charts
2.1, 2.3–
2.4, 2.6

🎧 CD1-17

A Circle the correct form of the verb. Then listen to the conversation and check your answers.

1. Liu Yang is the first female astronaut that China **ever sent / has ever sent** into space.

2. She **trained / has trained** to be a pilot at China's Air Force College, and then
she **joined / has joined** the Air Force.

3. She **flew / has flown** five different types of aircraft, and she **did / has done** 1680 hours
of flight time.

4. She **also participated / has also participated** in military exercises and emergency rescues.

5. Liu started training to be an astronaut. She **has never experienced / had never experienced**
anything so challenging.

🎧 CD1-18

B Listen to the next part of the conversation. Then work with a partner. Discuss the questions.
Then listen again and check your answers.

1. What has Liu Yang done in her life?
2. Had she always wanted to be an astronaut?
3. How have her coworkers described her?
4. How long had she been in the Air Force before becoming an astronaut?

Review the Grammar gives
students the opportunity to
consolidate the grammar in
their reading, writing, listening,
and speaking.

Connect the Grammar to Writing

1 READ & NOTICE THE GRAMMAR.

A What is a goal that you have achieved? How did it affect you? Tell a partner your ideas. Then read the narrative.

Achieving a Goal

About a year ago, I was watching the Olympics, and I decided that I wanted to become a runner. I knew I should set an achievable goal, so I decided to train for a 5K race.

My parents were surprised when I told them about my goal, because I had never been interested in running before. In fact, I had never run more than a mile, and I had always been very slow. My friends thought I was joking. Everyone assumed that I would quit after a week.

Fortunately, I proved them all wrong. I did two things to achieve my goal. First, I went online and researched a good training plan. I found a website that helps you plan workouts. You start by walking, and then you gradually start running. After that, I joined a local running group. We ran in the park twice a week, and I made friends who had also decided to run a 5K.

Three months later, I achieved my goal: I ran in my first race. I didn't win, but I ran the whole way, so I was proud of myself. Since then, I have run in several races. I have also started training for a longer run. My next goal is to run in a 10K race. My friends have stopped laughing at me, and a few of them have even asked me to help them start running!

GRAMMAR FOCUS

In the narrative in exercise **A**, the writer uses these verb forms:

Simple past	• to tell about the main event of the story (*About a year ago . . . I decided that . . .*)
Past perfect	• to discuss events that happ... (*I had never run more than*...)
Present perfect	• with *since* to tell about past... present (*Since then, I have*...)

B Read the narrative in exercise **A** again. Find and circle... past. Underline two past perfect examples, and double... examples.

Connect the Grammar to Writing provides students with a clear model and a guided writing task where they first notice and then use the target grammar in one of a variety of writing genres.

Write a Personal Narrative

C Complete the time line with information from the narrative in exercise **A**. Write the letter of the events in the correct order. Then compare your answers with a partner.

a. Ran in several other races

b. Was never interested in running

c. Joined a running club

d. Parents were surprised

e. Ran in 5K

f. Watched the Olympics

g. Found a good website

b. ___   ___   ___ ___ ___ ___ ___

Set a goal to run a 5K   Now

2 BEFORE YOU WRITE.

A Work with a partner. Make a list of goals that you have achieved. Discuss which goals would be the most interesting to write about.

B Create a time line for your personal narrative. Write the events of the story that you want to tell. Use the time line in exercise **1C** as a guide.

3 WRITE two or three paragraphs telling your story. Use your time line in exercise **2B** and the text in exercise **1A** as a guide. Remember to start your story with background information. At the end, tell how your life has changed.

WRITING FOCUS   Using *First* and *After that* to Show a Sequence

Notice *first* and *after that* in the narrative in exercise **1A**.

Use these words at the beginning of the sentence to explain the order of events in a text. Place a comma after *first* and *after that*.

First, I went online and . . .   *After that,* I joined a local running club.

4 SELF ASSESS. Underline the verb forms in your narrative. Then use the checklist to assess your work.

☐ I used the present perfect and the present perfect progressive correctly. [2.1, 2.2, 2.4, 2.5]

☐ I used the simple past correctly. [2.3]

☐ I used the past perfect and the past perfect progressive correctly. [2.6, 2.7]

☐ I used commas correctly with *first* and *after that*. [WRITING FOCUS]

The Passive

▲ Borneo red flying frog in
mushroom, Sabah, Borneo

EXPLORE

1   **READ** the article about oceanographer Sylvia Earle. What message is she trying to communicate to the world?

Sylvia Earle and the Deep Blue Sea

Ever since Dr. Sylvia Earle **was knocked over** by a wave as a young child, she **has been fascinated** by the ocean. She has led more than a hundred ocean expeditions and spent more than 7000 hours underwater. Her research **is guided** by her commitment to preserving ecosystems[1] and developing new technologies for exploring the sea.

People sometimes ask Earle, "Why is the ocean so important?" She explains how the natural cycles that balance Earth's water, air, and climate **are** all **regulated** by the ocean. She also notes our dependence on the ocean's food chain,[2] from the biggest fish to the tiniest organisms.[3] If just one link in the chain **is removed**, it will affect the whole system. For example, if the plants that feed the small fish **are destroyed** by pollution, the small fish will die. Then, the larger fish that depend on the small fish will disappear as well.

In the past, people behaved as though the ocean **could not be harmed**. However, today, the ocean **is being damaged** at a rapid rate, and it is clear that humans are responsible. More trash and chemicals **are being dumped** into the water. This damages delicate ecosystems, such as coral reefs, and all the life that they support. People are also overfishing. In fact, over 90 percent of big fish such as tuna **have been killed** for food.

Earle firmly believes that the ocean **must be protected** from further harm. She urges people around the world to help support what she calls "the blue heart" of the planet.

[1] **ecosystem:** the plants and animals living in an area together, and the relationship that exists between them and the environment
[2] **food chain:** a series of living things that are linked to each other because each feeds on the one next to it
[3] **organism:** an animal or plant, especially one that is so small that you can't see it without a microscope

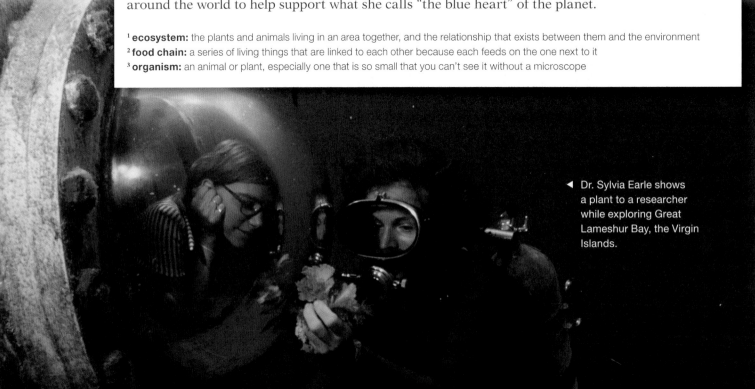

◀ Dr. Sylvia Earle shows a plant to a researcher while exploring Great Lameshur Bay, the Virgin Islands.

▶ Dr. Sylvia Earle

2 CHECK. Read the statements. Circle **T** for *true* or **F** for *false*.

1. Sylvia Earle became interested in the ocean when she was a teenager.   **T**   **F**

2. Earle studies the connections between living things in the ocean.   **T**   **F**

3. Smaller numbers of big fish will result in smaller numbers of little fish.   **T**   **F**

4. In the past, people thought that nothing could harm the ocean.   **T**   **F**

5. The condition of the ocean is changing slowly.   **T**   **F**

3 DISCOVER. Complete the exercises to learn about the grammar in this lesson.

A Look at the underlined verbs in the sentences based on the article in exercise **1**. Circle the forms of *be*.

1. Dr. Sylvia Earle (was) knocked over by a wave as a young child.

2. Earth's water, air, and climate (are) regulated by the ocean.

3. Ocean plants (are) destroyed by pollution.

4. The world's oceans (could be) harmed.

5. More trash and chemicals (are being) dumped into the water.

6. The ocean (must be) protected from further harm.

B Write the number of each sentence in exercise **A** in the correct column.

Simple Present Passive	Simple Past Passive	Present Progressive Passive	Passive with Modal
2, 3	1	5	4, 6

LEARN

9.1 Active and Passive

Active	Passive
Big fish **eat** small fish.	Small fish **are eaten** by big fish.
Object	Subject

	Active	Passive
	Subject + Verb (+ Object)	Subject + *Be* + Past Participle*
Simple Present	People **take** lots of pictures here.	Lots of pictures **are taken** here.
Simple Past	They **saw** a shark near the beach.	A shark **was seen** near the beach.
Present Progressive	People **aren't protecting** the whales.	The whales **are not being protected**.
Past Progressive	They **were washing** the elephants.	The elephants **were being washed**.
Present Perfect	I **haven't walked** the dog.	The dog **hasn't been walked**.

* See page **A1** for a list of irregular verb forms.

1. In an active sentence, the subject performs the action of the verb. The subject is the *agent* or *doer*.	Active: <u>The fishermen</u> **caught** ten bluefish. Subject/Agent
In a passive sentence, the subject receives the action of the verb. Sometimes *by* + the agent comes at the end of the sentence to show who or what is performing the action.	Passive: <u>Ten bluefish</u> **were caught** by <u>the fishermen</u>. Subject Agent
2. The passive occurs in different verb tenses. It always includes a form of *be* + the past participle form of the verb. The form of *be* shows the verb tense.	The animals **are being fed**. The research **has not been completed**. Seven new species of mushrooms **were identified**.
3. Only transitive verbs (verbs that take a direct object) can be used with the passive. Intransitive verbs cannot be made passive.	Transitive Verb: discover A new type of sea animal **was discovered**. Intransitive Verb: disappear ✗ Those birds <u>are disappeared</u>.
4. To make questions in the passive, put a form of the auxiliary *be* or *have* before the subject.	The applications **were completed**. **Were** the applications **completed**? The animals have been trained. **Have** the animals **been trained**?

4 Underline the verb in each sentence. Then write **A** if the sentence is *active* and **P** if the sentence is *passive*.

_P_ 1. During the expedition, Sylvia Earle's instructions <u>were followed</u> by the team.

_____ 2. Most of our oxygen on Earth is generated by the ocean.

_____ 3. The changes in the ocean ecosystem affect all of us.

_____ 4. Nearly half of the world's coral reefs have disappeared.

_____ 5. The sea around the Galápagos Islands is being polluted by boats.

_____ 6. In the last 50 years, more than 90 percent of the big fish in the sea have been eaten.

_____ 7. Many sea creatures have been dying from water pollution.

_____ 8. Action is being taken to protect the California and Oregon coasts.

_____ 9. An area of Antarctica is protected by scientists and international governments.

_____ 10. The efforts of researchers have increased public awareness of our ecosystem.

> **REAL ENGLISH**
>
> The passive is common in formal speaking and writing. The active is more common in informal situations.
>
> Formal: *Not a great deal **is known** about the ocean floor.*
>
> Informal: *We **don't know** a lot about the ocean floor.*

5 Read each sentence and underline the object of the verb. Then rewrite the sentences in the passive. Do not include the agent of the action. Use the correct form of the verb.

1. We protect <u>about 12 percent of the land on Earth</u> in some way.

   About 12 percent of the land on Earth is protected in some way.

2. Local officials are considering new guidelines for beach preservation.

   _____ for beach preservation.

3. The mayor has created a nature preserve near the river.

   _____ near the river.

4. Were guides giving tours yesterday at the nature preserve?

   _____ yesterday at the nature preserve?

5. Villagers have cut down all the trees in that forest.

   _____ in that forest.

6. Did swimmers see dolphins near the beach?

   _____ near the beach?

7. Is the parks department protecting the birds on the island?

   _____ on the island?

8. Volunteers cleaned up the trash on the riverbank.

   _____ on the riverbank.

9. Fishermen catch tens of thousands of fish every day.

   _____ every day.

10. Has anyone reported the environmental problems to government officials?

    _____ to government officials?

9.2 Passive with Modals

Active	Passive
They **should solve** the problem.	The problem **should be solved**.
Object	Subject

	Present and Future Passive
	Modal *(Not)* + *Be* + Past Participle
Present	The plans **must be approved**.
Future	The research **might be done** next month. The report **won't be seen** by the public.

	Past Passive
	Modal *(Not)* + *Have Been* + Past Participle
Past	The money **may have been taken**. She **should not have been told** the news.

1. The passive form with a modal is the modal + *be (not)* + the past participle of the verb.	The monkey **can be trained**. The elephant **couldn't be moved**.
2. For passive sentences with the modal expressions *be going to* or *have to*, use: a. *be going to* + *be* + past participle b. *have to* + *be* + past participle	a. The work **is going to be completed** soon. b. The project **has to be done** now.

6 Complete the sentences. Use the modal and the passive form of the verbs in parentheses.

1. Sea turtles ___must not be disturbed___ (must / not disturb) during the nesting season.

2. Rules about proper behavior around sea turtles _____ (should / follow).

3. Information about the turtles _____ (can / find) at nature preserves.

4. New beach rules _____ (be going to / post).

5. In many coastal towns, no street lights _____ (will / turn on) when the turtles are nesting.

6. Photographs _____ (should only / take) from far away.

7. The effects of human behavior on sea turtles _____ (might / understand) more clearly now.

8. Perhaps more sea turtles _____ (will / save) in the future.

PRACTICE

7 Read the sentences. Circle the correct verb form to complete each sentence.

1. The Grand Canyon **has shaped** / **has been shaped** by the once powerful Colorado River.

2. Now the great Colorado River **is drying up** / **is being dried up**.

3. About seventy percent of the water **uses** / **is used** to grow crops.

4. People in far-off cities, for example, Los Angeles, **are using** / **are being used** the water.

5. Miles of dried up river beds **can see** / **can be seen** now.

6. A lot of animals **have not survived** / **have not been survived** the dry conditions.

7. Climate change **is also harming** / **is also being harmed** the Colorado River.

8. In the next few decades, the amount of available water **may reduce** / **may be reduced** significantly because of climate change.

9. What **could do** / **could be done** to save the river?

10. More water **should conserve** / **should be conserved**.

8 Complete the exercises.

A Complete the questions with the words in parentheses. Use the correct passive forms of the verbs.

1. How many sharks _____are killed_____ (kill) every year?

2. How many people _____ (attack) by sharks every year?

3. When _____ (the megamouth shark / discover)?

4. How many shark species _____ (threaten) by human activity?

5. Which part of a shark _____ (sell) for food?

► A pregnant sand tiger shark swims over coral. Bonin Islands, Japan.

6. Where _____ (shark-fin soup / eat) the most?

7. When _____ (shark-fin soup / serve)?

8. How _____ (can / sharks / protect)?

B SPEAK. Work with a partner. Take turns answering the questions you wrote in exercise **A** with the choices in the box. See page A10 to check your answers.

Asia	at weddings	fewer than 100	More than 100
the fins	60 million	1976	stop hunting them

A: *How many sharks are killed every year?*

B: *Sixty million.*

9 SPEAK & WRITE.

A Work with a partner. Look at the map of Madagascar and some of the endangered species that live there on page 243. Do you know other endangered animals? Tell your partner at least one other endangered animal and where it lives.

B Write sentences about Madagascar using the words in parentheses. Use a correct active or passive form of each verb. Use negative forms when correct according to the map and information on page 243.

1. (Madagascar / locate / off the coast of Africa)

    Madagascar is located off the coast of Africa.

2. (Baobab trees and lemurs / find / in Madagascar)

    _____

3. (A few areas of Madagascar / protect / by the government)

    _____

4. (Most of the island / protect)

    _____

5. (Many of Madagascar's plants and animals / live / in small, unprotected areas)

    _____

6. (Many of these plants and animals / endanger)

    _____

7. (A lot of the rain forest areas in Madagascar / destroy)

    _____

8. (Some rain forest areas / preserve)

    _____

9. (Every year, they / cut down / more and more trees)

_____

10. (The rain forest in Madagascar / should / protect / to save endangered species)

_____

AFRICA

MADAGASCAR

▲ Grandidier baobab

▲ Silky sifaka (lemur)

▲ Lesser chameleon

▲ Long-tailed ground roller

INDIAN
OCEAN

▲ Harlequin mantella frog

■ Rain forest
■ Rain forest in bad condition because trees are being cut down
■ Other forest
⁄ Area where endangered animals live
□ Protected area

10 LISTEN.

CD3-03-06

A You will hear a tour guide talk about a cruise in Antarctica. Listen to each part of his story. Then choose the correct sentence for each item.

Part 1 1. a. The cruise ship rescued passengers from two other ships.

b. The passengers on M/S Explorer were rescued by two other ships.

Part 2 2. a. Fewer ships are coming to Antarctica than in the past.

b. Antarctica is visited by thousands of tourists every year.

Part 3 3. a. Some plants have been harmed.

b. Some animals have been bothering people.

4. a. Tours to Antarctica will be stopped.

b. Tours to Antarctica should be limited and controlled.

Part 4 5. a. Guidelines have been created to protect Antarctica.

b. The IAATO has promised to create guidelines to protect Antarctica.

6. a. Only twenty people can join each tour group.

b. One hundred people can be included in each tour group.

7. a. The situation is considered to be better now.

b. The situation is not any better now.

8. a. Tour companies are required to obey the new rules.

b. Tour companies don't have to obey the new rules.

CD3-03-06

B Listen again and check your answers.

▼ Cruise ship and iceberg at Deception Island, Antarctica

11 EDIT. Read the paragraph. Find and correct seven more errors with passives.

Three Gorges Dam: Success or Failure?

Construction on the Three Gorges Dam[1] on the Yangtze River began in 1994. It ∨^{was} completed in 2012. The dam is considered a great success because it has had some positive effects on the environment. In the past, a lot of coal is used for energy. Now, the dam generates water power, and the need for coal has been reduced. This means that there is less carbon dioxide in the air. Unfortunately, there have also been some negative effects. Many places were flood because of the dam. Over a million people had to being moved. Also, the dam located in a region with many plants and animals. Many plant species in this region have being harmed by the dam. More could be harm in the future. The dam has also caused changes to the temperature and increased the amount of pollution in the water. This has been threatened the freshwater fish in the area. Changes should been made to improve the situation soon. Authorities have promised to make these changes.

[1] **dam:** special walls built across rivers to stop the water from flowing; used to create electricity

12 APPLY.

A Work in a group. Discuss some environmental problems that you know about. Make a chart in your notebook like the one below and write notes for each category.

Problem	Cause	Changes in Environment	What Should Be Done?
river in my town has been polluted	chemicals from nearby factory	fish and plants are dying	make rules that control how factories get rid of chemical waste

B In your notebook, write five sentences about one of the problems your group discussed. Use the passive and the verbs in the box or your own ideas.

damage	endanger	improve	poison	preserve
destroy	harm	limit	pollute	rescue

C Exchange sentences with someone from a different group. Ask each other questions to learn more.

A: *Are any steps being taken to clean up the river?*

B: *Yes, the harmful chemicals are being removed with special equipment.*

A: *Have all the fish been killed?*

B: *No, some species have survived.*

EXPLORE

CD3-07

1 **READ** the article about night gardens. How are night gardens different from the gardens that we see during the day?

Night Gardens

Take a walk through a garden at night. You will probably notice that flowers look different from how they look during the day. At nighttime, colors **are transformed**[1] when they **are lit by** moonlight. White and yellow flowers shine, and reds and oranges glow.[2]

Glowing colors are especially important for plants that bloom[3] only at night, such as the cereus cactus plant and some tropical water lilies. Night-bloomers **are pollinated by** bats and moths. Most of these creatures are active only at night. They don't have good vision, but they can easily locate flowers that glow in the dark. In addition, night-bloomers have a sweet smell, so their pollinators **are attracted by** their scent as well as their color.

That's the scientific explanation for the colors and fragrance of night gardens, but it does not explain their peacefulness or the magical effect they have on us.

[1] **transform:** to change from one appearance to another
[2] **glow:** to give off light
[3] **bloom:** to flower

▶ A night-blooming cereus flower unfolds in Honolulu, Hawaii.

2 CHECK. Correct the error in each sentence according to the article.

different

1. Flowers look ~~the same~~ at night and during the day.

2. The colors of flowers change in sunlight.

3. Bees pollinate night bloomers.

4. Pollinators locate flowers that are hard to see in the dark.

5. Science can explain the effect that night gardens have on us.

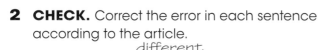
▲ Hummingbird hawk moth

3 DISCOVER. Complete the exercises to learn about the grammar in this lesson.

A Look at the sentences based on the article in exercise **1**. Underline the passive in each sentence.

1. At nighttime, the colors of flowers <u>are transformed</u>.

2. They <u>are lit</u> by moonlight.

3. Night-bloomers <u>are pollinated</u> by bats and moths.

4. Their pollinators <u>are attracted</u> by scent as well as color.

B Look at the sentences in exercise **A** again. Write **A** if the agent is mentioned. Write ✗ if the agent is not mentioned.

1. __A__   2. __A__   3. __A__   4. __A__
   ✗

C Look at the sentences in exercise **A** again. What word is used before the agent?

LEARN

9.3 Using the Passive

1. The passive can be used when you want to emphasize *what* happened more than *who* or *what* performed the action (the agent).	Coffee **is produced** in Colombia.
2. The passive can also be used when you do not know the agent.	Look! The car **has been stolen**!
3. The passive is sometimes used when it is not necessary to state or repeat the agent.	✓ My car was stolen. ✗ My car was stolen <u>by a car thief</u>.
4. The passive can also be used to avoid criticizing or blaming someone.	My manager told me in a nice way, "This report **was not done** correctly."

4 Rewrite the sentences in the passive. Do not include the agent.

1. People love flowers for their beauty and scent.

   Flowers are loved for their beauty and scent.

2. In Australia, people chose the golden wattle as the national flower.

   _____

3. You can see wax flowers in Western Australia.

   _____

4. The media reported an unusual story from Sydney, Australia.

   _____

5. Australian police discovered a destroyed flowerbed outside a museum.

   _____

◄ Gary the Goat with his owner, comedian Jimbo Bazoobi, outside an Australian courthouse

6. A goat named Gary had eaten the museum's flowerbed.

_____

7. The police ordered Gary's owner to pay a fine.

_____

8. The owner brought Gary to the courthouse for his trial.

_____

9.4   Using *By* with the Passive

1. In a passive sentence, use *by* + the agent when it is important to say who or what performed the action.	Her roses were destroyed **by insects**. *Agent*
2. Sometimes the agent is clear from the context, so you do not need *by* + agent.	Charles Dickens wrote many books. *Oliver Twist* **was written** in the 1830s.
3. It is common to mention the agent when it is: a. a number b. a person's name c. someone or something specific	a. This magazine is read **by millions of people**. b. The portrait was painted **by Picasso**. c. Many animal habitats are threatened **by pollution**. ✗ Many animal habitats are threatened <u>by something</u>.

5 Look at each verb and agent. Then complete the sentence with the correct form of the verbs. Use the passive. If the agent is important, include *by* + the agent. If the agent is not important, cross it out.

1. write / Jack London

   The Call of the Wild _was written by Jack London_ .

2. ~~pick / farm workers~~

   The peaches on this farm ___are picked___ in late summer.

3. release / ~~people~~

   The wolf ___was released   by people___ into the wild last week.

4. visit / millions of tourists

   The Taj Mahal in India ___is visited by millions of tourist___ every year.

5. steal / ~~someone~~

   My cell phone ___was stolen by someone___ last night.

6. give / the president of South Africa

   Tomorrow, an important speech ___will be given by the president of S.A.___

7. eat / birds

   Many baby sea turtles _are eaten by birds_ before they reach the ocean.

8. destroy / a forest fire

   Our house _was destroyed by a forest fire_ last year.

PRACTICE

6 Complete the article with the words in parentheses. Use the passive and the correct form of each verb.

Nearly one-third of parrot species (1) _are threatened_ (threaten) in the wild. The World Parrot Trust (2) _____ (start) in 1989 to help parrots survive and also to help protect parrots in captivity. Educational materials (3) _____ (post) on the World Parrot Trust's website. They teach the public about the dangers parrots face around the world.

The Cape Parrot of South Africa (4) _____ (endanger). This parrot (5) _____ (have to / protect) because of three problems. First, their population (6) _____ (reduce / by disease). Now only 1000 to 1500 of these parrots still live in the wild. Second, the parrots' natural habitat (7) _____ (damage / deforestation). The third problem relates to business. Although it is against the law, large numbers of these birds (8) _____ (catch / wild-parrot traders). Then they (9) _____ (sell) to people who want them as pets.

7 Complete the article about one of the natural wonders of the world with the words in parentheses. Use the active or passive and the correct form of the verbs. Add *by* when necessary.

Table Mountain (1) __is considered__ (consider) to be one of the most amazing places in South Africa. It (2) __is__ (be) in the beautiful city of Cape Town. The flat top of the mountain measures 2 miles (3 km) across. A tall pile of stones (3) __has been placed__ (place) on the highest point of the mountain. The pile of stones (4) __is called__ (call) *Maclear's Beacon*. Table Mountain (5) __is visited by__ (visit) many tourists who like to hike and bike there.

In 1926, Trygve Stromsoe, a Norwegian engineer, (6) __propose__ (propose) a plan for a cable car system on the mountain. The cableway (7) __was completed__ (complete) in 1929. Since the opening of the cableway, over 16 million people ✳(8) __have taken__ (take) the trip to the top of the mountain. Table Mountain offers visitors an incredible view of Cape Town. The mountain (9) __is also known__ (also / know) for something else: Mensa, a group of stars. These stars (10) __were named__ (name) after Table Mountain. (*Mensa* means "table" in Latin.)

▲ Table Mountain in
Cape Town, South Africa

8 Read the article. Then complete the sentences below. Use the active or passive and the correct form of the verb. Include *by* + the agent when necessary.

> Tourists who visit Cape Town, South Africa, shouldn't miss the Cape of Good Hope. It's a rocky piece of land that sticks out into the Atlantic Ocean. The Cape of Good Hope is a very important place because when ships reach the cape, they have to turn east to sail around Africa.
>
> Bartolomeu Dias was the first European explorer to discover the cape in the 15th century. He called it the Cape of Storms because it was very stormy there. Its discovery had opened up a trading route between Europe and Asia, so it got a new name: Cape Hope. Over the years, many European traders stopped at the cape to buy food and supplies from the local people. Eventually these traders built the city of Cape Town. Many ships also sank near the cape. People told stories about *The Flying Dutchman*. This was a ghost ship that tried to sail around the cape over and over again, but never succeeded.
>
> Nowadays, the Cape of Good Hope is part of Table Mountain National Park. You can find many unusual plants and animals at the cape, including African penguins. You can also see different kinds of whales in the waters around the cape.

1. The Cape of Good Hope _shouldn't be missed by tourists_ who visit Cape Town, South Africa.

2. Ships _____ east when they reach the Cape of Good Hope.

3. The Cape of Good Hope _____ in the 15th century.

4. At first, the cape _____ the Cape of Storms because it was very stormy there.

5. The cape _____ the Cape of Good Hope because it had opened up an important trading route.

6. European traders _____ food and supplies from the local people at the cape.

7. The city of Cape Town _____ these traders.

8. Stories _____ about *The Flying Dutchman*, a ghost ship.

9. Unusual plants and animals _____ at the Cape of Good Hope.

10. Whales _____ in the waters around the cape.

9 Read the headlines. Then complete the sentences using the passive. Use the correct form of the verb. Add *by* when necessary.

1. **LION-MEAT BAN PROPOSED**

   A ban on lion meat _was proposed by African authorities_

2. **SWORDFISH EYEBALL FOUND ON FLORIDA BEACH**

   A swordfish eyeball _was found_ on a Florida beach.

3. **SINGING MICE OBSERVED IN 2005 STUDY**

   Singing mice _was observed_ in a 2005 study.

4. **BRAZILIAN FAMILY RAISING TIGER**

   A tiger _is being raised by a brazilian family_

5. **THREE BILLION BIRDS KILLED EVERY YEAR; CATS TO BLAME**

   Three billion birds _have been killed_ every year.

6. **68 BURMESE PYTHONS CAUGHT IN FLORIDA**

   Sixty-eight Burmese python snakes _were caught_ in Florida.

7. **REPAIRMAN DISCOVERS BEAR IN BASEMENT**

   A bear _was discovered by a Repairman_ last Tuesday.

10 APPLY.

A Listen to the conversation. Which headline in exercise **9** is the conversation about?

B Complete the sentences. Use the passive form of six of the verbs from the box. Add *not* and *by* when necessary.

bite	catch	chase	contact
~~find~~	give	release	repair

Last Tuesday a 500-pound black bear (1) _was found_ in the basement of a home near the state park. A repairman discovered the bear while he was working in the basement. The repairman ran out, and fortunately he (2) _____ the bear or hurt in any other way. The animal control department (3) _____ and some officers came right away. They shot the bear with tranquilizers. The tranquilizers were not effective at first, and the bear managed to escape. The bear (4) _____ for nearly 45 minutes before it (5) _____ . The bear (6) _____ into the wild after it (7) _____ a medical exam.

C Work with a partner. Use your imagination to write a news report for another headline from exercise **9**. Use the report in exercise **B** as a model.

EXPLORE

CD3-09

1 READ the article about hurricane hunters. What important work do they do?

Hurricane Hunters

One September morning, Captain Chad Gibson boarded an airplane in Mississippi. A violent hurricane had been reported in Cuba. It was raining hard, and winds were over 110 miles per hour (177 kph). Gibson was planning to fly right through the storm.

Being caught in the middle of a storm was no problem for Gibson, because he is a hurricane hunter. His job is to collect information about powerful storms. Most of this information **gets collected** when the plane flies through the calm eye of the storm.[1] The pilots use a device called a dropsonde to record humidity,[2] temperature, and wind speed. With this information, they determine the strength of a hurricane and where it is heading. Then they send the information to weather forecasters.

After considering the data, the weather forecasters issue warnings about areas that they expect **to be affected**. Sometimes, people in these areas have to prepare **to be evacuated**.[3] Sometimes people do not want **to be evacuated**, but it is safer if they leave the area. That way, they can avoid **getting caught** in dangerous situations.

The damage caused by past hurricanes has been considerable, but without the work of the hurricane hunters, it would have been even worse. Pilots like Chad Gibson know that their work can save lives. They don't mind **being asked** to track dangerous storms. As Gibson says, "It's just a job. You know, a lawyer goes to his office. We get on our plane."

[1] **eye of the storm:** calm area in the center of a storm or hurricane
[2] **humidity:** the amount of water in the air
[3] **evacuate:** to move out of a place of danger for a period of time

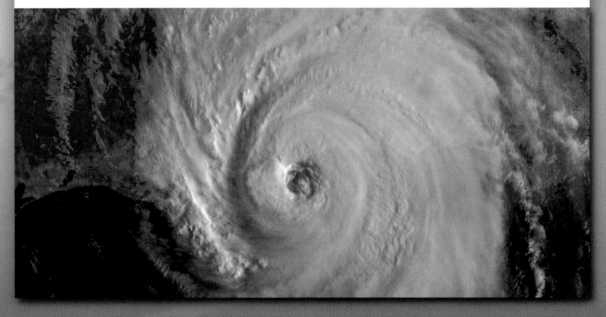

▲ A satellite image of Hurricane Katrina, which devastated New Orleans and the Gulf Coast of the US in August 2005.

2 CHECK. Write answers to the questions. Write complete sentences.

1. When do hurricane hunters collect information?

   Hurricane hunters collect information when they fly through the

   calm eye of the storm.

2. What are three things that a dropsonde checks?

   _____

3. What two important things about a hurricane do the pilots want to find out?

   _____

4. What do weather forecasters do with the hurricane hunters' information?

   _____

3 DISCOVER. Complete the exercises to learn about the grammar in this lesson.

A Read the sentences from the article in excercise **1**. Underline the passive in each sentence.

1. <u>Being caught</u> in the middle of a storm was no problem for Gibson.

2. The weather forecasters issue warnings about areas that they expect to be affected.

3. That way, they can avoid getting caught in dangerous situations.

4. They don't mind being asked to track dangerous storms.

B Look at the sentences in exercise **A** again. Then read the statements. Choose **T** for *true* or **F** for *false*.

1. You need to use a form of *be* in all passives.   **T**   **F**

2. Passives can be formed with both gerunds and infinitives.   **T**   **F**

3. The final verb form in passive phrases is always a past participle.   **T**   **F**

LEARN

9.5 Passive Gerunds and Passive Infinitives

Passive Gerunds	Passive Infinitives
(Not) Being + Past Participle	*(Not) To Be* + Past Participle
I dislike **being given** extra work. I don't mind **not being invited** to the picnic. I was angry about **being fired** from my job.	I want **to be invited** to the party. I tried **not to be caught** in the storm. I was happy **to be given** some extra work.

1. The passive form of a gerund is *being* + the past participle.	She dislikes **being asked** a lot of questions. He was upset about **not being told** the news.
2. Like gerunds, passive gerunds can: a. be the subject of a sentence b. follow verbs such as *avoid, dislike, mind, risk, understand*[1] c. follow a preposition	a. **Being questioned** about my work made me nervous. b. I **don't mind being interviewed**. c. Are you interested **in being called** if a job opens up?
3. The passive form of an infinitive is *(not) to be* + the past participle.	She is determined **to be elected** president. The information is **not to be discussed** with anyone.
4. Passive infinitives can follow verbs and adjectives normally followed by an infinitive. a. Verbs: *ask, expect, hope, prefer, wait*[2] b. Adjectives: *afraid, determined, lucky, ready*[3]	a. We **waited to be picked up** at the station. b. I was **lucky to be given** the award.

[1] See page **A2** for a full list of verbs and phrases followed by gerunds.
[2] See page **A3** for a full list of verbs followed by infinitives.
[3] See page **A3** for a full list of adjectives followed by infinitives.

4 Circle the correct form of the verb to complete each sentence.

1. When hurricanes develop, hurricane hunters get ready **being sent / to be sent** into the storm.

2. Hurricane hunters risk **being injured / to be injured** on the job.

3. Hurricane hunters never complain about **being expected / to be expected** to help weather forecasters.

4. Buildings are often in danger of **being damaged / to be damaged** during a hurricane.

5. When a bad storm is coming, people shouldn't wait **being evacuated / to be evacuated**.

6. Sometimes homeowners need **being told / to be told** that they can't return to their homes.

7. Everyone looks forward to **being allowed / to be allowed** back into their homes.

8. After a storm, people hope **being given / to be given** assistance by the government.

Why have you been surprised at showing you my new business).

9.6 Get Passives

1. You can use a form of *get* + the past participle to create a passive meaning. *Get* passives are commonly used:	
a. to describe something unwanted or unexpected	a. His dog **got hit** by a car. He's very upset.
b. to talk about something that will have a negative effect	b. Kim i**s going to get punished** for staying out too late.
c. with certain verbs such as *accept, deliver, fire, hire, invite, offer, pay, promote, show*	c. I'm so happy. I **got accepted** to the University of Iowa.
2. The gerund form of a passive with *get* is *getting* + the past participle.	I'm worried about **getting fired**.
The infinitive form of a passive with *get* is *to get* + the past participle.	I don't expect **to get fired**.

5 Complete the conversations with a correct form of *get* and the verbs in parentheses. In some cases, more than one form of the verb is possible.

Conversation A

Eve: Are tornadoes frequent where you live?

Al: Yes, they're pretty common. In fact, we (1) _____got hit_____ (hit) by one last month.

Eve: Were there any injuries?

Al: No, we were very lucky. Some windows (2) _____ (break) but no one (3) _____ (hurt).

Conversation B

Deb: Did you have any damage from the hurricane?

Vic: Our basement (4) _____ (flood), but the rest of the house was OK. Downtown (5) _____ (hit) much worse. Main Street was affected badly.

Deb: Why? Did the stores (6) _____ (damage)?

Vic: Yeah, especially the grocery store; a lot of food (7) _____ (ruin). I think it's going to take weeks before that store dries out.

Deb: Oh, no. So can you still buy food there?

Vic: Yeah, you can. There isn't much to buy there now, but I heard that more food (8) _____ (deliver) tomorrow.

► A bull tries to escape a running wildfire in Gradford, Texas.

PRACTICE

6 Read about the effects that weather has on wildlife. Complete the paragraph with the correct form of *get* or *be* and the verbs in parentheses. More than one answer is sometimes correct.

Many animals are in danger of (1) _____get harm_____ (harm) during storms, especially during hurricanes. Violent storms can affect a variety of species. Even fish are not safe. During a hurricane, for example, fish habitats often (2) _____ (damage) when tree limbs and branches break off and fall to the ground. The wetlands (3) _____ (fill) with the tree parts. This reduces the amount of oxygen in the water and fish die as a result. Birds are at risk, too. During a hurricane, many birds (4) _____ (blow) out to sea. (5) _____ (remove) from their natural habitats can be very dangerous for birds, and many of them (6) _____ (kill) when this happens. The Puerto Rico parrot population, for example, (7) _____ (reduce) greatly after Hurricane Andrew. Normally, large sea animals such as manatees (8) _____ (not affect) by hurricanes, and they do not need (9) _____ (rescue). However, there are exceptions. For instance, after Hurricane Andrew, one manatee (10) _____ (find) far away from its home in coastal waters.

7 Complete the exercises.

A Complete the questions with the passive. Use the correct form of *get* and a verb from the box.

bite	burn	~~catch~~	injure	rescue	sting

1. Have you ever ___gotten caught___ in a bad storm?

2. What should you do to avoid _____ in a wildfire?

3. Have you ever _____ from a dangerous situation?

4. Have you ever _____ in a car accident?

5. What do some people do when they _____ by a bee?

6. Have you ever _____ by an animal?

B **SPEAK.** Work with a partner. Ask and answer the questions in exercise **A**. Add details about your experiences.

8 **LISTEN** to the conversation about a camping trip. Then read the statements. Circle **T** for *true* or **F** for *false*.
CD3-10

1. Campers' garbage could bother some animals at the campground.   **T**   **(F)**

2. Julie woke up her friends when she heard a noise.   **T**   **F**

3. Julie and her friends hadn't thrown all the garbage away.   **T**   **F**

4. Skunks spray to defend themselves in the wild.   **T**   **F**

5. Julie was able to stop the skunk from spraying.   **T**   **F**

6. The campers felt lucky that their adventure only involved a skunk.   **T**   **F**

9 **EDIT.** Read the paragraph. Find and correct eight more errors with passives.

                                             shown
    When I was a child, I remember being ~~show~~ a bird nest in a tree in our yard. It was a robin's nest, and it was amazing. There were four blue eggs in the nest. The bird didn't seem to mind be watched, and I was careful not to get too close. I was very young, maybe four, but I never needed telling not to touch the nest. Somehow I knew that without being remind. One day, I looked and saw baby robins in the nest. I don't think they liked be left alone by their mother, but sometimes she had to fly away to get food. When she came back, the babies made a lot of noise while they were waiting to being fed!

    Since that time I have always loved birds, and I love to go on birdwatching trips. In recent years, I have traveled all over the world to observe birds. I sometimes get invite to speak at birdwatching conferences. Be asked to share my knowledge of birds with others gives me a lot of pleasure. Fortunately, birdwatching is a very safe hobby. I've never get injured while doing my favorite thing.

10 APPLY.

A Look at the photo. Then write sentences about it. Use your imagination. Use passive gerunds, passive infinitives, and *get* passives in your sentences.

1. This city _____ .

2. The taxi _____ .

3. The woman doesn't want _____ .

4. The dog doesn't mind _____ .

5. The woman and her dog don't need _____ .

6. _____ can be scary.

B Work in a group. Share your sentences from exercise **A**. Ask each other questions about your sentences. Try to use passive gerunds, passive infinitives, and *get* passives.

A: *This city got hit by a bad snowstorm.*

B: *Did anyone get hurt in the snowstorm?*

A: *No, no one got hurt, if I remember correctly.*

Charts
9.1–9.6

1 Circle the correct words to complete the conversation.

Elsa: I remember when I first started working at the animal preserve 40 years ago, one of my favorite animals was a young elephant named Lucy. But one day, (1) she **disappeared** / **was disappeared**, and she (2) **never saw** / **was never seen** again.

Paul: I remember Lucy. Then shortly after that, we (3) **noticed** / **were noticed** that every day another animal was missing. We realized that some thieves (4) **must have taken** / **must have been taken** them. Eventually, the thieves (5) **caught** / **were caught** by the police. If I remember correctly, they (6) **sent** / **got sent** to jail for three years.

Elsa: That's right. That was a harsh punishment at that time. I don't think those thieves expected (7) **to punish** / **to get punished** at all.

Paul: No, I don't think they did. But it was a good thing, because more and more animals (8) **are saving** / **are being saved** now. Since our departure, some of the animals (9) **have released** / **have been released** back into the wild.

Elsa: That's great news. It shows how much people (10) **have learned** / **have been learned** since we started our work.

Charts
9.1–9.4

2 Rewrite the sentences in the passive where possible. Begin each sentence with the underlined word(s). Use the correct form of the verb. Use *by* + the agent when necessary.

1. We find <u>bats</u> throughout most of the world.

   <u>Bats are found throughout most of the world.</u>

2. We can see <u>bats</u> all over the world.

   _____

3. In some parts of the world, <u>bats</u> live in caves.

   _____

4. Someone should stop <u>the destruction</u> of bat habitats.

   _____

5. A deadly disease has killed <u>more than 5.7 million bats</u>.

   _____

6. Organizations are investigating <u>the spread of the disease</u>.

   _____

7. The disease could threaten <u>the survival of bats</u>.

   _____

8. The government should have protected <u>these endangered animals</u> from this disease.

   _____

Charts
9.5–9.6

3 Complete the sentences with passive gerunds, passive infinitives, *get* passives and the correct form of the verbs in parentheses.

1. The old couple isn't worried about <u>being caught OR getting caught</u> (catch) in the hurricane. They aren't ready _____ (evacuate). They hope _____ (leave) alone in their home until the hurricane is over.

2. The baby monkey _____ (hurt) when it fell out of a tree. Now it wants _____ (pick up) by its mother. It's asking _____ (feed) some fruit.

3. _____ (trap) in a fire can be very dangerous. If you play with fire in your home, you risk _____ (burn) very badly. A fire _____ (start) in a house last week by five children who were playing with matches. Luckily, the children _____ (rescue) by a firefighter. The firefighter _____ (promote) after she saved the children.

Charts
9.1–9.6

4 **EDIT.** Read the text. Find and correct seven more errors with passives.

Good News for Gray Seals, or Is It?

                                                     _{been}

Good news for the gray seal population has ⌄announced. Seal populations are being grown off the north Atlantic coast of the United States. For many years, seals killed for their skins, oil, and meat. However, since 1972, they have be protected by U.S. law, and they cannot be killed. Many people worry, however, that the seal population is getting out of control, and that nothing will been done to manage it. Fishermen are complaining because large amounts of fish are eating by the seals. In addition, there is the shark problem. Sharks like to eat seals, so when seals move into an area, sharks usually follow. In fact, many more sharks can be seen in the areas where seal populations have increased. Naturally, swimmers are concerned about to be attacked by sharks. Swimmer Jon Turner says, "It's great that the gray seal population has come back, but now I have to be careful not to get bite by a shark!"

5 LISTEN & SPEAK.

Charts
9.1,
9.3–9.5

CD3-11

A Take the quiz. Circle the letters of the correct answers. Then listen and check your answers.

1. Which of the following is a major problem facing the world's oceans?

   a. Overfishing   c. Pollution

   b. Building in coastal areas   d. All of these things

2. Which of the following has been linked to climate change on Earth?

   a. Droughts (periods with little or no rainfall)   c. Melting ice caps

   b. Flooding   d. All of these things

3. On average, what are your chances of being struck by lightning in any given year?

   a. 1 in 7,000,000   c. 1 in 70,000

   b. 1 in 700,000   d. 1 in 7000

4. How many pounds of wild fish and shellfish are removed from the ocean every year?

   a. About 700,000 pounds   c. More than 170 billion pounds

   b. Less than 170 million pounds   d. About 100 million pounds

5. How big was the biggest wave that has ever been recorded?

   a. 12 feet (4 meters)   c. 75 feet (23 meters)

   b. 30 feet (9 meters)   d. 90 feet (27 meters)

CD3-11

B Listen again. Then write the answers to the questions in your notebook.

1. What is happening to Earth's oceans and the species that live in them?

2. What is happening to rainfall patterns and melting polar ice?

3. What role do activities such as golf and mountain climbing play during a thunderstorm?

4. Why are there fewer fish and shellfish in the ocean every year?

5. What caused the biggest wave?

C Work with a partner. Discuss your answers from exercise **B**.

A: *The ocean and its species are being harmed by pollution.*

B: *That's one problem. Another is overfishing.*

1 READ & NOTICE THE GRAMMAR.

A Look at the photo below. What do you know about this animal? Discuss with a partner. Then read the essay.

Senegal
Sierra
Leone

AFRICAN MANATEES

African manatees can be found in the rivers and coastal areas of western Africa. Unfortunately, the future of African manatees is uncertain. There are now fewer than 10,000 of these animals left. The destruction of their natural habitat and hunting are major threats.

A large part of the manatees' habitat is being destroyed by the building of dams. In Senegal, for example, manatees get stuck in the shallow water created by dams on the Senegal River. Pollution from boats on the river also damages their habitat, as does the clearing of wetlands.

Hunting is another problem. Hunting manatees is illegal, but their meat is still being sold in markets, and their bones are used to make parts of walking sticks. Because the laws are not strongly enforced, people who hunt manatees illegally do not get punished.

Although all manatees are endangered, the African manatees are especially at risk because of the serious problems they face. Many environmental groups are working to save African manatees. They hope that education and better law enforcement will help protect these animals.

GRAMMAR FOCUS

In this essay, the writer uses the passive with and without the agent.

• The agent is mentioned when it adds new information.
  *A large part of the manatees' habitat **is being destroyed by the building of dams**.*

• The agent *isn't* mentioned when it is already clear or obvious.
  *African manatees **can be found** in the rivers and coastal areas of western Africa.*

B Read the essay in exercise **A** again. Find two more examples of the passive. Indicate whether or not the agent is mentioned.

1. _____can be found_____   _____no agent_____

2. _____   _____

3. _____   _____

C Complete the chart with information from the essay in exercise **A**.

Endangered Species: _African Manatee_	
Threat	**Specific Examples**
Habitat is being destroyed	1. 2. 3. Clearing of wetlands
	1. Meat is sold in markets 2. 3.

2 BEFORE YOU WRITE.

A In your notebook, make a list of all the endangered animals that you have heard of. Then choose the animal from your list that you know the most about.

B Make a chart in your notebook like the one in exercise **1C**. Think about the animal you chose in exercise **A**. What are the two biggest threats to its survival? Write notes in your chart. Use the chart from exercise **1C** as a model.

3 WRITE an essay about the endangered animal you chose. Use the information from your chart in **2B** and the essay in exercise **1A** to help you.

> **WRITING FOCUS**   Using *Especially*
>
> Notice how the writer uses *especially* in the essay in exercise **1A**. *Especially* indicates that the writer is adding an important or particular example of detail to a sentence.
>
> *Although all manatees are endangered, African manatees are **especially** at risk because of the serious problems they face.*

4 SELF ASSESS. Read your essay again. Underline the passive. Then use the checklist to assess your work.

☐ I used the passive correctly. [9.1–9.5]

☐ I used *by* + the agent only when it was important. [9.4]

☐ I used *especially* to give additional information. [WRITING FOCUS]

UNIT 10 Beauty and Appearance

Causative Verb Patterns and Phrasal Verbs

A female io moth, Little Orleans, Maryland, USA

EXPLORE

CD3-12

1 **READ** the article about a popular annual event in Abu Dhabi. In what way does it celebrate the past?

Who's the loveliest of them all?

The contest participants come from near and far. They wear gold and silver and flutter[1] their long eyelashes. However, this is no ordinary beauty contest. The competition takes place in a remote part of Abu Dhabi, one of the United Arab Emirates. There are about 25,000 contestants and they all have large heads, floppy lips, and long legs. They come from all over the Arabian Peninsula for *Al Dhafra*, the annual beauty contest for camels. Yes, camels.

To prepare for the contest, experienced trainers **help owners to make their camels** look their best. The camels are fed special food to make them healthy and strong. They are also washed from top to bottom, which **makes their hair shine**. Sometimes the trainers **get the camels to loosen up** by massaging them. Then, the camels are decorated.

The beauty contest lasts ten days. Each day, the trainers **have the camels walk** in front of the judges. The judges evaluate the size of the camel's head, the length of the neck, and the size and shape of the hump.[2] The owners of top-scoring camels win millions of dollars. The most exciting day is the last one, when the judges choose the most beautiful camel of all.

A winning camel brings a lot of prestige[3] to an owner; however, the contest is about much more. Historically, the camel provided people of the desert with food, clothing, and transportation. *Al Dhafra* **lets this community celebrate** their traditional relationship with camels, the much loved "ships of the desert."

[1] **flutter:** to quickly move up and down
[2] **hump:** the large lump on a camel's back
[3] **prestige:** being admired or respected

▼ These long legged, floppy-lipped, big-eyed camels are getting ready for a big day.

2 CHECK. Correct the error in each sentence according to the information in the article.

1. The beauty contest is for camels from ~~Abu Dhabi~~. *all over the Arabian Peninsula*

2. Camel owners get help from family members before the contest.

3. A camel's hair shines after it is massaged.

4. The trainers evaluate the camels at the contest.

5. On the last day, the judges choose the most skillful camel.

3 DISCOVER. Complete the exercises to learn about the grammar in this lesson.

A Find these sentences in the article from exercise **1**. Write the missing words.

1. . . . experienced trainers _____ their camels look their best.

2. They are also washed from top to bottom, which _____.

3. Sometimes the trainers _____ by massaging them.

4. Each day, the trainers _____ in front of the judges.

5. *Al Dhafra* _____ their traditional relationship with camels . . .

B Look at the verb patterns in the phrases you wrote in exercise **A**. Then check (✓) the pattern that is used with each verb.

Verb	Object + Base Form of Verb	Object + Infinitive (*to* + verb)
1. help		
2. make		
3. get		
4. have		
5. let		

LEARN

Causative (handwritten)

10.1 *Have, Let,* and *Make*

Have/Let/Make + Object + Base Form
The teacher **has her students do** a lot of homework.
Amy **lets her children play** outside every day.
Jon's mother **makes him clean** his room once a week.

1. *Have/let/make* + object + the base form of a verb indicates that the subject causes or influences a person or thing to act.	The director **had the actor say** his lines again. He **made the actors wear** silly costumes. He **didn't let the actors choose** the costumes.
2. *Have someone do something* means to require or ask someone to do something.	The teacher **had the students** retake the test. Did you **have anyone read** your essay?
3. *Let someone do something* means to allow or permit someone to do something.	Jack's mother **lets him stay up** late.
4. *Make someone do something* means to force or cause someone to do something.	She **made the child drink** milk, but he hated it. That book **made me decide** to study history.

(handwritten left margin: Preguntar o pedir } lepido que; Permitir o dar permiso; Forzar Obligar (Causar en algo o alguien); Hace que)

4 Circle the correct answers to complete the paragraph about a camel market in Abu Dhabi.

Today, the huge number of cars on the streets of Abu Dhabi might (1) **have / (make)** you think that camels are a thing of the past. However, a trip to the camel market in Al Ain is likely to change your mind. You can (2) **have / make** someone give you a tour of the market, or you can look around by yourself. Camels of all colors and sizes are kept in wire pens. That (3) **lets / makes** you see them up close. There is lively competition among the traders. Each man tries to (4) **let / make** people believe that his camels are the very best. Some owners (5) **have / let** tourists enter the camel pens, but the visitors often have to pay to do this. The cutest camels are the wide-eyed babies. They (6) **have / make** everybody smile. Some traders won't (7) **have / let** you take pictures. They will (8) **let / make** you put your camera away, so be sure to ask permission first. Take your time and look around. Perhaps a visit to the market will (9) **have / make** you want a camel of your own. You probably won't be able to (10) **let / make** it behave like a prize-winner, but you will still love it.

▲ Mother and baby camel, Abu Dhabi, UAE

10.2 Get and Help

[handwritten: Causative]

[handwritten: Gramm {9C 10, L1   Read {9B]

Get + Object + Infinitive
I **get my friend to exercise** with me after work.

Help + Object + Base Form/Infinitive
I **help my son to do** his homework. I **help my son do** his homework.

1. *Get* + object + infinitive means to persuade or cause someone to do something. *[handwritten: Persuation]*	He **got his brother to lend** him some money. The classes **get me to think** differently about history.
2. *Help* + object + the base form of the verb or infinitive means to assist or guide. *[handwritten: Assitance Ayuda]*	The teacher **will help you do** the report. The teacher **will help you to do** the report.

[handwritten margin: Cuenta que me ayuda]

5 Complete the interview with a beauty contest participant. Use the correct forms of *get* or *help* and the words in parentheses. More than one answer is sometimes possible.

A: You entered your first beauty contest at age 16. Did your parents think you were too young?

B: Yes, at first, but I finally (1) ___got them to agree___ (them / agree). They knew how much I wanted to participate. But they (2) ___got me to promise___ (me / promise) to finish my college applications before I started preparing for the contest.

A: Was the contest all about appearance?

B: Absolutely not. We had to show we had talents and skills. Luckily, the trainers (3) ___helped us to prepare___ (us / prepare) for the contest. For example, my talent was tap dancing, so my trainer (4) ___helped me to practice___ (me / practice) six times a week.

A: What about your relationship with the other contestants? How was that?

B: It was great! I made lifelong friends with some of the other people. We always (5) ___helped each other do___ (each other / do) our best.

A: What's the secret to winning a contest?

B: Well, for one thing, you have to (6) ___get the judges to respect___ (the judges / respect) you. They have to realize that there is more to you than your appearance.

A: You've won several contests, haven't you?

B: Yes, and the scholarship money (7) ___helped me to pay___ (me / pay) for college.

A: That's great. A college degree will (8) ___help you to get___ (you / get) a good job. Do you know what you're going to study?

B: I want to study psychology, so I can (9) ___help people to solve___ (people / solve) their problems.

A: That's a good goal. Well, good luck!

PRACTICE

6 Complete the exercises.

A Put the words in the correct order to complete the questions about personal appearance.

1. gotten / change / your / appearance / to / you

   Has anyone ever _gotten you to change your appearance_ ?

2. get / your / cut / hair / to

   Who do you _____ ?

3. people / about / make / their appearance / worry

   Do you think that advertisements _____ ?

4. you / wear / make / certain clothes

   Did your parents _____ when you were young ?

5. your clothes / anyone / borrow / let

   Have you ever _____ ?

6. for new clothes / you / shop / help

   Does anyone _____ ?

B **SPEAK.** Work with a partner. Ask and answer the questions from exercise **A**. Explain your answers.

A: *Has anyone ever gotten you to change your appearance?*

B: *Yes. Once my sister got me to curl my hair.* OR *No. My friends and I aren't really interested in appearance.*

7 Circle the correct words to complete the paragraph.

Flower Power

Flowers are beautiful, but how do they (1) **get / help /** (**make**) people feel? Research has shown that flowers can (2) **get /** (**help**) **/ let** people to improve their mood and (3) **get / have /** (**make**) them smile. According to one study of older adults, receiving flowers (4) **got / had /** (**made**) 81 percent of the participants feel happier. Other studies showed that the smell of flowers can (5) **get / let /** (**make**) people feel more positive and might even (6) (**help**) **/ make / get** them to sleep better. There is also evidence that flowers (7) (**get**) **/ let / have** people to act friendlier toward one another.

So if you are feeling sad, take a walk in a garden. The owners probably won't (8) **get /** (**let**) **/ make** you pick the flowers, but you can still smell them. Better yet, you can (9) (**get**) **/ make / let** someone to send you some.

8 Read each conversation. Then complete the sentence about the conversation with the correct form of the verb in parentheses.

1. **Pam:** Alicia, can I borrow your sweater for the party tonight?

    Alicia: OK. But please be careful with it.

    Alicia is going to ___let Pam borrow___ (let) her sweater.

2. **Polly:** Jake, the kitchen needs a paint job.

    Jake: Yes, I'm going to call the painters today.

    Jake is going to ___have the painters___ (have) come to paint the kitchen.

3. **Jen:** I haven't had time to decorate the house for Cathy's birthday party yet.

    Andy: Don't worry. I can do it for you.

    Andy is going to ___help Jen to decorate___ (help) the house for the party.

4. **Chen:** Kyle got mud all over himself at the soccer game!

    Miki: I know, but he's clean now. I told him to take a shower.

    Miki ___makes Kyle take___ (make) a shower.

5. **Lily:** You looked great at the party last night! Where did you get that dress?

    Amy: At Magnim's. I asked a salesperson to choose a dress for me!

    Amy _____ (get) a dress for her.

6. **Nora:** Do you think children should participate in beauty contests?

    Rex: No. Their parents shouldn't allow them to do that.

    Rex thinks that parents shouldn't _____ (let) in beauty contests.

7. **Ana:** The lawn really needs mowing.

    Hector: I'll talk to Jorge about mowing it tonight.

    Hector is going to _____

    _____ (get) the lawn.

8. **Maria:** I think orchids are really beautiful flowers. Don't you?

    Rachel: Yes, I do. I feel happy when I look at them.

    Orchids _____

    (make) happy.

▶ The orchid *Ophrys apifera* looks like a female bee.

273

9 LISTEN.

A Listen to the conversation about a man who loves beautiful plants. Then read the statements. Circle **T** for *true* or **F** for *false*.

CD3-13

1. Visiting Bahia made Alex Popovkin want to live there.	**T**	**F**
2. Alex had a dream, and he made it happen.	**T**	**F**
3. Alex has scientists help him identify plant species.	**T**	**F**
4. Alex's photos let people see animals they would never see otherwise.	**T**	**F**
5. Alex does not let people download his photos of plants on the Internet.	**T**	**F**

B Listen again and check your answers.

CD3-13

10 APPLY.

A Use the prompts to write questions about yourself, someone else you know, or people in general.

1. why / flowers / make / _____people_____ / feel happy

   Why do flowers make people feel happy?

2. how / team sports / make / _your friends_ / act

   How do team sports make your friends act?

3. how / travel / help / _you_ / see things differently

   How does travel help you to see things differently?

4. what kind of music / get / _your sister_ / relax

   " " " " get your sister relax?

5. what / teachers / let / _students_ / do in the classroom

   What do teachers let students do in the classroom!

6. what things / help / _you_ / fall asleep

   " " do help you " "

B Work with a partner. Ask and answer your questions in exercise **A**.

A: *Why do flowers make people feel happy?*

B: *Looking at flowers helps people forget their troubles.*

EXPLORE

CD3-14

1 **READ** this excerpt from a book about ancient Egyptians. Which of their techniques for improving personal appearance do people still use today?

Looking Good in Ancient Egypt

Thanks to the work of archaeologists, today we know a great deal about ancient Egyptian life. Consider, for example, four small jars on exhibit at the Louvre Museum in Paris. Experts first thought that the jars had contained the internal organs[1] of a pharaoh.[2] It was common for Egyptians to store the organs of the dead this way. However, when officials at the museum **had the jars examined** by chemists, they discovered that the jars had actually contained cosmetics.[3] In fact, a great many combs, brushes, mirrors, cosmetic containers, and different types of makeup have been found in tombs and temples. Ancient Egyptians clearly cared a lot about appearance.

Queen Cleopatra is one ancient Egyptian who is known for her beauty. Cleopatra had her own beauticians, as many wealthy Egyptians did. Research shows that she **had her hair dyed** and **styled** into complex hairdos. She also **had her nails polished**. Her hands were decorated with henna, a reddish-brown dye. Another famous beauty was Queen Nefertiti. Her husband **had large images** of her **painted** on the walls of tombs and temples. This let him share his wife's beauty with the people and communicate her power at the same time.

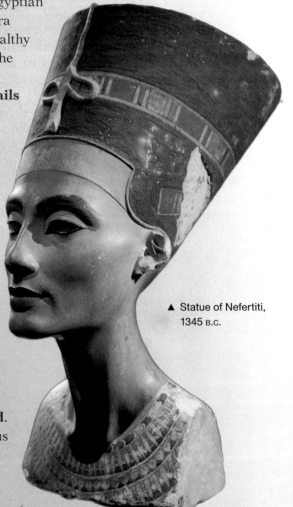
▲ Statue of Nefertiti, 1345 B.C.

Concern with appearance was not limited to women. Both men and women wore eye makeup to beautify themselves and prevent eye disease. (It seems that the chemicals in the makeup could fight infection.) Men also **had their hair cut**, and boys **got their heads shaved**. Evidently, the ancient Egyptians' focus on appearance was not very different from our own.

[1] **organ:** a part of the body that has a particular function such as the heart or lungs
[2] **pharaoh:** a ruler of ancient Egypt
[3] **cosmetics:** substances such as lipstick, powder, and skin cream that people put on their faces to look more attractive

2 CHECK. Read the statements. Circle **T** for *true* or **F** for *false*.

1. Scientists discovered that the jars at the Louvre contained ancient jewels.   **T**   **F**

2. The ancient Egyptians were buried with things that they used every day.   **T**   **F**

3. Wearing eye makeup benefited people's health as well as their appearance.   **T**   **F**

4. Women wore makeup, but men didn't.   **T**   **F**

5. Modern beauty techniques have little in common with those of
   the ancient Egyptians.   **T**   **F**

3 DISCOVER. Complete the exercises to learn about the grammar in this lesson.

A Find these sentences in the excerpt from exercise **1** on page 275. Write the missing words.
Do the subjects perform the actions? Discuss your answers with a partner.

1. Research shows that she _____
   into complex hairdos.

2. She also _____.

3. Her husband _____
   on the walls of tombs and temples.

4. Men _____ cut, and boys _____.

B What is the pattern of the verb phrases you wrote in exercise **A**? Circle the answer.

1. *have / get* + past participle

2. *have / get* + past participle + object

3. *have / get* + object + past participle

▼ Necklace of Princess Khnumit,
12th Dynasty 20th-19th B.C.;
Jewelry was popular among
Egyptian royalty.

LEARN

(handwritten margin notes)
I have my brother clean my house
" get "   "   to clean "   "
{ had
{ have   ??
will { get
translate

10.3 Passive Causative: *Have Something Done*

Have + Object + Past Participle
I **had my watch repaired** last week.
Did you **have the battery changed**?

1. Use passive causatives with *have* to talk about services that we have someone else do for us.	We **had the roof fixed** last year. (Someone else fixed the roof.)
2. The subject of a sentence with a passive causative did not perform the action. The action was done by someone else.	I **had the kitchen painted** by HMS Painters. (HMS Painters painted the kitchen.)
3. **Be careful!** The form of the verb *have* changes with different tenses and modal verbs.	I'm **having** the kitchen **painted** this week. I **have** the kitchen **painted** every two years. I **haven't had** the kitchen **painted** recently. I'm **going to have** the kitchen **painted** soon. **Should** we **have** the kitchen **painted**?
4. **Be careful!** The passive causative (*have something done*) looks similar to the present perfect (*have done something*), but the meanings are very different.	I never **have the house cleaned**. I **have never cleaned** the house.

(handwritten margin notes: Mice fine / Hayo fine / Haré fine)

4 Complete the paragraph about ancient Egypt. Use the correct form of *have* and the words in parentheses.

The pharaohs were very powerful rulers, and they (1) ___had many things done___ (many things / do) in their kingdoms to demonstrate their power. For example, they (2) ___had their portraits painted___ (their portraits / paint). They also (3) ___had their images puted___ (their images / put) on coins. In addition, the pharaohs (4) ___had large tombs built___ (large tombs / build) for themselves. Women of high status (5) ___had (their) heads shaved___ (heads / shave). They wore wigs instead of their own hair, and they (6) ___had the wigs dyed___ (the wigs / dye) different colors: black, blond, gold, blue, or green.

The Egyptians believed in life after death, so they (7) ___had their bodies preserved___ (their bodies / preserve) for the next life in a process called mummification. Because they believed that they would need many of their possessions in the afterlife, they (8) ___had their belongings placed___ (their belongings / place) near them in their tombs. These belongings included weapons, jewelry, food and drink, and cosmetics. They also (9) ___had special words written___ (special words / write) on their coffins to protect them from harm after death. Some pharaohs even (10) ___had their pets buried___ (their pets / bury) with them.

10.4 Passive Causative: *Get Something Done*

Get + Object + Past Participle
She **got** her hair **done**.
Did he **get** the car **washed**?
Why **have** you **gotten** the locks **changed**?

1. Use passive causatives with *get* to talk about services that people arrange for someone to do. *Have* and *get* usually have the same meaning in passive causatives.	**I got my teeth cleaned.** (The dentist cleaned my teeth.)
2. The form of the verb *get* changes with different tenses and modal verbs.	She**'s getting** her hair dyed right now. She **gets** her hair dyed every two months. She **hasn't gotten** her hair dyed recently. She**'s going to get** her hair dyed soon. She **shouldn't get** her hair dyed.

5 Complete the conversations. Use the correct form of *get* and the objects and verbs in parentheses.

1. **A:** Your hair looks great.

   B: Thanks. I ___got it cut___ (it / cut) last week at the new hair salon on First Street.

2. **A:** How's your eyesight?

   B: Excellent. I ___got my eyes checked___ (my eyes / check) last month.

3. **A:** These pants are too long. I need to ___get them shorten___ (them / shorten).

   B: You can take them to the tailor after work. He's open until seven o'clock.

4. **A:** Can you drive me to the mall?

   B: Sorry, my car is at the repair shop. I ___get it serviced___ (it / service) today.

5. **A:** I'll order a pizza. What time should we pick it up?

   B: Why don't we ___get it delivered___ (it / deliver)?

6. **A:** Do you have a credit card?

   B: No, but I'm going to get one. First, I have to ___get the application signed___ (the application / sign) by my parents.

7. **A:** Your car looks really clean. Did you wash it yourself?

   B: No, I ___got it washed___ (it / wash) at the local car wash.

8. **A:** I like the pharmacist at Green Street Pharmacy. He fills prescriptions quickly.

   B: Yes, I always go there to ___get my prescriptions filled___ (prescriptions / fill).

> **REAL ENGLISH**
>
> Use *by* + the agent when it is necessary to say who did the action.
>
> *Did you get the pictures taken **by your neighbor**?*
>
> *No, we had them taken **by a professional photographer**.*

PRACTICE

6 Look at the calendar for an Egyptian art exhibit. Today is April 10th. Complete the sentences. Use the correct form of *have* + object + past participle. More than one verb form may be used in some items.

APRIL	Staff Assignments for Egyptian Art Exhibit (✓ = done)			Jim Morton, Director, City Center Museum		
Sunday	Monday	Tuesday	Wednesday	Thursday	Friday	Saturday
	1 ✓ print exhibit catalog	2	3	4 ✓ record audio tour	5	6
7	8	9 ✓ paint gallery	10 TODAY	11 install lighting	12 unpack artworks	13
14	15	16	17 arrange art	18	19	20
21	22 write labels for artworks	23	24	25 take photographs of exhibit	26	27
28	29	30 design and print tickets				

1. On April 1st, the director, _had the catalog printed_ .

2. By the end of last week, he _had the audio tour recorded_ .

3. On April 9th, Mr. Morton _had the gallery painted_ .

4. Tomorrow, he _will have lighting installed_.

5. The day after the lighting is installed, _he will have the artworks unpacked_

6. The week of the 14th, he _will have the artworks arranged_

7. After the art is arranged and labeled, he _will have photographs taken of the exhibits_

8. At the end of the month, he _____ .

7 LISTEN & WRITE.

CD3-15

A Listen to the conversation about the exhibit. Decide who actually did each task. Check (✓) the correct column. Then compare your answers with a partner.

Task	The director did this.	Somebody else did this.
1. Painting the gallery		
2. Installing the lights		
3. Unpacking the artworks		
4. Arranging the artworks		
5. Preparing the labels		
6. Labeling the artworks		
7. Photographing the exhibit		
8. Designing and printing the tickets		

B Write three affirmative and three negative sentences about the museum director in exercise **A**. Use the correct form of *have* or *get*.

The director didn't paint the gallery. He had it painted by his assistants.

8 EDIT. Read the text. Find and correct five more errors with passive causatives.

The Maya Idea of Beauty

Thousand of years ago, the Maya often had things ~~do~~ *done* to themselves to improve their looks. This is shown in the Maya art that archaeologists have found. We can see from the art that Maya kings and nobles got holes to make in their teeth. Then they had pretty stones put in the holes. Ordinary Maya probably couldn't afford to have pretty stones in their teeth. Pictures show them with sharp, pointed teeth. They probably had their teeth make sharp to decorate themselves. Upper-class people had fancy tattoos on their bodies. Researchers believe that they didn't create the tattoos themselves. They must have had decorated their bodies with these designs. Today, some people do similar things to their bodies. For example, it is common for people to have their ears pierce. Other people get dyed their hair or their nails painted. They do these things to look good. Will people still be getting these things done hundreds of years from now, or will they think that people in the twenty-first century had some very strange habits?

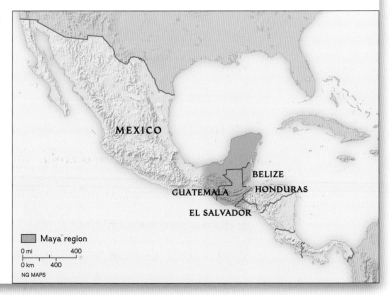

MEXICO

BELIZE

GUATEMALA   HONDURAS

EL SALVADOR

☐ Maya region

0 mi   400

0 km   400

NG MAPS

◄ This Maya sculpture may show Pacal, who ruled from 615 A.D. for 68 years.

9 APPLY.

A Circle the things that someone else usually does for you.

Clean:	home	car	teeth		
Cut:	hair	beard	nails	grass	
Do:	laundry	homework	dry-cleaning	nails	
Fix:	laptop	phone/tablet	TV	car	bike
Paint:	home				
Pay:	tuition	rent	medical bills		
Take Care of:	children	pets			
Wash:	hair	car	dishes		

B Work in a group. Ask and answer questions about the things your classmates have circled on the list.

A: *Who do you get to cut your hair?*

B: *I go to a hairdresser on Center Street.*

C Write four or five sentences about your group's responses. Use *have* and *get*.

Felipe gets his sister to cut his hair.

Last week Charles had to get his laptop fixed. He had it fixed at the Tech Center.

EXPLORE

CD3-16

1　READ the article about an animal researcher who is interested in more than good looks. What is Lucy Cooke's message for the world?

Funny looking or beautiful?

It is often said that beauty is in the eyes of the beholder.[1] That is certainly true for zoologist[2] Lucy Cooke. While most people prefer cute pandas and kittens to odd-looking frogs and sloths, Cooke does not. Instead of being **turned off** by less attractive creatures, she is fascinated by them. She looks beyond their appearance and tries to **find out** as much as possible about how they behave and adapt to their environments.

Consider the sloth. This slow-moving animal lives in the tropical forests of South and Central America. It often hangs upside-down in trees, **holding on** with its long claws. Most people think that the sleepy sloth is lazy, dirty, and stupid. However, Cooke is quick to **point out** that sloths have been greatly misunderstood. In fact, their behavior **helps** them **out** in the wild. Their slow metabolism[3] helps protect them from poisons in the leaves they eat, and moving slowly keeps them hidden from predators.[4]

Cooke is concerned that attractive animals get all the attention. It troubles her that there is much less research on "uncute" animals such as sloths and frogs, yet many of these animals are in danger of **dying out**. Cooke wants to show the world how some of the strangest-looking creatures deserve attention and protection. To **get** her message **across**, she takes advantage of the Internet. People can watch humorous videos online about her adventures with the unloved species of the world. Just watch Cooke's video about sloths—you will probably **end up** loving them as much as she does.

Fun Sloth Facts

- Sloths are great at hiding.
- Sloths spend up to 70% of their time resting.
- Sloths can take up to a month to digest a meal.

[1] **beauty is in the eye of the beholder:** people have different ideas about what is beautiful
[2] **zoologist:** a scientist who studies animals
[3] **metabolism:** the processes in the body that cause food to be used for energy and growth
[4] **predator:** an animal that lives by killing and eating others

point out = notice

▼ Sleeping sloth

▶ Lucy Cooke's goal is to save ugly and unloved creatures that are dying out.

2 CHECK. Answer the questions. Write complete sentences.

1. What kind of animals are most interesting to Lucy Cooke?

   _____

2. What quality of the sloth helps it survive in its environment?

   _____

3. According to Cooke, what is the problem with attractive animals?

   _____

4. How does Cooke communicate her message to the world?

   _____

3 DISCOVER. Complete the exercises to learn about the grammar in this lesson.

A Find these bold words in the article in exercise **1**. Write the missing words to complete the phrase.

1. **turned** ___off___   4. **dying** _____

2. **point** _____   5. **get** her message _____

3. **helps** them _____   6. **end** _____

B Look back at the article and find the verbs in exercise **A**. Then read the statement. Circle **T** for *true* or **F** for *false*.

When you add a preposition to a verb, it can change the meaning of the verb.   **T**   **F**

LEARN

10.5 Phrasal Verbs: Transitive and Intransitive

Phrasal Verbs	
Transitive	He **looked over** the contract carefully. _____Direct Object_____
Intransitive	We **grew up** quickly.

1. Phrasal verbs usually mean something different from the two or three words that are used to form them.	Phrasal Verb: **Look out!** (_look out_ = be careful) Regular Verb: **Look** out the window. Do you see the bird?
2. **Remember:** A transitive phrasal verb is followed by an object.	Could you **turn off the light**? _____Object_____
3. An intransitive phrasal verb cannot be followed by an object.	He **came over**.
4. Three-word phrasal verbs (_come up with_, _put up with_, _look forward to_) are always transitive.	Have you **come up with** an idea for project? I can't **put up with** his behavior. It's very bad. I'm **looking forward to** the party this weekend.
5. Phrasal verbs are more common in spoken English and informal writing. They are often used in place of one or more words that express the same meaning.	Informal: _put off_ The party was **put off** until next week. Formal: _postpone_ I have to **postpone** the meeting until next week.

See page **A4** for a list of transitive and intransitive phrasal verbs.

4 Complete the exercises.

A Circle the correct phrasal verb to complete each sentence.

1. Can you **make out /** (**point out**) a website with information about sloths?

2. My friend and I once visited a sloth sanctuary in Costa Rica. We had planned to spend an hour there, but we **looked up /** (**ended up**) staying all day.

3. The people who **look after / look for** the sloths in the sanctuary are kind.

4. The sanctuary does important work by preventing sloths from **dying out / helping out**.

5. Would you like to (**help out /** turn out) the sloth rescue group in your free time?

6. Lucy Cooke has **come after / come up with** many great ways to communicate her message.

7. I recently **found out / got out** how to join the Sloth Appreciation Society, which tries to help sloths.

8. I'm going to **keep out of /** (**keep up with**) the society's activities through its website.

B **ANALYZE THE GRAMMAR.** There are six sentences with transitive phrasal verbs in exercise **A**. In your notebook, write the number of each sentence and the transitive phrasal verb + object.

1. point out a website

10.6 Transitive Phrasal Verbs: Separable and Inseparable

Separable	Inseparable
He **looked over** the report. Direct Object He **looked** the report **over**. Direct Object	We can't **get over** the changes. Direct Object

1. Most transitive phrasal verbs are separable. The object may come after the phrasal verb or between the two parts of the phrasal verb.	Who **picked out** the birthday card? Who **picked** the birthday card **out**?
2. When the object is a pronoun (*me, you, him, . . .*), it comes between the two words.	✓ She didn't **pick** it **out**. I did. ✗ She didn't <u>pick out it</u>.
3. In an inseparable phrasal verb, the object or object pronoun comes after the two parts of the phrasal verb.	✓ I **came across** an interesting article. ✓ I **came across** it while doing research. ✗ I <u>came it across</u> yesterday.
4. Three-word phrasal verbs are always inseparable.	✓ Gary **looked up to** his older brother. ✗ Gary <u>looked up</u> his older brother <u>to</u>.

See pages **A5–A8** for a list of separable and inseparable phrasal verbs and their meanings.

Con pronombres van siempre en el medio (from no pueden ir al final) pero en el medio pueden ir pronombres u objetos

5 Complete the conversations with the correct form of the phrasal verb in parentheses and *her, him, it,* or *me.* You can check the meanings of the verbs on pages **A5–A8**.

1. **A:** Do you know the expression "Beauty is in the eye of the beholder"?

   B: Yeah. I ___looked it up___ (look up) on the Internet.

2. **A:** I saw an ad for a cool motorcycle. It's on sale. You should ___check that out___ (check out).

   B: No, thanks. Motorcycles ___turn me off___ (turn off).

3. **A:** Remember Jim from our high school? I ___run into him___ (run into) yesterday.

   B: Yes, I ___get together with him___ (get together with) sometimes. We play golf.

4. **A:** The first time my grandfather saw my grandmother, he ___fell for her___ (fall for). At first she didn't like him, and she refused to ___go out with him___ (go out with). He was really disappointed, and it took him a while to ___get over it___ (get over). But when they met again a few years later, she liked him a lot better . . . and eventually they got married!

   B: That's so romantic!

5. **A:** Vera, would you come with me to look for a wedding dress? I need someone to help me ___pick it up___ (pick out).

   B: Sure, I'd love to.

6. **A:** Colin, I see something strange on this X ray. I've never ___come across___ (come across) before in any other X ray.

   B: Let's ask Dr. Voltman to take a look.

PRACTICE

6 Circle the correct phrasal verbs to complete the paragraphs. You can check the meanings of the words on pages **A5–A8**.

What is beauty?

I read an interesting article about beauty the other day. I (1) **came across** / came up with it when I was (2) **looking after** / **looking up** something online. The article (3) **pointed out** / **picked out** that people around the world have different ideas about what beauty is. So many different things can be considered beautiful—human beings, works of art, music, and nature. Even if people (4) **go along with** / go over the idea that art, for example, is beautiful, they may not like the same kind of art. One person might love modern art, but it might (5) **turn off** / turn up another person.

One thing we do know is that beauty in all its different forms is something people just can't (6) give in / **give up**. People need beauty just like they need oxygen or water. It (7) **cheers them up** / shows them up when they are feeling sad, and it calms them down when they are feeling anxious.

Nobody can say for sure what beauty is, but some people have tried to (8) **figure it out** / think it up. One artist wanted to discover something that everyone in the world agreed was beautiful. He (9) **came up with** / came over an interesting idea, and he did experiments to test it. His research (10) **ended up** / made up showing that people around the world share at least one idea: a springtime scene with lakes, rivers, and forests is beautiful.

▲ Caryatids of Athens, Greece, show the classical Greek idea of beauty.

7 Match each bold phrasal verb with its correct meaning.

_c_ 1. They **put** their paintbrushes **away** after art class.

_j_ 2. Don't **give up**. You'll solve this problem if you keep trying.

_a_ 3. My winter coat was getting old, so I **gave** it **away**.

_b_ 4. He **put** his favorite shirt **on** to look his best.

_g_ 5. I asked the movie star for her autograph, but she **turned** my request **down**.

_h_ 6. In one fairy tale, a magician **turns** a frog **into** a handsome prince.

_f_ 7. **Turn on** the lights. I can't see anything.

_i_ 8. Lynn borrowed my laptop, but she **gave** it **back** last night.

_e_ 9. She doesn't like horror movies. They **turn** her **off**.

_d_ 10. I can't hear the TV. Can you **turn up** the volume?

a. give without charging money

b. place clothing, jewelry, or makeup on one's body

c. put something in its usual place

d. increase

e. make someone feel disgust

f. make equipment or lights start working

g. refuse

h. change to something different

i. return

j. quit

8 WRITE & SPEAK.

A Look at the meanings of the phrasal verbs in exercise **7**. Then complete the chart with an object for each phrasal verb. If the phrasal verb is separable, write the phrasal verb + object two ways.

give away	give away money	give money away
give back		
give up		
put away		
put on		
turn down		
turn into		
turn on		
turn up		

B Complete the sentences with your own ideas.

1. When I go to a special event, I put on _my favorite sneakers_.

2. I turn down invitations to parties when _I lost my day_.

3. When I'm at a party, I turn into a _good dancer_ person.

4. I once put aside money for _my first business_.

5. When _really want something for me_ something difficult, I don't give up.

6. I sometimes give away _my advices_.

7. When you _smell something strange in ur food_, you should always give them back.

8. People should turn on their phones when _they are in a party_.

C Work with a partner. Compare the sentences you wrote in exercise **B**.

9 EDIT. Read the conversation. Find and correct five more errors with phrasal verbs.

A: The other day I came ~~over~~ _across_ an interesting article. It was about a beautiful bird called the Gouldian finch.

B: What was so interesting about it?

A: Well, when a male finch chooses a mate, he uses his right eye to pick out her. For some reason, his right eye helps him choose a better mate.

B: That's strange. How did they figure that up?

A: They covered the finch's right eye. They noticed that with its left eye, the finch chose any bird as a mate.

B: Wow. It's amazing how animals and plants choose mates in different ways.

A: Well, choosing a mate is really important. If animals and plants choose the wrong mates, their species could die over.

B: What does that say about the way that people choose mates?

A: The article points that human beings also choose mates to keep their species alive.

B: So when people go over with each other for a while and then break up, are they really trying to stay alive?

A: You could look at it that way.

B: Or maybe they just can't put up each other with anymore!

A: That's possible, too.

Unit 10: L3

▼ Gouldian finches, Australia

10 APPLY.

A Write responses to the questions. Replace the <u>underlined</u> words with the correct form of the phrasal verbs from the box.

| fall for | figure out | ~~get across~~ | look up to | run into | stand out |

1. What idea about beauty do you want to <u>make others understand</u>?

   I want to get across the idea that beauty involves more than appearance.

2. Can beauty alone make a person <u>fall in love with</u> someone else?

   _____

3. What problem have you <u>understood after thinking about it</u> recently?

   _____

4. Have you ever <u>unexpectedly met</u> a friend in another country?

   _____

5. Do most young people <u>admire</u> famous people?

   _____

6. What kind of people <u>do you notice</u> in a crowd?

   _____

B Work in a group. Discuss your answers to the questions in exercise **A**.

A: *I want to get across the idea that beauty involves more than appearance.*

B: *I agree.*

Charts
10.1, 10.2,
10.5, 10.6

1 Complete the paragraph with six of the eight words from the box.

across	let	make	have	out	point	them	to

◀ A stick insect

Many animals are able to (1) _____ themselves look like their surroundings. This ability is called camouflage. Camouflage lets animals find food, and it also helps (2) _____ hide from predators. Scientists often (3) _____ out that stick insects are masters of camouflage.

Because of their stick-like shape and color, these tiny bugs of the forest look just like the leaves and twigs of trees and plants. They don't stand (4) _____ from the background, and this helps (5) _____ protect them. Sometimes the insects look harmless, but they are not. If you come (6) _____ an American stick insect, be careful. They're poisonous.

Charts
10.1–10.4

2 Complete each sentence with the correct form of the verb in parentheses.

1. Hundreds of years ago in Venice, rich people had fancy masks _____ (make) for big parties.

2. They got others _____ (make) their masks. They didn't make them themselves.

3. Some had mask makers _____ (design) the masks to look like famous characters.

4. Some got masks _____ (design) to show emotions such as jealousy and anger.

5. Nowadays some people have masks _____ (decorate) with feathers.

6. Others get artists _____ (decorate) their masks with jewels.

7. Sometimes people like to have costumes _____ (create) to go with the masks.

8. When they have experts _____ (create) the designs, the results can be incredible.

290 CAUSATIVE VERB PATTERNS AND PHRASAL VERBS

3 **LISTEN** to the conversation between two people in a costume store. Then circle the correct verb according to what you hear.

1. The customer **(lets)** / **helps** the salesperson see the invitation to the party.

2. The salesperson **makes** / **has** the customer walk over to the display of masks.

3. The Venetian mask **helps** / **lets** the wearer eat, drink, and talk.

4. The mask with the feathers always **makes** / **has** people feel beautiful and exciting.

5. The tiger mask will probably **help** / **have** the customer feel good.

6. The salesperson **had** / **made** the assistant wrap up the mask.

4 **EDIT.** Read the text. Find and correct six more errors with causative verb patterns and phrasal verbs.

The Mystery of Masks

Wearing masks lets people ~~to~~ hide their identity from others. This can help to create a feeling of mystery at a masquerade ball, a dance where people wear costumes. In a normal situation, you might be able to come up with some ideas about people's qualities because you can see their faces and expressions. You think about whether they are good looking and how often they smile. Their appearance gets you form certain opinions about them. It may help you to decide if you want to talk to them.

Some masks stand up from all the rest because they are so fancy. People may pay a lot of money to have made these masks. Do such amazing masks make you to want to meet the people who are wearing them? Once a friend of mine fell her husband for at a costume party before she ever saw his face. She loved his voice and personality, and she didn't think about his appearance at all. Sometimes a masquerade ball can turn it out to be a very special day.

5 **SPEAK.** Work in groups. Discuss the answers to these questions.

1. Why do some people enjoy putting on costumes? Why do others dislike it?

2. When was the last time you wore a costume? Describe it. How did it make you feel?

3. What kinds of costumes stand out at a party?

4. Give examples of animals or insects that use camouflage. How does it help them?

Connect the Grammar to Writing

1 READ & NOTICE THE GRAMMAR.

A What do people in your culture do to make themselves more attractive? How do they prepare themselves for special events? Tell a partner. Then read the blog.

Here comes the bride!

Hello, everyone. The last time I wrote, everyone in my family was looking forward to my sister's wedding. Well, the big day finally arrived, and it was my job to help her get ready. It is traditional for an Indian bride to wear elaborate[1] makeup and clothes.

My sister got her hair done at a salon, but she let me do her makeup. I used mascara and eyeliner to make her eyes stand out. Indian brides also have beautiful patterns painted on their hands with a reddish-brown dye called *henna*. I am not skilled enough to do this, so she had a professional henna artist paint her hands.

I helped her put a traditional *bindi* on her forehead, and then my mother and I helped her get dressed. My mother let my sister borrow some fancy gold jewelry.

My sister was stunning on her wedding day, and her husband looked attractive, too. He had gotten his hair cut, and his face was clean-shaven to show off his jawline and cheekbones. He was dressed in a modern suit. He also had on a cool expensive watch. He made his brother lend it to him for the wedding.

I'll write more about the wedding in my next post!

¹ **elaborate:** very fancy

GRAMMAR FOCUS

In the blog in exercise **A**, the writer uses the following types of causative verbs:

Have, let, and make	• show when one person causes someone to do something or gives permission to do something (. . . she **let me do** her makeup.)
Help	• shows when someone assists someone else (It was my job to **help her get** ready . . .)
Passive causatives	• talk about services that others do for someone (My sister **got her hair done** at a salon . . .)

B Read the blog in exercise **A** again. Underline the examples of causative verbs.

C Complete the diagram with information from the blog in exercise **A**. What did the bride and groom get or have done to look attractive for the wedding? Discuss your answers with a partner.

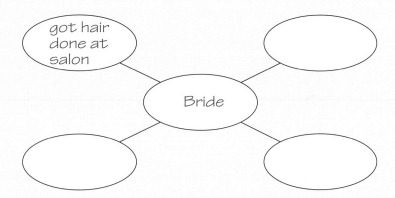

2 BEFORE YOU WRITE.

A Work with a partner. Brainstorm ways that men and women change their appearance to go to parties and weddings or to job interviews. Use exercise **1A** for ideas.

B Make a diagram like the one in exercise **1C**. Write ways that people from your culture make themselves look more attractive.

WRITING FOCUS   Gender and Adjective Choice

In English, some adjectives that describe appearance are more commonly used only for men or women. Some adjectives are used for either.

beautiful, pretty, stunning (for women)
handsome (for men)
attractive, striking, good looking (women or men)

---

3 WRITE a blog entry describing a time when you helped someone prepare for a special event. Write two or three paragraphs. How did you make this person look different? Use your diagram from exercise **2B** and the blog in exercise **1A** to help you.

4 SELF ASSESS. Read your blog entry. Underline the verb forms. Then use the checklist to assess your work.

☐ I used causative verbs with objects correctly. [10.1, 10.2]

☐ I used the passive causative correctly. [10.3, 10.4]

☐ I used phrasal verbs correctly. [10.5, 10.6]

☐ I used appropriate adjectives for men and women. [WRITING FOCUS]

UNIT 11 The Power of Images

Relative Clauses

▲ A time-exposure image shows star trails over Geghard Monastery, Armenia.

EXPLORE

CD3-18

1 READ the web page and comments on a photography site. Then write your own comment below.

Myphotospace
share like post

Photo by Dipanjan Mitra

This photo was taken in the Sundarbans in West Bengal, India. The Sundarbans is an area **that is famous for its mangrove forest and royal Bengal tigers**. In this photo, the farmers **that live in the area** had recently experienced a devastating storm **that flooded the fields and destroyed crops**. You can see the water from the flood. However, the scene is not sad. Maybe that's because the boy, **whose feet dangle over the water**, seems untouched by the flood. We feel his calm.

Comments:

Greta M. Beautiful picture. I like the way it captures the child, **who seems to be living in the moment**.

Raul O. This photo, **which shows the highs and lows of life in the Sundarbans**, sends a powerful message. It shows how people, especially children, can survive even in the most difficult circumstances.

Post a comment _____

2 CHECK. Answer the questions about the web page in exercise **1**. Write complete sentences.

1. Where was the photo taken?

   _____

2. What is this area known for?

   _____

3. What weather recently affected this region?

   _____

4. How did it affect the region?

   _____

3 DISCOVER. Complete the exercises to learn about the grammar in this lesson.

A Write the missing words in each sentence from the Web page. Then draw an arrow to the word they describe.

1. In this photo, the farmers _who live in the area_ had recently experienced a devastating storm that flooded the fields and destroyed crops.

2. Maybe that's because the boy, _____, seems untouched by the flood.

3. I like the way it captures the child, _____.

4. This photo, _____, sends a powerful message.

B Look back at the words *which*, *who*, *whose*, and *that* in the clauses you wrote in exercise **A**. Complete each statement with the correct word/s.

1. _____Who_____ and _____ are in clauses that describe people.

2. _____ and _____ are in clauses that describe things.

3. _____ is in clauses that describe possession.

LEARN

11.1 Subject Relative Clauses

After the Main Clause

This is the website. The website sells photos by Russian photographers.

This is the website that sells photos by Russian photographers.
Subject Relative Clause

Inside the Main Clause

The tourists were from Hawaii. The tourists took photos of the ski slopes.

The tourists who took photos of the ski slopes were from Hawaii.
Subject Relative Clause

1. A relative clause describes a noun or indefinite pronoun (*someone, anyone, something*) in a sentence. The relative clause* comes after the noun or pronoun it describes.	The people **that took the photos** are my friends. Someone **who was at the party** took this photo.
2. A subject relative clause starts with a relative pronoun (*that, which,* or *who*). The relative pronoun is the subject of the relative clause.	The people left. The people were here an hour ago. The people **that** were here an hour ago left.

3. In a subject relative clause, use:
   a. *that* or *who* as a subject for people
   b. *that* or *which* as a subject for places, things, animals, or ideas
	a. That's the student **who got the scholarship.**
	b. Phones **that have computing ability** are called smartphones.

4. The verb in a subject relative clause agrees with the noun it describes.	There is **an app** that **shows** the weather forecast. There are **apps** that **show** the weather forecast.
5. **Remember:** The subject and verb in the main clause must agree.	**The photographer** who photographs animals **is going** to the Serengeti.

*Relative clauses are also called *adjective clauses*.

4 Underline five more relative clauses in the paragraph. Then draw an arrow from the relative pronoun to the noun or pronoun it describes.

Today anyone who has a digital camera can produce a clear photo. However, that is not enough to make it a great photo. Photographers who want to take powerful shots have to make sure that the photo has good composition. In photography, composition is the way that things or people in a picture are placed, or positioned. Look at some photos of your friends or family, and you'll see what I mean. Where are the people in the photo? Are they standing in the center with a lot of empty space in the background? If so, the picture probably isn't very interesting. Photographs are more striking when they show someone or something that is on the right or left, or off-center. In addition, a picture that does not have too many details will not have a clear focus. So think carefully about how you take your photos. Photos that have good composition will be the most successful.

5 Complete the exercises.

A Complete the advice for photographers. Write *who* or *which* and the correct form of the verb in parentheses.

1. When you're just starting out, don't buy equipment ___which costs___ (cost) a lot.

2. People _____ (keep) their camera with them at all times will get better photos.

3. Places _____ (not seem) unusual at first might still make great photos.

4. Look at photography magazines and websites _____ (can offer) you a range of information on technique.

5. Look closely at a photo _____ (demonstrate) strong composition and lighting.

6. Take a workshop from a photographer _____ (do) interesting work.

7. Copy the style of someone _____ (take) pictures that you admire.

8. Avoid subjects _____ (might be) extremely difficult to photograph.

B **SPEAK.** Work with a partner. Read the sentences in exercise **A** aloud, but change the relative pronouns to *that*.

> **REAL ENGLISH**
>
> The relative pronoun *that* is more common than *which* in subject relative clauses.

6 Read the sentences about photos from this book. Circle the correct words.

1. The leopard seal that **was playing** / **were playing** with Paul Nicklen **was** / **were** gentle. (pages 32–33)

2. The photo which **shows** / **show** mountains of Kauai **are** / **is** especially beautiful. (page 39)

3. The woman who **are sitting** / **is sitting** at the floor of the ice cave **has been taking** / **have been taking** pictures of ice formations with a special camera. (pages 90–91)

4. The old woman and girl who **appear** / **appears** in this picture **is from** / **are from** the Navajo tribe. (pages 114–115)

5. The girls that **are facing** / **is facing** away from us **lives** / **live** in Kabul, Afghanistan. (pages 142–143)

6. The sea turtle that **are drifting** / **is drifting** by the scuba diver **has never injured** / **have never injured** anyone. (page 179)

7. The volunteers who **work** / **works** for WWOOF **have been collecting** / **has been collecting** heather from a flower garden. (page 192)

8. The flowers that **has bloomed** / **have bloomed** on the cereus cactus **comes out** / **come out** only at night. (pages 246–247)

11.2 Non-Identifying Subject Relative Clauses

1. A non-identifying relative clause* gives extra information about a noun in the sentence. You don't need this information to understand who or what the noun refers to.	Cy went to Peru, **which is a beautiful place to visit.**
2. The relative pronoun *that* cannot be used in a non-identifying subject relative clause. Use *who* or *which*.	✓ Dave's father, **who lived in Peru**, always liked meeting people. ✗ Dave's father, <u>that</u> lived in Peru, always liked meeting people.
3. Use a comma before and after a non-identifying relative clause that is within a main clause.	✓ Facebook, **which started in 2004**, has over a billion users. ✗ Facebook <u>which started in 2004</u> has over a billion users.
4. Identifying and non-identifying clauses can change the meaning of a sentence.	My uncle who lives in New York owns a restaurant. (I also have an uncle in Los Angeles.) My uncle, who lives in New York, owns a restaurant. (I have only one uncle.)

*Non-identifying relative clauses are also called *non-restrictive relative clauses*.

7 Write the correct relative pronoun and add one or two commas to each relative clause.

1. Photo sharing, ____which____ is now extremely popular, has changed over time.

2. Websites like Flickr _____ became available in 2010 offered lots of space.

3. Facebook _____ started in 2004 allows people to share messages and photos.

4. College students _____ were the first users of Facebook were later followed by users of all ages.

5. I just bought the latest smartphone _____ has a powerful built-in camera.

6. Kevin Systrom and Mike Kreiger _____ wanted a way to edit photos started Instagram in 2010.

7. Instagram _____ was originally an application for iPhones is now available for Android devices.

8. Have you ever met Dr. Jones _____ teaches Photography 101?

9. Amsterdam _____ is the capital of the Netherlands is a wonderful city to photograph.

10. The photography exhibition was created by my friend Laura _____ is a professional artist.

8 Complete the exercises.

A Combine the sentences. Make the second sentence of each pair a relative clause with *which* or *who*. Use correct punctuation.

1. Photography is a highly competitive profession. Photography can be very creative.

   Photography, which can be very creative, is a highly competitive profession.

2. My friend Erin is a great photographer. Erin has just started his own business.

   _____

   _____

3. Online photography classes can be a great way to learn the basics. Online photography classes are often free.

   _____

   _____

4. Disposable cameras are popular with tourists. Disposable cameras are usually good for one use only.

   _____

   _____

5. Digital storytelling is popular with Professor Wong. Professor Wong has experience telling stories with photos.

   _____

   _____

6. Displays on cameras give you valuable information. Displays on cameras can be difficult to use.

   _____

   _____

7. Camera reviews can help you choose a good camera. Camera reviews are easy to find online.

   _____

   _____

8. Digital photographs are extremely popular. Digital photographs are inexpensive.

   _____

   _____

B Work with a partner. Compare your answers from exercise **A**.

11.3 Relative Clauses with *Whose*

> The photographer has a great website. His photos feature wildlife in Africa.
>
> The photographer **whose photos feature wildlife in Africa** has a great website.
>   *Relative Clause*

1. Use *whose* + a noun in a relative clause to show possession. *Whose* replaces a possessive adjective or noun (*his, her, its, their, Jim's, . . .*).	I know the woman. Her son has won the award. I know the woman **whose son has won the award.**
2. *Whose* is used for people. It is also used for places, things, animals, and ideas.	New Zealand is a country **whose** official languages include English and Maori.
3. Relative clauses with *whose* can be identifying or non-identifying. Non-identifying clauses must have a comma before and after them.	People **whose seats are up front** can go in first. Mr. and Mrs. An, **whose seats are up front**, can go in first.
4. **Be careful!** Do not repeat the possessive pronoun in a relative clause with *whose*.	✓ Will the person **whose cell phone is ringing** please turn it off? ✗ Will the person <u>whose his</u> cell phone is ringing please turn it off?

9 Underline the relative clause in each sentence. Then draw an arrow from *whose* to the noun it modifies.

1. The statues, <u>whose faces are difficult to see</u>, show a king and gods. (pages 196–197)

2. Does the frog, whose face peeks out from the mushroom, feel the rain? (pages 234–235)

3. Jimbo Bazoobi is an Australian citizen whose goat Gary has become famous. (page 249)

4. An insect whose wings display beautiful colors is a hawk moth. (pages 266–267)

5. The sloth, whose eyes are closed, sleeps peacefully. (page 282)

6. The starry night picture was taken in Armenia, whose sky shows a meteor. (pages 294–295)

7. The photographer, whose image captures star trails, used time exposure. (pages 294–295)

10 Complete the exercises.

A Combine the sentences. Make the second sentence in each pair a relative clause with *whose*. Add punctuation if necessary.

1. The woman in the photo is from the Maori tribe. Her name is unknown.

   The woman in the photo, whose name is unknown, is from the Maori tribe.

2. The Maori woman in the photo has a mysterious expression. Her eyes are deep brown.

   _____

   _____

3. New Zealand is 14.6 percent Maori. New Zealand's population is mostly European.

_____

_____ .

4. The Maori still live there today. Their ancestors came to New Zealand around 1250–1300 CE.

_____

_____ .

5. The Maori mainly speak English. Their native language is close to Polynesian.

_____

_____ .

6. New Zealand is a beautiful country. Its terrain is mountainous.

_____

_____ .

7. The Maori have lost some of their traditions. Their culture has changed.

_____

_____ .

8. We should try to respect people. Their cultures are different from ours.

_____

_____ .

B Work with a partner. Compare your answers from exercise **A**.

◄ a Maori woman

PRACTICE

11 Complete the exercises.

A Complete the paragraph with relative clauses. Use *that, who, which,* or *whose* and the words in parentheses. Use the simple present.

Photography helps us to understand human psychology. The photographer is important because it is his or her (1) ___viewpoint that comes___ (viewpoint / come) through in the photo. (2) _____ (the people / appear) in the photo are also relevant. People (3) _____ (expressions / show) more than one emotion are the most interesting. The way people interact can also say a lot. (4) _____ (people / influence) others or (5) _____ (people / be) powerful often stand in the center or in front. (6) _____ (groups of people / stand) together sometimes show a close relationship. (7) _____ (individuals / be) not comfortable with the group may stand off to the side or look away. A person (8) _____ (eyes / meet) the camera shows a connection with the photographer. Colors are also important. (9) _____ (red and orange / be) warm colors, attract our eyes first. (10) _____ (green and blue / be) cool colors, seem to move away from us. The photographer's choices are important in creating the mood of the picture.

B Write the numbers of the two non-identifying relative clauses in exercise **A**.

_____ , _____

12 Combine the sentences with relative clauses. Use *that, which, who,* or *whose*. Sometimes more than one relative pronoun is possible.

1. Photography can capture moments. The moments will be remembered forever.

   Photography can capture moments that will be remembered forever.

2. Photography is an activity. The activity will always hold your interest.

   _____

   _____

3. A photograph can communicate ideas. The ideas are hard to express in words.

   _____

   _____

4. Photos of loved ones become important possessions. The loved ones are far away.

   _____

   _____

5. With photography, we speak to people. Their language is different from ours.

_____

_____

6. Sharing photos allows you to connect to people. People are important to you.

_____

_____

7. Photography is an art. Its origins go back to the mid-1820s

_____

_____

8. The first surviving photograph shows a landscape. The photograph was taken in 1825 or 1826.

_____

_____

13 **PRONUNCIATION.** Read the chart and listen to the examples. Then complete the exercises.

CD3-19

PRONUNCIATION	Pauses with Non-Identifying Relative Clauses

Speakers pause before and after non-identifying relative clauses. The pauses make the information easier to understand. In writing, commas are used to indicate the pauses.

Examples:

Colors, which affect our feelings, are important in photography.
Black and white, which are not colors but tones, are important for contrast.

CD3-20

A Listen to the sentences about a photo contest on the Internet. Insert commas where you hear pauses. Not all of the sentences contain non-identifying relative clauses.

1. The contest which is held once a year has a $5000 cash prize.

2. Many people who have won the prize have gone on to be successful photographers.

3. The judges who are professional photographers consider the creativity of each photo.

4. The judges who do not always agree have a difficult task.

5. The contestant whose photo gets the highest score is the winner.

6. The photo which won last year's prize was taken by a 15-year-old.

B Work with a partner. Take turns reading the sentences from exercise **A**.

14 LISTEN.

CD3-21

A Look at the two images from a photography contest and listen to the judges discuss them. Which photo is the winner, photo 1 or photo 2?

Photo 1

Photo 2

B Listen to the conversation again. Circle the correct answers.

1. Where was the photo with the buildings and the sea taken?

   a. In Malé, in the Republic of Maldives.   b. In a Mexican town.

2. What is bothering the judge about Photo 1?

   a. It's not realistic.   b. The composition.

3. What part of Photo 1 does the judge want to look at?

   a. The buildings in the back.   b. He is not sure what to look at.

4. What should Photo 1 have shown more of to provide a better perspective?

   a. The buildings.   b. The sea.

5. What makes Photo 1 powerful?

   a. Its warmth and liveliness.   b. The way the photographer uses space.

6. Why is the photographer of the Mexican buildings the winner?

   a. The color in his photo is intense.   b. His technical abilities and composition are excellent.

C Listen to the sentences and complete the relative clause in each. Add commas where necessary. Then listen again and check your answers. Listen for pauses where you put commas.

1. The photo _that shows the buildings and the sea_ was taken in Malé.

2. Malé _____ of the Republic of Maldives is located in the Indian Ocean.

3. Let's talk about the photo _____ in a small Mexican town.

4. We see a hand _____ .

5. The photographer has excellent technical abilities and a composition _____ the viewer's attention.

15 APPLY. Work in a group. Look through this book and choose three or four photos to discuss. Use relative clauses where appropriate. Then write the sentences in your notebook.

I really like the photo (on pages 294-295) that shows the star trails. In this picture, which was taken in Armenia, the photographer used time exposure to show the meteor moving in the sky.

EXPLORE

CD3-23

1 **READ** the article about photojournalist Michael "Nick" Nichols, whose work takes him deep into the wilderness. What is his goal?

A LOOK INSIDE

Shooting the Real Story

Michael "Nick" Nichols started taking pictures in his Photography 101 class over thirty years ago, and he hasn't stopped since. His passion has always been to photograph the things **that he cares about**. Today, Nichols is an award-winning photojournalist whose powerful images in *National Geographic Magazine* tell real stories about endangered lands and wildlife.

For Nichols, telling the real story is key. He takes pictures of animals and places whose future is threatened. He wants the photos to motivate people and governments to protect these endangered animals and lands. Thanks to Nichols's extraordinary skill and determination, he has been successful. His work with conservationist Michael Fay in Central Africa is a good example. Fay walked 2000 miles (3219 kilometers) from Congo's deepest rainforest to the Atlantic Coast of Gabon. Nichols and Fay studied Africa's wilderness and listed 13 areas that were critical habitats. As a result, the president of Congo made the 13 endangered areas **that Fay and Nichols had identified** into national parks. Over the years, Nichols's pictures have told the stories of several species that are rapidly disappearing in the wild. His images of lions, tigers, elephants, and gorillas in their natural habitats are unforgettable.

Nichols knows his photos need to be realistic. If they aren't, people won't believe the stories **that the images tell**. "I can't stand a photograph **that I've made**, no matter how cool it is, if I set it up,"[2] he says. The wild and unpredictable nature of the animals is a great challenge. However, Nichols has a special ability to work in rough environments **which others find too difficult**. Time and time again, he shows the way life truly is in some of the most remote parts of the world.

¹ **set up:** arrange or create something

2 CHECK. Correct the error in each sentence to make it true according to the article.

1. Michael "Nick" Nichols is concerned about the future of zoo animals.

2. Fay walked a total of 500 miles through Africa's wilderness.

3. Nichols thinks it is most important for his photos to look cool.

4. The subjects of Nichols's photographs are usually easy to manage.

5. Nichols works in some of the most populated parts of the world.

3 DISCOVER. Complete the exercises to learn about the grammar in this lesson.

A Look at the bold relative clauses in the sentences from the article. Write the missing relative pronoun.

1. His passion has always been to photograph the things _____ **he cares about**.

2. The president of Congo made the 13 endangered areas _____ **Fay and Nichols had identified** into national parks.

3. People won't believe the stories _____ **the images tell**.

4. "I can't stand a photograph _____ **I've made**, no matter how cool it is, if I set it up," he says.

5. Nichols has a special ability to work in rough environments _____ **others find too difficult**.

B Work with a partner. Look at the relative pronouns you wrote in exercise **A**. Are they the subjects of the relative clauses?

◄ A pride of African lions walks through tall savanna grass. Masai Mara National Reserve, Kenya.

LEARN

11.4 Object Relative Clauses

After the Main Clause

We liked many works in the photo contest. Zeyna won <u>the contest</u>.
— Object

We liked many works in the photo contest **that Zeyna won**.
Object Relative Clause

Inside the Main Clause

The photo tells a story. Ricardo posted <u>the photo</u> on the Internet.
— Object

The photo **that Ricardo posted on the Internet** tells a story.
Object Relative Clause

1. In an object relative clause, the relative pronoun is the object. The relative pronoun may be *that, who, whom,* or *which.*	The wallet belongs to her. You found <u>the wallet</u>. Object The wallet **that you found** belongs to her. Object Relative Clause
2. The verb in an object relative clause agrees with the subject of the relative clause.	The trip **that Joe is taking** will be fun. The trip **that Joe and Ann are taking** will be fun.

3. Object relative clauses can be identifying or non-identifying.
  a. In identifying object relative clauses, the relative pronoun can be omitted.
  b. In non-identifying object relative clauses, use commas, but do not omit the relative pronoun.
	a. The man **that she was interviewing** is famous.
	   The man **she was interviewing** is famous.
	b. Vietnam, **which my family left over 30 years ago**, has changed a lot.
	✗ Vietnam <u>my family left over 30 years ago</u> has changed a lot.

4. Do not use *that* as the object relative pronoun in a non-identifying relative clause.	✓ Dr. Tam, **who(m) we have met**, is a surgeon. ✗ Dr. Tam, <u>that</u> we have met, is a surgeon.
5. Do not repeat the object at the end of an identifying object relative clause. The relative pronoun is the object.	✓ Where's the man **you were helping**? ✗ Where's the man you were helping <u>him</u>?

4 Complete the exercises.

A Complete each sentence with *that, who, whom,* or *which.* Sometimes more than one answer is possible.

1. Michael "Nick" Nichols has photographed 27 stories for *National Geographic Magazine*. This is work
   _____that_____ he has enjoyed.

2. He photographed orphan elephants _____ he saw in an elephant nursery in Nairobi.

3. The elephant nursery has created a home for the elephants _____ it has saved.

> **REAL ENGLISH**
>
> In formal English, *whom* is sometimes used instead of *who* in object relative clauses.
>
> *The employees* **whom the director dismissed** *had all worked at the bank for over 15 years.*

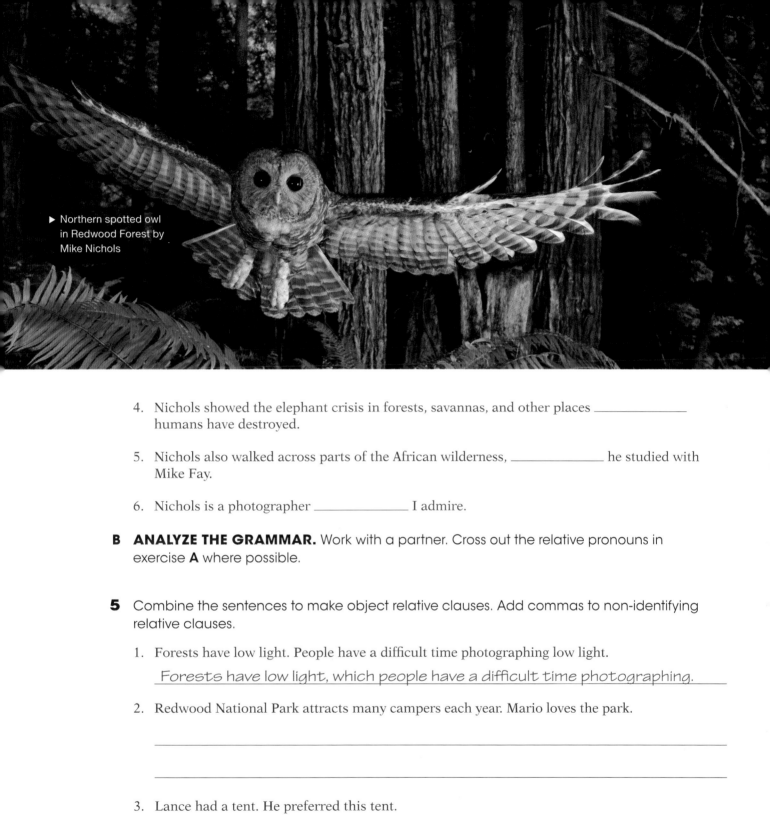

▶ Northern spotted owl in Redwood Forest by Mike Nichols

4. Nichols showed the elephant crisis in forests, savannas, and other places _____ humans have destroyed.

5. Nichols also walked across parts of the African wilderness, _____ he studied with Mike Fay.

6. Nichols is a photographer _____ I admire.

B ANALYZE THE GRAMMAR. Work with a partner. Cross out the relative pronouns in exercise **A** where possible.

5 Combine the sentences to make object relative clauses. Add commas to non-identifying relative clauses.

1. Forests have low light. People have a difficult time photographing low light.

   Forests have low light, which people have a difficult time photographing.

2. Redwood National Park attracts many campers each year. Mario loves the park.

   _____

   _____

3. Lance had a tent. He preferred this tent.

   _____

   _____

4. Emin ate the dinner. He had cooked the dinner over an open fire.

   _____

   _____

5. Joe was very knowledgable. Nancy asked him for directions.

_____

_____

6. The redwood trees were beautiful. The campers saw them.

_____

_____

11.5 Object Relative Clauses with Prepositions

After the Main Clause	Inside the Main Clause
I like the professor. I spoke to <u>him</u>. I like the professor **who I spoke to**. Relative Clause	The student left the program. I met with <u>him</u>. The student **that I met with** left the program. Relative Clause

1. A relative pronoun (*that, which, who,* or *whom*) can be the object of a preposition. The preposition usually comes after the verb in an object relative clause.	The movie **that we were talking about** won an award. The photos **that we were looking at** were amazing.
2. **Remember:** We often omit object relative pronouns from identifying relative clauses in conversation and informal writing.	The meeting **that I forgot about** was important. The meeting **I forgot about** was important.
3. In formal English, the preposition can come at the beginning of the object relative clause, before *whom* (for people) or *which* (for things).	My father, **after whom I was named**, died before I was born. The article **to which you are referring** is no longer available.
4. **Be careful!** Do not use a preposition + *who* or *that*.	✗ The person <u>to who</u> I sent the message isn't here. ✗ The club <u>of that</u> she is a member is private.

6 Complete the sentences. Use *that, which, who,* or *whom* or a preposition (*about, for, in, with*).

1. The profession _____ I'm going to tell you about is quite challenging.

2. Portrait photography, which most people don't know much _____, is my job.

3. The people for _____ I work are called clients.

4. Clients describe the kind of portraits they're looking _____ when I meet them.

5. I enjoy the children whom I work _____.

6. The contract on _____ we agree gets finalized.

7. I go to the home _____ which the photo shoot will take place early in the day.

8. I have to get the people _____ I take pictures of to relax.

9. My clients review the photographs _____ I take.

10. I always thank the people _____ I take pictures of.

7 Combine the sentences to make object relative clauses with prepositions. Use *that, which,* or *who(m)*. More than one answer is possible.

1. Take photos of areas. Endangered animals are found in the areas.

   Take photos of areas that endangered animals are found in.

2. Look up information on the animals. You take pictures of the animals.

   _____

3. Volunteer for a citizen science project. You care about the project.

   _____

4. Take photos for environmental groups. You want to contribute to the groups.

   _____

5. Take photos of environmental projects. You have volunteered for these projects.

   _____

6. Write information about the scientists. You work with the scientists.

   _____

7. Be respectful of natural areas. You work in the areas.

   _____

8. Collect stories of the subjects. You have taken pictures of the subjects.

   _____

9. Know the issues. People often argue about these issues.

   _____

10. Start a blog about current topics. People will be interested in these topics.

   _____

PRACTICE

8 Complete the sentences. Circle all the correct answers.

1. Photographers _____ include Annie Griffiths.

   (a.) who National Geographic works with

   b. that Griffiths which National Geographic works with

   (c.) that National Geographic works with

   (d.) National Geographic works with

2. Griffiths was one of the first women _____.

   a. to whom National Geographic gave an assignment

   b. National Geographic gave an assignment to her

   c. National Geographic gave an assignment to

   d. that National Geographic gave an assignment to

3. Some of the countries _____ include Australia, New Zealand, and Jordan.

   a. that Griffiths has worked in

   b. Griffiths has worked in

   c. in which Griffiths has worked

   d. which Griffiths has worked

4. Many of the strangers _____ have been friendly.

   a. Griffiths has met with

   b. that Griffiths has met with

   c. who Griffiths has met with

   d. to which Griffiths has met with

5. The people in Pakistan _____ were always warm and hospitable.

   a. which she stayed with

   b. that she stayed with

   c. she stayed with

   d. whom she stayed with

◀ A child peers between her sisters' robes in southern Pakistan.

6. The Zambian natives _____ allowed her to take the pictures.

   a. with whom she went swimming   c. who she went swimming with

   b. which she went swimming with   d. she went swimming with

7. Griffiths wants people to understand the women _____.

   a. she has taken photos of   c. of whom she has taken photos

   b. whom she has taken photos of them   d. of which she has taken photos

8. Griffiths and an organization _____ help women and girls in developing countries.

   a. that she started   c. which she started

   b. whom she started   d. she started

9 Complete the nature photographers' website with object relative clauses. More than one answer is possible.

Frequently Asked Questions

1. **What parts of your job do you like the most?**

   The parts of my job _____*that I like the most*_____ are meeting new people and doing something artistic every day.

2. **What do you eat when you are on assignment?**

   The food _____ isn't very good. In fact, sometimes it's absolutely awful.

3. **Do you usually take your family with you?**

   No, my trips are not fun for them. The only people _____ are assistants to help with the lighting on complex assignments.

4. **Do you work with local guides and translators, or do you use assistants for that kind of work?**

   The guides and translators _____ are always local people.

5. **Have you ever been frightened by a wild animal?**

   One time there was a gorilla _____. It came very close and looked at me. I didn't know what it was going to do.

6. **What do you most enjoy taking pictures of?**

   The subjects _____ are endangered species.

7. **Has the average person heard of the animals you photograph?**

   Probably not. I like to photograph unusual creatures, the ones _____

   _____. Photographs of uncommon animals can increase people's awareness of them.

8. **Do you ever observe other photographers?**

   Yes. I learn something from every photographer _____, from wildlife photographers to celebrity photographers.

10 LISTEN.

A Complete the paragraph about Joel Sartore, a longtime photographer for *National Geographic Magazine* and other publications. Use the information in the box to write relative clauses. Add commas where necessary.

> They may never see certain animals.
> He has great passion for his projects.
> ~~He has photographed many subjects.~~
> He is deeply committed to the Photo Ark project.
> He has traveled all over the world for his magazine assignments.

Joel Sartore is known for his ability to tell compelling stories about a wide range of topics. The subjects (1) _he has photographed_ range from beekeepers to soccer fans. He is also deeply concerned about animals that are in danger of extinction. Therefore, in addition to his magazine assignments (2) _____,

he has initiated a few projects of his own. One is called the Photo Ark. The goal of the Photo Ark project (3) _____ is to bring people eye to eye with certain animals (4) _____ and to make them care about these creatures. Take a look at some of Sartore's photos online. You will begin to appreciate the great passion (5) _____.

B Listen to the professor and the students discuss Joel Sartore. Check your answers.

CD3-24

▶ Sartore photographed this female Diana monkey as part of his Photo Ark project.

11 **EDIT.** Read the text. Find and correct five more errors with relative clauses. There is more than one way to correct some errors.

▲ Artist JR with exhibit

whose
JR is a French street artist ~~who~~ public photography exhibits have appeared in over 100 countries. His project, which JR calls it _Inside Out_, requires the general public to interact with his pictures. The idea is for people to share photos of themselves in public spaces to support ideas about that they care. Here is how it works: special photo booths in which people can take their own pictures there are set up. The self-portraits are then printed and made into huge posters are displayed on the street. These photos attract attention to the causes, such as human rights.

JR, for who _Inside Out_ is a way to make the world a better place, believes in the power of ordinary people. He is convinced that they can create positive change in the world. In JR's words, "Together, we'll turn the world inside out."

12 APPLY.

A Match the photojournalists with the issues that are most important to them.

_____ 1. Annie Griffiths   a. endangered species

_____ 2. Michael Nichols   b. life in the wild

_____ 3. Joel Sartore   c. women and children

B Write sentences in your notebook to describe the work of each photojournalist in exercise **A**. Include information that you learned in this lesson. Use relative clauses.

Annie Griffiths, who tries to help women and children in developing countries, has met many people in her travels.

C Imagine that you are a photojournalist who is concerned about a global issue, such as world hunger. What do you want to photograph and why? Write sentences using relative clauses in your notebook.

I want to take pictures of natural disasters, which can change people's lives In a single minute.

EXPLORE

CD3-25

1 READ the website about films in India. How are Bollywood films powerful for Indians living outside of their country?

Bollyblog
news

like   share   post

The Changing Face of Bollywood

The Indian film industry has been an important part of Indian cultural life for many years. The center of the industry, **nicknamed Bollywood**, is located in Mumbai (formerly Bombay). Bollywood, **where mostly Hindi language films are made**, makes over 1000 films a year. These days, the films are enjoyed by people around the world.

In the past, the movies were set in India and included singing and dancing, acting, romance, and always a happy ending. This type of film, **mixing all of these elements together**, was called *masala*. In Hindi this means a mixture of spices.

Modern times brought changes. Large numbers of Indians were living in other places: Asia, Africa, the Caribbean, Australia, Europe, and North America. In the late 1990s, **when new technology was developing**, Bollywood filmmakers realized they could make films for this diaspora[1] with satellite television, DVDs, and the Internet. The films were made with modern life in mind. The main characters were often Indians **living outside their country**. The films were shot where these Indians lived and in India. The new films were a bit different from *masala*s, but still about Indian values and traditions.

Bollywood films have had a powerful effect on the Indian diaspora. Even for Indians living far away, the films connect them to their homeland. Thanks to Bollywood, there is now a stronger sense of identity and community among Indians all over the world.

[1] **diaspora:** people who come from a particular nation, but who now live in many different parts of the world

2 CHECK. Read each statement about the article. Write **T** for *true* or **F** for *false*.

_____ 1.   Bollywood has made a total of 1000 films.

_____ 2.   The capital, Delhi, is the center of the Indian movie industry.

_____ 3.   *Masala* films usually end sadly.

_____ 4.   It is not unusual to see scenes outside of India in today's Bollywood films.

_____ 5.   Indian films help connect Indians living in other countries to India.

3 DISCOVER. Complete the exercises to learn about the grammar in this lesson.

A   Complete the sentences to match the sentences from the website. Change the underlined words.

1.   The center of the industry, <u>which is nicknamed Bollywood</u>, is located in Mumbai.

The center of the industry, <u>nicknamed Bollywood</u>, is located in Mumbai.

2.   This type of film, <u>which mixed all of these elements together</u>, was called *masala*.

This type of film, _____ all of these elements together, was called *masala*.

3.   The main characters were often Indians <u>who live</u> outside their country.

The main characters were often Indians _____ outside their country.

B   Underline the relative clauses that begin with *when* or *where* in the article. Circle the nouns that *when* and *where* refer to.

LEARN

11.6 Reduced Relative Clauses

The woman <u>who stars in the movie</u> has a beautiful voice.

The woman **starring in the movie** has a beautiful voice.

1. A subject relative clause can be reduced or shortened to a relative phrase.	The girl <u>who was riding the bike</u> fell off. The girl **riding the bike** fell off.
2. In a relative phrase, the relative pronoun (*who, that, which*) and any form of *be* is omitted.	People <u>who are driving hybrid cars</u> like them. People **driving hybrid cars** like them. The film <u>that was shown last night</u> was exciting. The film **shown last night** was exciting. He is the person <u>who is most interested in the job</u>. He is the person **most interested in the job**.
3. With some verbs other than *be*, you can omit the relative pronoun and add *-ing* after the base form of the verb.	Anyone <u>who wants to learn about film history</u> should read this book. Anyone **wanting to learn about film history** should read this book.
4. Use commas when a non-identifying relative clause is reduced.	The film festival, <u>which was held in Brazil</u>, attracted people from all over the world. The film festival, **held in Brazil**, attracted people from all over the world.

4 Complete the exercises.

A Complete each sentence with a reduced relative clause.

1. Nollywood, which was named after Bollywood, is the Nigerian film industry.

   Nollywood, __named after Bollywood__, is the Nigerian film industry.

2. Nollywood films, which are mostly made in English, are shown around Africa and overseas.

   Nollywood films, _____, are shown around Africa and overseas.

3. Some Somali films are made in Eastleigh, which is a neighborhood in Nairobi, Kenya.

   Some Somali films are made in Eastleigh, _____.

4. Last night we saw a film that was set in Nairobi.

   Last night we saw a film _____.

5. A Somali production company that is known as Eastleighwood is popular in many parts of the world.

   A Somali production company _____ is popular in many parts of the world.

6. Anyone who is interested in world politics would enjoy the movie.

   Anyone _____ would enjoy the movie.

B Complete each sentence with a reduced relative clause.

1. My favorite Indian movies are films that have a lot of singing and dancing.

   My favorite Indian movies are films __having a lot of singing and dancing__ .

2. The African film festival has movies that feature beautiful scenery.

   The African film festival has movies _____ .

3. That Nigerian director only produces films that promote social awareness.

   That Nigerian director only produces films _____ .

4. I enjoy movies that star my favorite actors.

   I enjoy movies _____ .

5. We want to see the thriller that is showing at midnight.

   We want to see the thriller _____ .

6. The critic loved the new film that shows life in Mumbai.

   The critic loved the new film _____ .

5 Complete the exercises.

A Underline the relative clause in each sentence. Then check (✓) the sentences that contain relative clauses that can be reduced.

___✓___ 1. Bollywood, which was named after Hollywood, makes different kinds of films.

_____ 2. Bollywood, which is also referred to as Hindi cinema, is one of the largest film producers in India.

_____ 3. Bollywood films, which many people enjoy, do not pretend to show reality.

_____ 4. Bollywood, which inspired many cinema movements, was followed by Nollywood.

_____ 5. Bollywood's production studio, which the government built, is called Film City.

_____ 6. The actors who appear in Bollywood movies come from all over India.

B In your notebook, write reduced relative clauses for the sentences you checked in exercise **A**.

▼ The Nairobi skyline. Some Somali films are made in Nairobi, Kenya.

11.7 Relative Clauses with *Where* and *When*

> We visited the region **where the film was made.**
> I remember the day **when I first saw a lion in the wild.**

1. Use *where* in a relative clause to describe a place (for example, *home, neighborhood, city, country, place*).	Istanbul is a city. Europe and Asia meet there. Istanbul is a city **where Europe and Asia meet**.
2. Use *when* in a clause to describe a time (for example, *day, weekend, year, time*).	I'll never forget the summer. Our team won the championship then. I'll never forget the summer **when our team won the championship**.
3. *Where* and *when* can be used in identifying and non-identifying relative clauses. They can be omitted only in identifying relative clauses.	Do you remember the time **when we met**? Do you remember the time **we met**? The movie is in Paris, **where we first met**.
4. **Be careful!** Do not use a preposition in a relative clause with *where* or *when*.	✓ The late 1920s was the time **when talking films replaced silent films.** ✗ The late 1920s was the time <u>during when</u> talking films replaced silent films.
5. Instead of *where*, you can use a preposition: a. before *which* b. following the verb in the relative clause	a. The apartment building **in which I was born** no longer exists. b. The apartment building **which/that I was born in** no longer exists.
6. Instead of *when*, you can use *in which* in identifying relative clauses.	Last year was the year **when they got married**. Last year was the year **in which they got married**.

6 Combine the sentences about silent movies. Use *when, where,* or a preposition with *which*. Add commas where necessary.

1. The history of film starts in the late nineteenth century. Movies had no sound then.

   The history of film starts in the late nineteenth century when movies
   had no sound.

2. People wanted to go to a relaxing place. They could escape from their troubles there.

   _____

   _____

3. Moviegoers saw silent movies in theaters. There were usually pianos or organs in the theaters.

   _____

   _____

4. The age of silent movies ended in the late 1920s. Talking movies became popular then.

    _____

    _____

5. The movie *The Artist* (2011) takes place during the last years of silent films. People were losing interest then.

    _____

    _____

6. Today, there are a few silent film festivals. People show modern silent movies there.

    _____

    _____

PRACTICE

7 Complete the blog with the words in the box. Some words can be used more than once.

meaning	showing	when	which	where

Tips for Independent Filmmakers

Are you a new independent filmmaker starting out? Here are some tips to help you set up your movie and find a good location (1) _____*where*_____ you can make your film.

First, think about what scenes you need to film. You should probably make a storyboard, (2) _____ a series of drawings in (3) _____ you visualize your scenes. You can draw sketches of scenes or use computer software to make it. The storyboard will help you plan your film. Now you are ready to decide on your location and schedule.

To save money, think about places (4) _____ you might be able to film for free. For example, perhaps you can use a warehouse, a field, a back alley, or a quiet restaurant. Don't forget that you can't film in a location without permission. Be sure to contact the owner first. You will need to be flexible about the hours (5) _____ you will be at the location. A restaurant might let you film for free in the middle of the night, but not at 6:00 p.m.

For more information (6) _____ you how to make a basic film, visit www.grexfilms.com.

8 Look at the information and the notes in the filming schedule. Then complete the conversation between two production assistants. Use *when* or *where* and the correct form of the words in parentheses.

Preliminary Filming Schedule for *The Talented Mr. Ripley*					
Day	Scene	Description	Location	Characters	Requirements
SHOOT DAY 1 (October 8)					
9:00–10:00	10	Tom Ripley gets off bus	Ischia Ponte, Italy	Tom, crowd	bus
10:30–2:30	10	Tom introduces himself to Richard and Marge	Bagno Antonio (Antonio Beach)	Tom, Richard, Marge, crowd	bathing suits, towels, shoes
BREAK FOR LUNCH					
3:00–4:15	13	Tom, Marge, and Richard have coffee	Marge's house	Tom, Richard, Marge	coffee cups
4:15–6:00	30	Tom gives Marge a letter	Marge's house	Tom, Marge	letter, perfume
6:00–7:15	31	Marge reads letter	Marge's house	Marge	letter

1. A: Do you know the first day _____when filming begins_____ (filming / begin)?

   B: Yes, it starts on October 8.

2. A: Is Ischia Ponte the place _____ (the bus scene / happen)?

   B: Yes, on the Ischia Ponte bridge.

3. A: Can you tell me the location _____ (Tom, Richard, and Marge / meet)?

   B: Bagno Antonio.

4. A: Do you remember the scene _____ bathing suits? (we / need)

   B: Scene 10.

5. A: Do you know the time of day _____ (we / stop) for lunch?

   B: Yes, we'll have lunch at two o'clock.

6. A: Did the director tell you the area _____ (Marge's house / be) located?

   B: No. I'll ask.

7. A: Can you remind me of the crowd scenes _____ (the director / want) extras?

   B: Yes, we need extra people for the scenes at Ischia Ponte and Bagno Ischia.

8. A: Do you know the hours _____ (Tom / be) on camera today?

   B: Most of the day. He's in scenes 10, 13, and 31.

9. A: The moment _____ (Tom / give) Marge the letter is always such a bad scene.

   B: I know! It's a really serious part of the movie.

10. A: Are the actors staying on the island _____ (the film / take) place?

    B: The actors are, but it's so expensive there that the film crew is staying somewhere else.

9 Complete the sentences about movie extras. Use the information in the box to write reduced relative clauses.

> Particular clothes are required for scenes.
> Information about your age is requested.
> Photographers' fees are posted on websites.
> Extras should not talk while filming.
> ~~Some people want to be an extra in a movie.~~
> Jobs are listed on movie studio websites.
> Being an extra requires long hours.

1. Anyone __wanting to be an extra in a movie__ should get a professional photo made.

2. Call photographers to find out how much they charge. Don't rely on the fees _____.

3. You can find jobs _____.

4. Be honest when you send the information _____.

5. Extras usually use their own clothing. Make sure you have the particular clothes _____.

6. Being an extra is a job _____. You might be on set for up to 14 hours.

7. Don't talk during filming. Extras _____ will have to leave and won't get paid.

10 EDIT. Read the memory about a scary movie. Find and correct five more errors with relative clauses.

A Memorable Movie

I will never forget how I felt the night ~~where~~ when I saw the movie "The Birds." I was watching it on TV with my family in the house where grew up. The movie, was directed by Alfred Hitchcock, was made many years ago, but to this day just thinking about it scares me to death. I'll never forget the moment in when the woman was locked in a room with all the birds attacking her. My oldest brother, who wanting to be funny, started making loud bird noises and moving his arms like wings. The shadows created by his moving arms frightened me even more. Since then I have never been able to look at a lot of birds are sitting on a telephone wire or on tree branches without getting scared. I will never forgive Alfred Hitchcock, or my brother, for that.

11 APPLY.

A Read the description of the movie. Underline the reduced relative clauses and the relative clauses with *when* and *where*.

What movie is it?

This is a horror movie <u>directed by Alfred Hitchcock</u>. The film, released in 1963, is based on a short story written by British author Daphne du Maurier. It takes place in a northern California town where birds start attacking people for no obvious reason. The main characters are Melanie and Mitch. Melanie Daniels, played by actress Tippi Hedren, is a rich young woman who follows a San Francisco lawyer named Mitch Brenner to the coastal town of Bodega Bay, where his mother and sister live. Strangely, on the day when Melanie arrives to town, birds start attacking people. At the end of the movie, Melanie hears noises coming from the attic of the Brenner home. Hundreds of birds rush at her as she opens the attic door. It's a terrifying movie!

The Birds
introducing Tippi Hedren

B Think about a movie you remember well. Write a description of the movie. Use the model in exercise **A** and the questions in the box to help you. Include at least three reduced relative clauses and three relative clauses starting with *where* or *when*.

Who are the main characters?	Where does the story take place?
Who starred in the movie?	Who directed the movie?
When was the movie released?	What is the most memorable scene in the movie?
Is the movie based on a book?	How does the movie end?
Is the movie a true story?	What happens to the main character(s)?

C Work in a group. Listen to your classmates read their movie descriptions. Try to guess the movie. Ask questions if you aren't sure.

A: *Is the movie* The Birds?   B: *Yes, it is.*

1 Read the paragraph. Then complete the statements with *that, who, whom, when, where, which,* or *whose.*

> Shirin Neshat is a visual artist from Iran. She came from a wealthy family. She left Iran in 1974 at age 17 to study art in Los Angeles. Neshat now lives in New York and makes visual art, photographs, and films. Her works look at the role of women in the Islamic world. In 2010 she was named the Artist of the Decade by the *Huffington Post*. Her work explores religion, human rights, and women's identity. Her works have been shown in many museums across the world, including New York, Greece, and Istanbul. Neshat says that artists are there to bring hope and become the voice of the people.

1. Shirin Neshat, _____ is from a wealthy family, is a visual artist from Iran.

2. In 1974 Neshat traveled to Los Angeles, _____ she planned to study art.

3. Neshat, _____ work explores women in Islamic society, has become famous.

4. Neshat makes different kinds of art, _____ include photographs and films.

5. Places _____ Neshat's works have appeared include museums in the west and east.

6. Neshat, _____ many people find a source of hope, wants to speak for people _____ can't speak for themselves.

Charts
11.1–11.5,
11.7
2 Add *that, which, who, whom, whose, when,* or *where* to complete the relative clause in each sentence.

1. In classrooms ⌄*where* presentations are done well, images can be a powerful teaching tool.

2. In the past, professors used fewer images, students had to rely on listening skills.

3. Most people remember things they see better than things they listen to.

4. The images hold an audience's attention are the most successful.

5. During presentations, are done in all kinds of classes, presenters use images in different ways.

6. There are many presentations use still or moving images to illustrate a difficult concept.

7. Other presentations use images encourage discussion and debate.

8. Sometimes a presenter's goal is to surprise students with an image gets them to look at an issue in a new way.

Charts
11.1–11.7

3 EDIT. Read an excerpt from a class lecture about the role of images in advertising. Find and correct seven more errors with relative clauses. There is more than one way to correct some errors.

How do images influence our actions?

Images communicate meanings ˅*that* can't always be expressed as quickly in words. That's why images are so important in advertising. We see ads everywhere, and they affect us in ways in we don't realize. For example, we might see an ad for a candy bar before a movie is shown at the local theater. Maybe a few days later, we're in the supermarket and we buy the same candy bar, that we didn't plan to buy. When we put it into the shopping cart, we probably aren't thinking about the candy we saw it in the movie.

Some people think they're not influenced by advertising because they don't buy products from ads whom they see. They don't realize that ads don't usually lead us to act immediately. This is the way ads work, though—they give us ideas that we act on them later.

Consider this photo of someone selling flowers and other products in Thailand, floating markets are common. What kinds of thoughts do you associate with the image? Do you think this is a better advertising image for a travel company or for a company that sells products made in Thailand?

Charts
11.1–11.6

CD3-26

CD3-26

4 LISTEN.

A Listen to the radio ad. What product is it advertising?

B Listen again. Complete each sentence with a relative clause that answers the question in parentheses.

1. The coconut is a fruit _____ .

   (What can coconuts provide you with?)

2. This tropical fruit, _____

   (How long have humans been using coconuts?)

   _____ , is a great source of iron and other minerals.

3. It's the perfect drink for people _____ on a hot summer day.

   (Who is coconut milk the perfect drink for?)

4. Just take one sip and you'll be transported to a beautiful tropical island _____

   _____ .

   (What will you see on the tropical island?)

5. The Hoolehua post office, _____ of these postcards each

   (How many coconut postcards does the post office

   year, is in Hawaii.   ship each year?)

6. Send some coconuts to your friends, _____ with such

   (How will your friends feel about the gift of coconuts?)

   a tasty and unusual gift.

Charts
11.1–11.7

5 WRITE & SPEAK.

A Work in a group. Choose a product and write an ad for it in your notebook. Include at least three relative clauses.

| a car | perfume | hiking boots | a smartphone | your idea: _____ |

Try on a pair of our XXG6 boots, and you'll love them. These boots, which are lightweight and waterproof, will be comfortable from the moment you put them on . . .

B Discuss one or two images that might be effective in your ad. Use a relative clause in your answer.

We'd like to illustrate our ad with a photo showing a hiker who is on a trail that goes through a beautiful forest. The focus should be on the hiker's boots . . .

Connect the Grammar to Writing

1 READ & NOTICE THE GRAMMAR.

A Have you recently seen a movie that had a big impact on you? Exchange ideas with a partner. Then read the review.

> ### MOVIE REVIEW: *The Deep*
>
> *The Deep* is a 2012 Icelandic film directed by Baltasar Kormákur. It is based on the true story of a fisherman whose boat sank at sea in 1984.
>
> Gulli, played by Ólafur Darri Ólafsson, is stranded in freezing cold waters after he survives an accident that sinks his fishing boat. In an instant, he changes from an ordinary person to a man who must make a heroic effort to survive. The movie is a beautiful and moving reflection on human endurance.
>
> The whole movie does not take place only in the icy waters where Gulli floats and tries to swim (although these are certainly the most dramatic parts). We also see many scenes of the town where he lives, both before and after the accident. The gray colors and tough, weather-beaten look of everything really give viewers a taste of a different world; it is one in which people must work hard and take great risks living. Scenes from the real life event, shown at the end of the film, add to the emotional impact.
>
>
>
> *The Deep* reminds us of the simple and at times dangerous lives that many people must live and the incredible choices that they sometimes have to face. It will leave you with a deep respect for Icelandic fishermen. Unsurprisingly, Kormákur dedicated the film to them.

GRAMMAR FOCUS

In this movie review, the writer uses the following types of relative clauses to describe or give extra information about a noun.

Subject relative clause	. . . *an accident* **that sinks his fishing boat**.
Object relative clauses	. . . *the incredible choices* **that they sometimes have to face**.

B Read the movie review in exercise **A** again. Find and underline three more relative clauses (including one reduced relative clause) and label what type each one is. Then circle the noun that the relative clause describes or gives extra information about.

C Complete the chart with information from the review in exercise **A**. Then discuss your answers with a partner.

Title of movie: _____The Deep_____   Year movie was released: _____

Director: _____

Main character: _____   Actor: _____

Plot/Story: An Icelandic fisherman must try to survive after his fishing boat sinks.

Setting (place) or visual effects: _____

This is a powerful/interesting movie because _____

_____

2 BEFORE YOU WRITE.

A Work with a partner. Create a list of the three best movies that you have seen in the past year. Help each other remember the actors in each one.

B Choose one movie from your list and prepare to write a review of it. In your notebook, make a chart like the one in exercise **1C** and fill in as much information as you can.

3 WRITE two or three paragraphs about the movie that you chose. Tell the basic plot and the setting. What made the movie powerful or interesting? Use your chart from exercise **2B** and the review in exercise **1A** to guide you. Use at least three relative clauses in your review.

> **WRITING FOCUS   Discussing Plot in the Simple Present**
>
> When we discuss the plot (the basic storyline) of a movie or a novel, we usually use the a present form of the verb. Even though we saw the movie or read the book in the past, the events in the story continue to exist. Every time we watch the movie or read the novel, the same events will occur. Notice the simple present in the first sentence of the plot summary:
>
> *Gulli, played by Ólafur Darri Ólafsson, **is stranded** in freezing cold waters after he **survives** an accident that **sinks** his fishing boat.*

4 SELF ASSESS. Underline the relative clauses in your review. Then use the checklist to assess your work.

- [ ] I used identifying and non-identifying subject relative clauses correctly. [11.1, 11.2]
- [ ] I used relative clauses with *whose*, *when*, and *where* correctly. [11.3, 11.7]
- [ ] I used object relative clauses correctly. [11.4, 11.5]
- [ ] I used the simple present when describing the plot of the movie. [WRITING FOCUS]

Adverb Clauses

Skyscrapers in New York
City's Financial District,
New York, USA

EXPLORE

CD3-27

1 **READ** the book review. According to Edward Glaeser, why do many people want to live in cities?

Triumph of the City by Edward Glaeser

We are becoming an urban species. More than half of the world's people live in cities today, and cities are still growing. For economist Edward Glaeser, this is good news. In his fascinating book, *Triumph of the City*, Glaeser explains why cities continue to attract people.

Glaeser sees great advantages to urban life. **Whenever people live close together**, they can exchange ideas, from business to technology to the arts. This exchange makes cities exciting and productive centers of opportunity.

> "Cities are our species' greatest invention."
> —Edward Glaeser

He also believes that cities are good for the planet because they reduce pollution. **Since urban residents don't drive much**, cities have fewer carbon emissions.[1] For example, fewer than one third of New York City residents drive to work as compared with 86 percent of people living elsewhere in the United States.

Glaeser thinks that cities are good for everyone—for people of all incomes. He does not believe that cities make people poor. He writes that we should build more skyscrapers **so that large numbers of people can live in relatively small areas**. Then housing will be affordable. However, **even though Glaeser has some interesting suggestions**, he underestimates the high cost of city living. Millions of urban residents can't afford food, clothing, and housing **because they are too expensive**. It is a serious problem.

Triumph of the City is a thoughtful book. **Although you may not agree with all of Glaeser's ideas**, you will probably enjoy his lively discussion.

[1] **carbon emissions:** the release of carbon dioxide into the air

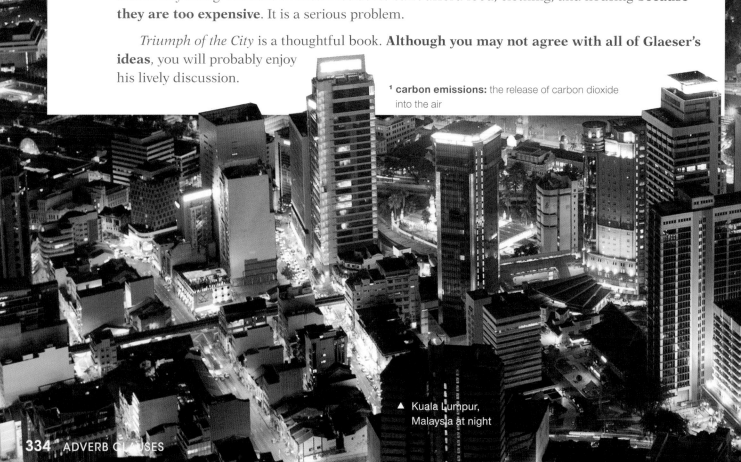
▲ Kuala Lumpur, Malaysia at night

2 **CHECK.** Correct the error in each sentence to make it true according to the book review.

1. About one third of the world's population lives in cities.

2. Cities today are decreasing in size.

3. According to Glaeser, cities cause pollution.

4. Eighty-six percent of New York City residents drive to work.

5. The reviewer agrees with all of Glaeser's ideas.

3 **DISCOVER.** Complete the exercises to learn about the grammar in this lesson.

A Find these sentences in the book review from exercise **1**. Write the missing words.

1. _____Whenever_____ people live close together, they can exchange ideas.

2. _____ urban residents don't drive much, cities have fewer carbon emissions.

3. He writes that we should build more skyscrapers _____ large numbers of people can live in relatively small areas.

4. Millions of urban residents can't afford food, clothing, and housing _____ they are too expensive.

5. _____ you may not agree with all of Glaeser's ideas, you will probably enjoy his lively discussion.

B Look at the words you wrote in exercise **A**. Write the words that show:

1. a contrasting idea: _____   3. reasons: _____ , _____

2. a purpose: _____   4. a time relationship: _____

LEARN

12.1 Adverb Clauses of Time

> <u>Whenever I hear that song</u>, I get sad.
>   Adverb Clause   Main Clause
>
> It started to snow **just as we were leaving the theater**.
>   Main Clause   Adverb Clause

1. Adverb clauses of time begin with a time word or phrase (*when, whenever, as, as long as, as soon as*). They tell when the action or event in the main clause happens.	**As I was leaving my dormitory**, I ran into an old friend.
2. *As* means when or while something is or was happening.	**As I was walking home**, it started to thunder.
Just as means that an action or event happened at exactly the same moment as another action or event.	My roommate called **just as I was leaving**.
3. *As long as* means from beginning to end.	I'll never forget that day **as long as I live**.
4. *Whenever* means any time or every time.	**Whenever she tells a story**, I laugh a lot.
5. Time clauses can come before or after the main clause. The meaning is the same.	We went on vacation **as soon as we finished classes**.
Remember: Use a comma after the time clause when it comes first in the sentence.	**As soon as we finished classes**, we went on vacation.

4 Underline five more adverb clauses of time in the paragraph. Add commas where necessary.

Singapore

<u>As you fly over Singapore</u> you'll see enormous skyscrapers. Five million people live in just 270 square miles (700 sq. km) there, so most people live in tall buildings. <u>Whenever</u> people think of skyscrapers they usually think of crowded spaces. However, this is not true of the Pinnacle@Duxton in Singapore. The Pinnacle is a huge skyscraper with 1800 apartments. You'll be amazed as you walk around it. <u>As soon as</u> you reach the 20th floor you'll see a 2625-foot (800 m) jogging track. You'll feel like you're running in the clouds <u>whenever</u> you go there to exercise. The skyscrapers in Singapore look like something from a science fiction movie. They're truly amazing works of architecture. You'll remember them <u>as long as</u> you live!

◀ The Singapore skyline

5 Circle the correct word(s) to complete each sentence.

1. Some people use elevators **as long as / whenever** they leave the building.

2. **As soon as / As** the new skyscraper was completed, people started complaining about it.

3. The power went out **as long as / just as** the elevator reached the twelfth floor.

4. **Whenever / As** people live close to each other, there is less privacy.

5. **Just as / Whenever** our neighbors have a party, they invite us.

6. **As / As soon as** I was driving home, I saw that new apartment building.

7. I'll remember my trip to Singapore **whenever / as long as** I live.

8. Oleg got to the station **just as / as long as** the train was leaving.

9. Please call me **as along as / as soon as** you get to Hong Kong.

10. **Whenever / As** we go to New York City, we always visit the Empire State Building.

12.2 Adverb Clauses of Contrast

<u>Although I've studied a lot</u>, I'm still nervous about the exam.
     Adverb Clause   Main Clause

I'm still nervous about the exam **even though I've studied a lot**.
     Main Clause   Adverb Clause

1. Adverb clauses beginning with *although*, *even though*, and *though* introduce a contrast. The information may be unexpected or surprising.	**Although Joe studied a lot**, he's still nervous about the exam. **Even though she loves him**, she is not going to marry him. **Though I slept well last night**, I'm very tired today.
2. *Even though* shows more contrast than *though*.	He bought a new car **even though he has trouble paying his rent every month**.
3. *Though* is more common in informal English.	Informal: **Though** I have the qualifications, they're not going to give me the job. Formal: **Although** you have the right qualifications, I'm afraid we can't offer you the position.
4. **Be careful!** Do not use *but* in sentences with *although*, *even though*, and *though*.	✓ **Though it was raining**, I went for a walk. ✗ Though it was raining, <u>but</u> I went for a walk.
5. **Remember:** Use a comma after the adverb clause when it comes first in the sentence.	**Although we enjoy the countryside**, we prefer city life.

6 Choose the best ending for each sentence. Then add commas where necessary.

1. Singapore has a population of five million although _____.

   (a.) it is only 270 square miles (700 sq. km) wide

   b. it has a lot of interesting architecture

2. Even though Chicago is a large city, _____.

   a. it has a lot of tall buildings

   b. it has a lot of parks and gardens

3. Some of the world's oldest cities are in Egypt although _____.

   a. Greek cities are not as old

   b. there are many ancient cities and towns in China

4. Toronto is the largest city in Canada although _____.

   a. it is not the country's capital

   b. it has a population of about 5.6 million

5. Although Yamoussoukro is the capital city of the Ivory Coast _____.

   a. it is the political capital

   b. it began as a very small village

6. Even though many ancient cities had walls around them _____.

   a. the walls did not always stop invaders

   b. the walls protected the city from invaders

▼ The walled city of Dubrovnik, Croatia

7. Shanghai, China has the largest population of any city in the world though _____.

    a. almost as many people live in Beijing

    b. far fewer people live in Jaipur, India

8. Though some large cities such as Tokyo and London have skyscrapers _____.

    a. their streets are inhabited by millions of people

    b. tiny streets in some sections show their ancient beginnings

12.3 Adverb Clauses of Reason and Purpose

Since I don't know how to get there, I'm going to use my GPS.
       Adverb Clause   Main Clause

Now that I have a GPS, I never get lost.
   Adverb Clause   Main Clause

We're going to leave early so that we can avoid traffic.
    Main Clause   Adverb Clause

1. *Because* and *since* show reasons.	**Because I didn't do well on the exam**, I'm going to take it again. **Since we're late**, let's take a taxi.
2. **Be careful!** *Since* can also refer to time.	**Since I got here**, I've done very little work.
3. *Now that* shows a reason. It means *because . . . now.*	**Now that I know English**, I can get a good job. **Now that Ed's retired,** he's going to have more free time.
4. *So that* shows a purpose. It means *in order to.* Modal verbs (*can, could, would*, etc.) are often used with *so that.*	I'm putting on my glasses **so that I can read the menu.** We studied hard **so that we would do well on the exam.** Max moved to the front of the classroom **so that he could see better.**

REAL ENGLISH

In conversation, *that* is often omitted after *so.*

   I texted Bill **so he could get the information fast**.

7 Circle the correct word(s) to complete each sentence.

1. (**Because**) / **So that** people live close together in cities, they can interact more.

2. **Since / So that** our city has excellent public transportation, we don't need a car.

3. More people want to live in big cities **now that / so that** they are safer and cleaner.

4. Cities need police **so that / since** they will be safe places to live.

5. Cities are important **now that / because** they are economic, political, and cultural centers.

6. **Now that / So that** I have a bike, I don't have to take the bus to work.

7. **So that / Since** the world population is growing, cities are becoming larger.

8. Some people move to big cities **so that / now that** they can live more exciting lives.

8 Complete the conversation with *because, since, now that,* or *so that.* More than one answer is sometimes correct.

Ali: How was your trip to Malaysia? Did you get to see much of Kuala Lumpur?

Bill: Yes, I did. The weather was nice. It was really warm (1) _____ Kuala Lumpur has a tropical rainforest climate. There's a lot to see there, especially religious sites. A lot of people go there (2) _____ they can visit the mosques and the Batu Caves outside the city.

Ali: What are the Batu Caves?

Bill: They're an important religious site. The Batu Caves are a group of cave temples cut into the side of a hill. Some people climb all 272 steps (3) _____ they can see all of the caves, but I didn't get to see many of the caves (4) _____ I didn't have that much time.

Ali: It sounds interesting. I've never heard of them.

Bill: A lot of people have never heard of them. But (5) _____ they have become famous, they attract a lot of tourists.

Ali: Really? So, what else did you do there?

Bill: Well, we visited Putrajaya (6) _____ it is so close to Kuala Lumpur. That was nice, too. It's a new city. The government built it not long ago.

PRACTICE

9 Circle the correct words to complete the sentences about Putrajaya, Malaysia.

1. Putrajaya was created **because / so that / though** Kuala Lumpur would be less crowded.

2. **Because / Just as / Although** there are a lot of government offices in Putrajaya, many government workers live there.

3. **Even though / Just as / Now that** many government workers live in Putrajaya, there is less traffic there than in Kuala Lumpur.

4. Government workers enjoy living in Putrajaya **even though / since / whenever** it has good public services.

5. You can see attractive buildings, parks, and bridges **as / even though / since** you walk down the streets of Putrajaya.

6. **As long as / So that / Although** Putrajaya does not have historical buildings, it does have interesting places, such as Wasana Park.

7. **Even though / So that / Since** Putrajaya is a big city, it also has a lot of green space, such as parks and botanical gardens.

8. **Although / Since / Whenever** people visit Putrajaya, they are surprised by its natural beauty.

▶ Tanguá Park,
Curitiba, Brazil

10 Read the sentences about Curitiba, Brazil. Then combine each pair of sentences into one sentence with an adverb clause. Use the word in parentheses. Add a comma where necessary. Sometimes there is more than one way to combine the sentences.

1. Curitiba is an attractive city. It has historic buildings and beautiful woods around it. (because)

   Because Curitiba has historic buildings and beautiful woods around it, it _is an attractive city._ OR _Curitiba is an attractive city because it has_ _historic buildings and beautiful woods around it._

2. Curitiba has a diverse population. Immigrants from Europe and Japan have made it their home. (since)

   _____

   _____

3. The population began to grow rapidly. Curitiba's mayor tried to reduce crowding. (as)

   _____

   _____

4. There are no cars on "The Street of Flowers." It's a nice place to walk and shop. (because)

   _____

   _____

5. Many people own cars in Curitiba. Two million people take public transportation every day. (although)

   _____

   _____

6. Curitiba developed a good recycling program. It can keep the city clean. (so that)

_____

_____

7. Children bring cans and bottles to recycling centers. They receive small gifts. (whenever)

_____

_____

8. Not all of the city's garbage is recycled in Curitiba. Seventy percent of it is. (though)

_____

_____

11 WRITE & SPEAK.

A Complete the blog entry with *since, because, although, even though, though, whenever,* or *so that*. Sometimes more than one answer is correct.

World Traveler

April 12

Rome and Dubai are two of my favorite cities, (1) _____ they are very different. (2) _____ there are a lot of huge skyscrapers in Dubai, it has a very modern look and feel. The architecture is amazing. In fact, many people go there (3) _____ they can visit the Burj Khalifa—the tallest building in the world. (4) _____ Dubai is well known for its impressive buildings, there are also many beautiful parks and gardens there. My favorite park is Dubai Miracle Garden, which has over 45 million flowers! Dubai is also a great city for shopping. (5) _____ I visit Dubai, I always go to the famous Wafi shopping mall.

Rome is my other favorite city. Like many other people, I to go there (6) _____ I can visit the historical sites and see the famous art. (7) _____ Rome is one of the most ancient cities in Europe, there is a lot to see, such as Renaissance palaces, the Pantheon, the Colosseum, and the Spanish Steps. Also, (8) _____ many of the sites in Rome are close together, it's a very walkable city. And the food in Rome is fantastic! (9) _____ I go to Rome, I gain weight!

Rome and Dubai are two wonderful cities with very different atmospheres. I highly recommend visiting them both!

B Complete the sentences to make them true about yourself and your city.

1. Although my city __is very crowded and noisy__ , __it's a great place to live__ .

2. _____ is the best time of year to visit my city since _____ .

▼ Rome, Italy

3. _____ is my favorite city because _____ .

4. Even though _____ is a _____ city,

   it's _____ .

5. Many people visit my city so that _____ .

6. Whenever I travel, I always _____ .

7. I want to visit _____ someday so that I _____ .

8. Whenever I visit my family, _____ .

C Work with a partner. Share your sentences from exercise **B**. Ask follow-up questions.

A: *Although my city is very crowded and noisy, it's a great place to live.*

B: *Really? What do you like about it?*

12 LISTEN & SPEAK.

CD3-28

A Listen to the conversation. Then answer the questions.

1. What is the Eurosky Tower? _____

2. Where is it? _____

3. Is Sergio's opinion of the Eurosky Tower positive or negative? _____

CD3-28

B Listen again. Choose the correct answer to complete each sentence.

1. In the past, Rome had _____ .

   a. no skyscrapers   b. only a few skyscrapers

2. The Eurosky Tower _____ .

   a. does not use sustainable energy   b. uses solar energy

3. Sergio believes that skyscrapers in Rome _____.

    a. destroy its beauty   b. add to its beauty

4. The Eurosky tower is a new tower _____ of Rome.

    a. in the residential and business district   b. in the old city

5. Sergio does not think that _____ will live in the Eurosky Tower.

    a. only rich residents   b. regular residents of Rome

6. Sergio's feeling about skyscrapers is that they _____.

    a. are bad for most cities   b. need to be a proper fit with cities

13   **EDIT.** Read the paragraph about urban sprawl. Find and correct five more errors with adverb clauses and commas. There is more than one way to correct some errors.

Urban Sprawl

Even *though* a lot of people who work in cities would prefer to live closer to their jobs, not all can afford to do so. Although the cost of housing in cities is usually very high, a lot of people have to live outside of the city in the suburbs and commute to work. The spread of cities into outside areas is called urban sprawl. Unfortunately, urban sprawl can have serious consequences. For example, in Mexico City, developers built new buildings as fast as possible so that could make money. They also built new housing, but it was far away from the city center. It can take two to five hours to get to work every day, so a number of people have moved in with family members who live in the city. Since they are now more crowded, they are closer to their jobs. Even though many people have moved back to Mexico City, there are now a great number of empty homes in the suburbs. It will take time and careful planning to solve this problem. People will have to be patient just as urban planners try to find a solution.

14   **APPLY.**

A   Work in a group. Imagine that you are going to build an ideal city together. Choose one of the topics from the box. Discuss your decisions and preferences. Use adverb clauses.

> **Geography:** mountains, hills, beaches, oceans, lakes, islands
> **Buildings:** skyscrapers, low buildings, historical, modern, futuristic buildings
> **Transportation:** car, bus, subway, bicycles, futuristic vehicles
> **Industries:** tourism, finance, technology, arts, restaurants

Our city is only going to have public transportation. There won't be any roads for cars. Even though cars are convenient, they use too much energy . . .

B   Present your group's ideas to the class.

EXPLORE

1 READ the article about Amsterdam. What makes this city so safe for cycling?

Amsterdam: A Cyclist's Dream

On a Monday morning in Amsterdam, the workday began as usual for Rokus Albers. **While finishing his coffee**, Albers checked messages on his phone. Then, he grabbed his backpack and headed for the nearest railway station. He wasn't there to take the train, though. Instead, Albers chose one of the public bicycles lined up outside the station. **After unlocking the bike with a smart card,**[1] he set out for his job on the other side of the city. He joined dozens of other cyclists in the bike lanes, safely apart from car traffic.

Amsterdam wasn't always bicycle friendly. In fact, cycling used to be dangerous, especially during the second half of the twentieth century. This was a time of rapid economic growth in the Netherlands. As people's incomes rose, they were able to afford expensive goods such as cars for the first time, and driving became popular. Highways were built to accommodate all of the cars. This meant there was less space for cyclists. **Having had a long tradition of cycling**, this was a big change for the country. Unfortunately, as car traffic increased, so did the number of fatal biking accidents. Many of the cyclists were children.

The Dutch were outraged.[2] They organized huge protests in the city streets. Government officials and urban planners listened. **Hoping to solve the problem quickly**, they started to think of ways to make the city safe for cyclists again. Soon there were separate bike lanes, and some areas were permanently closed to cars. The changes were so effective that today Amsterdam is a model of biking safety for other cities around the world.

[1] **smart card:** a small plastic card that can store and process computer data
[2] **outraged:** extremely angry and shocked

► Herengracht Canal, Amsterdam, Netherlands

2 CHECK. Read the statements. Circle **T** for *true* or **F** for *false*.

1. Rokus Albers rode his own bicycle to work.   **T**   **F**

2. Bike riding in Amsterdam was safe throughout the twentieth century.   **T**   **F**

3. Driving became popular when the Dutch economy improved.   **T**   **F**

4. Highways helped cyclists get around the city.   **T**   **F**

5. The Dutch people helped make biking safe again in their country.   **T**   **F**

3 DISCOVER. Complete the exercises to learn about the grammar in this lesson.

A Find these sentences in the article from exercise **1** on page 345. Write the missing words.

1. _____, Albers checked messages on his phone.

2. _____,
he set out for his job on the other side of the city.

3. _____, this was a big
change for the country.

4. _____, they started to think of
ways to make the city safe for cyclists again.

B Look at the reduced adverb clauses you wrote in exercise **A**. Then answer the questions.

1. Which clauses give information about time? Write the numbers of the sentences. _____, _____

2. Which clauses express a reason? Write the numbers of the sentences. _____, _____

3. Which words show that two of the clauses are about time? _____, _____

4. Do the clauses about reason include a reason word? _____

◄ A woman rides
a bicycle in
Amsterdam.

LEARN

12.4 Reduced Adverb Clauses of Time

> I saw the accident <u>while I was walking down the street</u>.
> Adverb Clause
>
> I saw the accident **while walking down the street**.
> Reduced Adverb Clause

1. An adverb clause of time can be shortened or reduced when the subject of the adverb clause and the main clause are the same. To reduce an adverb clause of time, omit the subject and use the *-ing* form of the verb.	I always have coffee <u>before I leave home.</u> I always have coffee **before leaving home.** Lois has been very busy <u>since she started college</u>. Lois has been very busy **since starting college.**
2. When an adverb clause of time is in the progressive, omit the subject and *be* and use the *-ing* form of the verb.	I got tired <u>while I was riding my bike</u>. I got tired **while riding my bike.**
3. Adverb clauses of time that begin with *after, before, since,* and *while* can be reduced.	**After seeing me do the trick,** Mike did it, too.
4. **Be careful!** It is not possible to reduce an adverb clause if the subject of the main clause and the subject of the adverb clause are different.	✓ **After the dog barked,** I opened the door. ✗ <u>After barking,</u> I opened the door.
5. **Remember:** Use a comma when the reduced adverb clause comes first in the sentence.	**Before leaving for work,** I watered the plants.

4 Rewrite each sentence. Change the adverb clause to a reduced adverb clause. Add commas where necessary.

1. Since Amsterdam started a bike-share program, the city has improved conditions for cyclists.
   <u>Since starting a bike-share program,</u> Amsterdam has improved conditions for cyclists.

2. After the city closed the downtown area to cars, it opened the area to bikes.
   _____ the city opened the area to bikes.

3. Dutch people spend years learning bike safety rules before they get their driver's licenses.
   Dutch people spend years learning bike safety rules _____.

4. After they get a bike diploma, Dutch children can ride their bikes alone.
   _____ Dutch children can ride their bikes alone.

5. While they are taking a road test, drivers show how they watch out for cyclists.
   _____ drivers show how they watch out for cyclists.

6. Drivers must turn and open the door with their right hands before they exit the car.
   Drivers must turn and open the door with their right hands
   _____ .

7. While drivers are turning to open their doors, they look for any cyclists on the road.

_____, drivers look for any cyclists on the road.

8. After Amsterdam improved its road safety, it has become one of the world's best places to bike.

_____, Amsterdam has become one of the world's best places to bike.

12.5 Reduced Adverb Clauses of Reason

<u>Because he felt tired</u>, he went to bed early.
      Adverb Clause

Feeling tired, he went to bed early.
Reduced Adverb Clause

1. In many cases an adverb clause of reason can be reduced. Omit the subject and *because* or *since*. Then change the verb to the *-ing* form. Put *not* before the *-ing* form of the verb to make a negative.	<u>Because she is an only child</u>, she is often lonely. **Being an only child**, she is often lonely. <u>Because she was an only child</u>, she was often lonely. **Being an only child**, she was often lonely. <u>Since I don't know Chinese</u>, I can't understand him. **Not knowing Chinese**, I can't understand him.
2. To reduce an adverb clause of reason in the present perfect or past perfect, change *have* or *had* to *having*.	<u>Since she has spent all her money</u>, she needs more. **Having spent all her money**, she needs more. <u>Since she had spent her money</u>, she needed more. **Having spent her money**, she needed more.
3. **Remember:** In order to reduce an adverb clause, the subject of the adverb clause and the main clause must be the same.	✓ **Because Jake won the race**, his sister was happy for him. ✗ <u>Having won the race</u>, his sister was happy for him.

5 Complete the sentences about the subway system in Seoul, Korea. Change the adverb clauses in parentheses to reduced adverb clauses.

1. _____Having 316 miles of track_____, Seoul's subway system is one of the longest. (because it has 316 miles of track)

2. _____, the trains make travel around Seoul easy. (because they run every two minutes during rush hour)

3. _____, the stations are a great source of information. (since they provide digital maps and schedules)

4. _____, the mayor of Seoul lowered the price of subway fares. (because he had heard complaints about high subway fares)

5. _____, the subway cars are excellent for winter travel. (since they have heated seats)

6. _____, the subway is very convenient. (since it has opened a lot of new stations)

7. _____, the Seoul subway provides passengers with easy Internet access. (because it offers free wi-fi in stations and on subway cars)

8. _____, I want to ride the subway when I go to Seoul. (because I have read about it)

PRACTICE

6 WRITE & SPEAK.

A Read the statements. Check (✓) the statement if the adverb clause can be reduced.

   ✓ 1. After they arrived in London, Pam and Emily took a bus to their hotel.

      2. After he had spent a year in Mexico, Matt spoke Spanish fluently.

      3. Before Linda left for Australia, we had a party for her.

      4. After he saw the pyramids outside Cairo, Ed wanted to learn more about them.

      5. Jackie learned some Turkish before she moved to Istanbul.

      6. Since Claudia loves to dance, her trip to Brazil during Carnival was wonderful.

      7. While Cara was driving to the airport, her car broke down.

      8. Because she's an art history major, Tanya really enjoyed her trip to Florence.

      9. After he left Lisbon, Scott went to Madrid.

      10. Since she had never been to Iceland, Anita was excited to spend a day there on her way to Moscow.

B In your notebook, rewrite the sentences you checked in exercise **A** with reduced adverb clauses.

   After arriving in London, Pam and Emily took a bus to their hotel.

C In your notebook, write two more sentences with reduced adverb clauses about other cities, but don't include the names of the cities. Read your sentences to the class. Your classmates will try to guess the cities.

   A: *After arriving in this city, I visited Shinjuku.*

   B: *The city is Tokyo!*

7 In your notebook, combine each pair of sentences into one sentence with a reduced adverb clause. Use the words in parentheses when they are provided. Add commas where necessary.

1. She had driven everywhere for years. Ella wanted to move to a more walkable neighborhood.

   Having driven everywhere for years, Ella wanted to move to a more walkable neighborhood.

2. Ella made a decision. Ella looked for a website about walkability. (before)

3. Ella was doing some research online. She found a "walkability" website. (while)

4. The website considers factors such as walking distance to stores and public transportation. It gives a walkability score. (after)

5. Some communities had gotten bad walkability scores. These communities made changes to improve their scores.

6. They have everything they need nearby. That's why Ella's family is happy in their new home.

7. Ella's children walk home from school. Her children can stop at a park and play. (while)

8. Ella had been dependent on a car for years. Ella is happy that she doesn't need one now.

8 **EDIT.** Read the paragraph. Find and correct six more errors with reduced adverb clauses and commas. There is more than one way to correct some errors.

City Life

After ~~grow~~ ^growing up in the suburbs, many young people in the United States are choosing to live in cities. Have attended college in lively cities, a lot of young people don't want to give up their urban lifestyles after they graduate. Cities offer a variety of interesting things to do plus the convenience of having everything nearby. After experience city life, many young people find living in the suburbs boring. Transportation is another factor that makes cities attractive to them. Having spent their early years riding around in the family car a lot of young people prefer to get around on public transportation, by bike, or on foot. These forms of transportation give them more independence. Being more independent, their parents are proud of them. There are other benefits, too. For example, walking can be a social activity. While friends are walking together, they can have a conversation or stop and have coffee. Since there are sidewalks, bike lanes, and public transportation, there's no need to have a car in many cities. Not own cars, young people don't have to spend money on parking and gas. Whenever they want to leave the city they can rent a car or take a bus or train. Cities offer everything that many young people want these days.

9 APPLY.

A Look at the walkability map of San Francisco, California. In your notebook, write answers to the questions below. Use reduced adverb clauses and the words in parentheses in your answers. More than one answer may be possible.

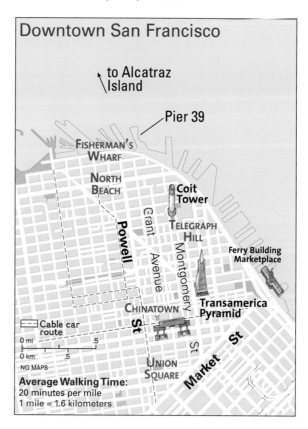

1. I'm leaving the Transamerica Pyramid now. How long will I need to walk to Coit Tower? (after)

   After leaving the Transamerica Pyramid, you will need about 15-20 minutes to walk to Coit Tower.

2. I want to go to Fisherman's Wharf after I leave Union Square. How can I get there quickly? (after)

3. What will I see while I am traveling from Union Square to Fisherman's Wharf? (while)

4. I'm going to walk from Powell Street to Telegraph Hill. Which streets or avenues will I cross on my way there? (while)

5. I'm planning to walk from Ferry Building Marketplace to Chinatown. What will I see before I arrive there? (before)

6. I'm having dinner with a friend tomorrow night at Pier 39. I hear there are a lot of nice shops there. Should we plan to spend some time shopping there before we have dinner? (yes)

B In your notebook, draw a map of part of your city or hometown. Label some of the main streets and important places.

C Work with a partner. Ask and answer questions about your maps from exercise **B**. Use reduced adverb clauses and the questions in exercise **A** to help you.

A: *What will I see while I'm walking along the river?*
B: *Some boats and a lot of cyclists.*

Review the Grammar UNIT 12

1 Read the sentences about the city of Pontevedra in Spain. Underline the adverb clauses and circle the reduced adverb clauses. Add commas where necessary.

1. Although Pontevedra has only around 85,000 people, traffic congestion used to be a problem.

2. Being the major city in the region it has attracted a lot of commuters.

3. Since it now has a free bike-lending service the city has set a new lower speed limit for cars.

4. The city council designed a special map with walking times so that the city would become more walkable.

5. People can leave their cars at one of the free parking lots whenever they visit the city.

6. Though people disliked the new policies at first they now support them.

7. Being a small city Pontevedra was never very well known outside of the region.

8. Now that it is such a walkable city it has become popular with urban planners.

2 Read the sentences about London, England. Circle the correct word(s) to complete each sentence.

1. London started making drivers pay to enter the city **so that / just as** there would be less traffic.

2. **Whenever / Although** you plan to drive into London, try to pay the charge before you go. It's cheaper.

3. **As long as / Just as** people had gotten used to the charge, the price increased.

4. **So that / Though** drivers have to pay on weekdays, they don't pay on weekends.

5. Most drivers pay the charge **so that / whenever** they avoid a large fine.

6. **While spending / Having spent** hours in traffic in the past, taxi drivers like the charge.

7. **Even though / Since** there was less traffic in London after the charge, it seemed like it was working well.

8. **Although / Since** there were fewer cars in London at first, the amount of traffic has been increasing lately.

3 LISTEN & SPEAK.

🎧 CD3-30

A Listen to the podcast. Check (✓) the names of smart cities you hear.

☐ Amsterdam   ☐ Detroit   ☐ St. Petersburg   ☐ Beijing

☐ Cairo   ☐ Dubai   ☐ Stockholm   ☐ Yokohama

B Listen again. Choose the correct answer to complete each statement.

🎧 CD3-30

1. Smart cities have certain things in common _____.
   a. since people agree on everything   b. although people don't agree on everything

2. Whenever a city invests in its people and new communication technology, _____.
   a. it becomes more expensive   b. it creates more jobs and improves the quality of life

3. Smart cities want to offer a good quality of living _____.
   a. so that more skilled professionals move to them   b. even though they pay workers less money

4. Being a smart city, _____.
   a. Stockholm pays its workers a little less than most cities   b. Stockholm offers its residents a good quality of life

5. Smart cities try to use natural resources carefully _____.
   a. so that they will last a long time   b. although they show few signs of running out

C Work with a partner. Compare your answers from exercise **B**.

Charts 12.1, 12.2, 12.4, 12.5

4 **EDIT.** Read the paragraph about Melbourne, Australia. Find and correct seven more errors with adverb clauses, reduced adverb clauses, and commas. There is more than one way to correct some errors.

Melbourne, Australia

     Even Sydney is more famous, Melbourne, Australia is one of the most livable cities in the
though (inserted above "Even Sydney")

world. What makes a city livable? Excellent education, quality health care, good roads, and public transportation are essential. People need to feel safe that they can walk around day or night without feeling afraid. Even though it has a great tram system, people can get around Melbourne easily. Having so many restaurants, unique shops, and music festivals Melbourne offers a wide variety of leisure activities. Although it's located on the beautiful Yarra River, it's perfect for water sports. Melbourne has great weather, too. Whenever they are in the mood residents can go to the beach. Though Melbourne has so much to offer, it has visitors from all over the world. After come to the city, people don't want to leave.

Charts 12.1–12.5

5 **SPEAK & WRITE.**

A Work in a group. Discuss the city or town that you are in now. As a group, write as many sentences as you can about the city. Use adverb clauses and reduced adverb clauses.

Although Washington, DC, is a big, crowded city, it feels very livable to me.

B Share your sentences with the class. Ask and answer follow-up questions.

1   READ & NOTICE THE GRAMMAR.

A   Think about a city you know well. What is your favorite place in that city? What is your least favorite part of it? Tell a partner about it. Then read the text.

A Vital Restoration

Like any city, Seoul can be a stressful place to live. City residents living with crowds and pollution need outdoor spaces to experience nature. This is why the Cheonggyecheon project, a new park built around an ancient stream, has a great design.

Before the park was built, the stream was covered by a big, noisy highway. Having lived near the highway at that time, I remember it. It was not a nice place to walk around because there was so much traffic. In 2003, the city began removing the highway and building a park next to the stream.

Whenever I go for a walk in that area now, I feel refreshed. Seeing the greenery and flowing stream, I can leave behind the stress of city life. It's a great place to hang out with friends or to sit and relax. Now that Cheonggyecheon is such a nice park, people visit it more often and take more walks.

Even though the project cost a lot of money, I think it was worth it. Having brought beautiful scenery to Seoul, Cheonggyecheon was good for the city. Other cities should build similar parks so that their residents can have a beautiful place to go and relax.

GRAMMAR FOCUS

In the text, the writer uses the following types of adverb clauses:

Clauses of time to tell when the action or event in the main clause happens.
   Before the park was built, *the stream was covered by a big, noisy highway.*

Clauses of contrast to express an idea that is the opposite of the idea in the main clause.
   Even though the project cost a lot of money, *I think it was worth it.*

Clauses of reason to explain the idea in the main clause.
   *It was not a nice place to walk around **because there was so much traffic.***

Clauses of purpose to express a reason or purpose for something.
   *Other cities should build similar parks **so that their residents can have a beautiful place to go and relax.***

B Read the text in exercise **A** again. Notice the adverb clauses. Find and write two more reduced adverb clauses in the the first column of the chart. Then write each as a full adverb clause in the second column as full clauses in the chart. Then work with a partner and compare your answers.

Reduced Adverb Clauses	Changed into Full Adverb Clauses
Having lived near the highway . . .	Since I lived near the highway . . .

C Read the text in exercise **A** again. What are the positive and negative aspects of the project? Write them in the chart. Then discuss your ideas with a partner.

Positive Aspects	Negative Aspects
adds beauty to the city	was very expensive

2 BEFORE YOU WRITE.

Choose a city project, for example, a park, a bridge, a plaza, or a building. What are the positive and negative aspects about it? In your notebook, make a chart like the one in exercise **1C**. Complete the chart with your ideas.

3 WRITE about the city project you chose. Write three or four paragraphs. Do you think it has improved the city? Explain why or why not. Use your chart from exercise **2** and the text in exercise **1A** to help you.

> **WRITING FOCUS**   Using *Like* to Make a Comparison
>
> Use *like* + a noun phrase to tell your reader that the subject in the main clause and the noun after *like* are similar. Remember to put a comma after the phrase with *like*.
>
> **Like any city,** *Seoul can be a stressful place to live.*

4 SELF ASSESS. Read your text. Underline the adverb clauses. Then use the checklist to assess your work.

☐ I used adverb clauses of time and contrast correctly. [12.1, 12.2]

☐ I used adverb clauses of reason and purpose correctly. [12.3]

☐ I used reduced adverb clauses of time and reason correctly. [12.4, 12.5]

☐ I used *like* in a prepositional phrase to show similarity. [WRITING FOCUS]

Conditionals

▶ People trying to decide which way to go in the middle of multiple waterfalls (Plitvice Lakes National Park, Croatia)

EXPLORE

CD4-02

1 **READ** the article about why people do not always make logical decisions. What often influences the decisions we make?

Making Decisions: Are you in control?

It's vacation time. You are planning a trip to visit your family, so you compare airlines. You learn that 87 percent of Flyright flights arrive on time and that Skyway flights are late 13 percent of the time. Which airline will you choose the next time you fly?

If you are like most people, you will probably choose Flyright. It seems more efficient than Skyway. However, **if you stop and think, you will find no difference between the two flight records**. Then, why did Flyright seem better at first? Psychologists explain that we are greatly influenced by the way we see information. For example, **if an option[1] is presented in a positive way, people usually prefer it**. That's why an 87 percent success rate seems better than a 13 percent failure rate. **Unless we think carefully, we don't realize the facts** are the same. Instead, we make a decision based on our first reaction.

The way we perceive[2] information greatly affects our decisions whether we are buying toothpaste or a car. It also has a powerful effect in politics and on the way people vote. Studies show that in the United States, people prefer candidates who talk about political issues in positive, encouraging ways. A politician's physical appearance matters, too. Voters like people who appear to be good leaders.

Even if we think our decisions are completely rational,[3] they are not. We make a lot of choices because information is presented in a certain way. However, **if we know this, we will be able to do something about it in the future**. We can try to think more seriously about our choices and consider them from different points of view. In that way, we can better control our decisions, both large and small.

[1] **option:** a choice
[2] **perceive:** become aware of something through the senses; understand something
[3] **rational:** showing clear, logical thought

2 CHECK. Read the statements. Circle **T** for *true* or **F** for *false*.

1. Flyright has a better flight record than Skyway.   **T**   **F**

2. We often make decisions because the options are presented to us in certain ways. **T**   **F**

3. A politician's appearance is not important to voters.   **T**   **F**

4. We think our decisions are rational, but they aren't always.   **T**   **F**

5. There is nothing that we can do to control our decision making.   **T**   **F**

3 DISCOVER. Complete the exercises to learn about the grammar in this lesson.

A Find these sentences in the article from exercise **1**. Write the missing words.

1. _____ like most people, you will probably choose Flyright.

2. However, _____ , you will find no difference between the two flight records.

3. . . . _____ in a positive way, people usually prefer it.

4. _____ our decisions are completely rational, they are not.

5. However, _____ ,we will be able to do something about it in the future.

B Look at the sentences in the box. Then answer the questions.

> a. Unless we think carefully, we don't realize the facts are the same.
> b. However, if we know this, we will be able to do something about it in the future.

1. Which sentence talks about a future result.   Sentence a.   Sentence b.

2. Which sentence talks about a fact that is generally true?   Sentence a.   Sentence b.

3. Which verb form is used after *if* and *unless*?

   a. *will* + the base form of the verb   b. the simple present

▲ Sunrise in Times Square, New York City

LEARN

13.1 Present Real Conditionals

1. A conditional sentence describes a condition and a result. The *if* clause gives the condition. The main clause tells the result.	<u>If I eat late at night,</u> <u>I don't sleep well.</u> *If Clause (Condition) Main Clause (Result)*
Present real conditionals describe facts, general truths, habits, or routines.	If it's very cold, my car doesn't start. If I take the train, I always bring a book. If the weather is nice, I walk to work.
2. A present tense verb is used in both clauses.	If you **talk** to friends, you **make** better decisions. **Do** you **make** better decisions if you **get** advice? If Tom **is** on the phone, he**'s talking** to Joe.
3. The *if* clause can come before or after the main clause with no change in meaning. Use a comma when it comes first.	I listen to the news in the morning **if I have time**. **If I have time in the morning**, I listen to the news.
4. A conditional clause can also begin with *unless*. *Unless* has the same meaning as *If . . . not*.	If I don't sleep ten hours, I feel tired. **Unless I sleep ten hours**, I feel tired.
5. A conditional clause can also begin with *even if*. *Even if* is used when the information in the main clause is unexpected or surprising.	**Even if Ari sleeps only five hours,** he has a lot of energy. I feel tired **even if I sleep for eight hours**.
6. In real conditionals, *when* can be used instead of *if*. The meaning is similar.	**If he has time**, he practices the piano. **When he has time**, he practices the piano.

4 Complete the exercises.

A Read each statement. Then choose the statement that is closest in meaning.

1. If my friends are wearing a certain brand of jeans, I buy the same brand.

   a. My friends wear a certain brand of jeans, so I wear the same brand.

   b. I buy a certain brand of jeans, so my friends wear them, too.

2. I don't go in a store if it is empty.

   a. When a store is empty, I don't go in.

   b. When I don't go into a store, nobody else does, either.

3. If I make a bad decision once, I don't make the same decision a second time.

   a. When I make a bad decision, I don't do it a second time.

   b. Once I made a bad decision, but I didn't make the same mistake again.

4. When I need advice, I ask a friend.

   a. My friends know I need advice when I ask.

   b. If I have a problem, I ask my friends for advice.

B Complete each sentence with the correct form of the verbs in parentheses.

1. If my friends _____*drive*_____ (drive) nice cars, I _____*want*_____ (want) one, too.

2. If a store _____ (have) an attractive window display, I _____ (go) in.

3. If I _____ (see) designer labels, I _____ (not be) impressed.

4. When my dad _____ (make) a mistake, he _____ (try) to correct it.

5. If my sister _____ (need) to make an important decision, she always _____ (think) carefully first.

6. If I _____ (buy) something that doesn't fit, I _____ (return) it.

7. When I _____ (have) a question about a product, I _____ (ask) a salesperson.

8. If I _____ (shop) when I'm tired, I _____ (not make) good decisions.

C **SPEAK.** Work with a partner. Look at the statements in exercises **B**. Are these statements true for you? Why, or why not?

Statement 1 is not true for me. If my friends have nice cars, I don't care. I want a car that's safe and doesn't use a lot of gas.

5 Complete the exercises.

A Circle the correct word(s) to complete each sentence.

1. **(If)/ Unless** you think you make rational decisions, you are mistaken.

2. Some people go shopping every weekend **if / even if** they don't need anything.

3. We often make decisions based on our emotions **when / unless** we don't have a lot of information.

4. We often buy brands that we know **even if / if** others are less expensive.

5. People often do something **if / even if** they see other people doing it.

6. **If / Unless** the salespeople in a store are rude to me, I leave.

7. **If / Unless** we understand the influences on our decisions, they continue to influence us.

8. I have friends who always wear stylish shoes **even if / if** they hurt their feet.

B **SPEAK.** Work with a partner. Complete the sentences with information about yourself.

1. When I need to make an important decision, I . . .

2. If someone gives me a gift I don't like, I . . .

3. Unless . . ., I don't buy it.

4. Even if I'm very tired, I . . .

When I need to make an important decision, I ask my friends and family for advice.

13.2 Future Real Conditionals

1. Future real conditionals describe possible conditions in the future and real results.	If he passes the exam, he will be very happy. 　　Condition　　　　　　　Future Result He won't graduate unless he passes. 　Future Result　　　　　Condition
2. Use the simple present in the *if* clause. Use *will* or a form of *be going to* in the main clause.	If you **go** to Caracas next year, you **will like** it. If I **finish** by 8:00, I'**m going to meet** my friends.
3. Other modals (*can, have to, could, may, might, must, should*) can be used in the *if* clause or main clause.	If I don't have to work late, I **may go** to a movie. If I **can't do** the work, I'll tell you.
4. Imperatives can also be used in the main clause.	If you go to the store, **buy some coffee.**
5. **Remember:** *Unless* means *If . . .not.*	**Unless** we leave soon, we'll be late.

6 Complete the exercises.

A Complete each sentence with the correct form of the verbs in parentheses. Use *will*.

1. Unless you _____make_____ (make) a decision, someone else
   ____will choose____ (choose) for you.

2. If you _____ (make) the wrong decision, it _____ (hurt)
   your future.

3. If a person _____ (worry) too much about always making the right
   decision, it _____ (not be) good for his or her health.

4. If someone _____ (think) too much about making the best decision, he or
   she _____ (have) a hard time making any decision at all.

5. If you _____ (not sleep) enough, it _____ (be) harder
   for you to make important decisions.

6. Unless you _____ (ask) someone who knows you for advice, you
   _____ (not get) advice that is right for you.

7. If you _____ (be) afraid of change, you _____ (not try)
   anything new.

8. If a person _____ (keep) an open mind, he or she _____
   (learn) new things.

B **SPEAK.** Work with a partner. Compare your answers from exercise **A**. Then discuss where other modals can be used in the sentences.

I think "might" can be used in number 1. Unless you make a decision, someone else might choose for you.

7 Paulo is trying to decide whether or not to do an internship. Use the words to write future real conditionals. Add commas where necessary.

1. Condition: Paulo / take the internship   Result: he / get some useful job experience

   If _Paulo takes the internship, he will get some useful job experience_ .

2. Condition: his coworkers / teach him new skills   Result: he / be interested

   _____ if _____ .

3. Condition: he / do the internship   Result: it / be good for his résumé

   If _____ .

4. Condition: he / accept the position   Result: he / meet new people

   If _____ .

5. Condition: the work / be physically demanding   Result: he / not get in shape

   _____ unless _____ .

6. Condition: he / have a paying job   Result: he / not be able to pay his bills

   _____ unless _____ .

7. Condition: his work hours / be 7:00 a.m. to 7:00 p.m.   Result: he / not accept the offer

   _____ if _____ .

8. Condition: he / enjoy the internship   Result: he / apply for the job

   If _____ .

PRACTICE

8 Put the words in the correct order to make sentences. Put the conditional clause first in 2–4. Put the conditional clause second in 5–8. Add commas where necessary.

1. a career that matches your talents / you / your job / will be more enjoyable / choose / if

   If you choose a career that matches your talents, your job will be more
   enjoyable. OR Your job will be more enjoyable if you choose a career that
   matches your talents.

2. have / don't realize it / we each / we / a personal work style / even if

   _____

   _____

3. a set schedule / you / will be happier / in a job that has flexible hours / if / don't like

   _____

   _____

4. you / a job that requires travel / don't take / to be away from home / don't like / if

_____

_____

5. helps you to succeed / if / a stressful job / a lot of pressure / good for you / might be

_____

_____

6. if / don't choose / important to you / making a lot of money / is / a low-paying career

_____

_____

7. you / excited about the job / the interviewer / won't be / seem / interested in you / unless

_____

_____

8. it / you / is / know all of your career possibilities / hard to make a decision / unless

_____

_____

9 WRITE & SPEAK.

A In your notebook, write three sentences about the careers in the box. Then write one sentence about another career that you know about. Use conditionals.

| accounting | business | computer science | education | engineering | medicine |

If you are good with numbers, you might like to work in accounting.

B Work with a partner. Share your sentences from exercise **A**. Do you agree with your partner's ideas? Why, or why not?

10 EDIT. Read the paragraph. Find and correct six more errors with conditionals.

If
∨
~~Even if~~ you don't want to work in an office every day, you should consider starting your own business. That's right, you can be your own boss! If you have a hobby that you are very good at, you might be able to earn a living doing it. For example, if you will have a talent for web design, you could sell your services to small companies. To get started, choose a company that you know about and show them some examples of web pages you've designed. Unless they like your work, offer to design a web page for them for a small fee. If you will do a good job the first time, they will probably hire you again. They may also recommend you to other businesses. Soon you'll have a lot of customers contacting you, and you'll be running your own business. If you don't make a lot of money, you'll feel satisfied and successful. You will also be doing something you love. Running your own business can be a lot of work, but it's worth it. If people will enjoy their jobs, they are usually happier. You won't know for sure unless you are going to try.

11 WRITE & SPEAK.

A Look at the information in the chart about the advantages and disadvantages of having your own business. In your notebook, write 6–8 sentences. Use present and future real conditionals and the information from the chart.

Having Your Own Business	
Advantages	Disadvantages
be your own boss	work 60–80 hours a week
have a lot of freedom	not have much free time
do something you love	take risks
make a lot of money	not have any paid vacation time

If you have your own business, you can be your own boss.

B Work in a group. Discuss this question: Would you prefer to have your own business or work for someone else? Give reasons. Use present and future real conditionals.

12 LISTEN.

CD4-03

A Listen to the talk about making decisions. Check (✓) the things that the speaker says may influence the decision-making process.

☐ the place   ☐ eating   ☐ too many choices   ☐ color

☐ the time of day   ☐ advice from friends   ☐ exercise   ☐ language

CD4-03

B Listen again. Then read the statements. Circle **T** for *true* or **F** for *false*.

1. It's often not helpful to spend a long time making a decision.   **T**   **F**

2. The best time to make decisions is early afternoon.   **T**   **F**

3. People should take a relaxing break before they make a decision.   **T**   **F**

4. Eating before making a decision will make you tired.   **T**   **F**

5. It's better to make emotional decisions in your native language.   **T**   **F**

13 APPLY.

A Read each situation. Then in your notebook, write 2–3 sentences about each situation. Use conditionals.

1. Harry is thinking of getting a motorcycle. It's less expensive than a car, but a car is safer.

   He'll save money if he gets a motorcycle.

2. Sophia is about to graduate from college. She would like to do volunteer work abroad for a year. However, her friends are going to graduate school or are getting jobs.

3. Veronica is taking a semester off from college to travel around Brazil for five months. She doesn't speak Portuguese. She is trying to decide if she should travel alone, with a friend, or with a tour group.

B Work in a group. Discuss the consequences for each situation in exercise **A** and the best decision for each person.

EXPLORE

CD4-04

1 READ the article about the debate over animals from the past. What is the main question in this debate?

Back to Life

Woolly mammoths, saber-toothed cats. These animals went extinct[1] thousands of years ago. Today, more animals continue to go extinct, and every year the number increases. **Scientists wish they could change the situation**. Some of them would like to bring extinct animals back to life. Experiments with a few species of birds and frogs suggest that this might be possible someday. Is it a good idea to revive[2] extinct animals? Some people say yes, but others don't agree.

The Argument for Revival

Reviving some species could help the environment. Consider, for example, the woolly mammoths. They lived on grass-covered land in Siberia, Russia, 12,000 years ago. However, after mammoths disappeared, the land turned into tundra.[3] Not many plants can grow there now. **If large numbers of mammoths were brought back, they could improve the land**. Scientists would also benefit. **If researchers could study a large variety of revived animals, they would learn a lot**; and much of the information could be used to help living species.

The Argument against Revival

Natural habitats change over time. **Would animals survive if they were revived? Would they die without their old habitats? Would they be a danger to creatures living in those regions now?** Perhaps they would be harmed by hunting or pollution and die out again. In addition, **if scientists focused on extinct species, they might not have time to spend on living species**.

There are still many questions about extinct species revival. **Even if scientists had more answers, people would continue to debate the issues**.

[1] **extinct:** no longer living
[2] **revive:** bring back to life
[3] **tundra:** treeless flat land found mostly in the Arctic Circle

▶ A museum worker checks the hair on this woolly mammoth replica. (Victoria, British Columbia, Canada)

2 **CHECK.** Answer the questions. Write complete sentences.

1. What do woolly mammoths and saber-toothed cats have in common?

   _____

2. What is happening to more animals every year?

   _____

3. How has the ancient woolly mammoth's habitat changed?

   _____

4. What are some dangers that revived species might experience today?

   _____

3 **DISCOVER.** Complete the exercises to learn about the grammar in this lesson.

A Read each sentence from the article in exercise **1**. Then read the statements below. Write **T** for *true* or **F** for *false*.

1. Scientists wish they could change the situation.

   _____ Scientists are not sure that they can change the situation.

2. If large numbers of mammoths were brought back, they could improve the land.

   _____ It is certain that large numbers of mammoths will be brought back.

3. If researchers could study a large variety of revived animals, they would learn a lot.

   _____ Researchers can't study a large variety of revived animals now.

4. Even if scientists had more answers, people would continue to debate the issues.

   _____ Scientists don't have all of the answers now.

B Look at sentences 2–4 in exercise **A** again. Circle **T** for *true* or **F** for *false*.

1. In sentences 2 and 4, the simple past is used in the *if* clause.   **T**   **F**

2. In sentences 2–4, the simple past is used in the main clause.   **T**   **F**

3. In sentence 2, the verb form in the *if* clause describes an action in the past.   **T**   **F**

4. In sentences 2–4, the sentences are about real situations.   **T**   **F**

▲ Yamal Peninsula,
Siberia, Russia

LEARN

13.3 Present and Future Unreal Conditionals

1. Present and future unreal conditionals describe situations that are untrue, impossible, or imaginary.	**If I lived in Rio de Janeiro,** I would go to the beach every day. (I don't live in Rio de Janiero.)
2. The *if* clause gives the condition, and the main clause gives the result.	If I lived downtown, I would walk to work. *If Clause (Condition) Main Clause (Result)*
Use the simple past in the *if* clause. Use *would* + the base form of the verb in the main clause. (*Could* and *might* can also be used in the main clause. *Could* is sometimes used in the *if* clause.)	**Would** we **save** money if we **bought** a smaller car? What **would** you **do** if you **won** the lottery? If you **didn't have to work**, you **could go** with us. If I **could travel** anywhere, I'**d go** to Peru.
3. **Be careful!** The verb after *if* is simple past, but the situation or event refers to the present or future.	If I **had a dog**, I would name it Rufus. If you **came here tomorrow**, we would have fun.
4. Use *were* for all subjects in the *if* clause. In informal conversation, *was* is often used for *I, he, she,* and *it*.	If **I were** rich, I would live somewhere different.
5. **Be careful!** The contracted *'d* has two meanings: *would* and *had*.	**He'd come** with us if he had the time. **He'd already left** when we arrived.
6. **Remember:** Use a comma when the *if* clause comes first in a sentence.	She'd take art classes **if she had more free time.** **If she had more free time,** she'd take art classes.

4 Complete the sentences with the correct form of the verbs in parentheses. Use *would*.

1. If extinct animals _____*were*_____ (be) brought back to life, there _____*would be*_____ (be) consequences.

2. Most people _____ (not believe) it if they _____ (see) a dinosaur.

3. Animals that have gone extinct _____ (cause) problems if they _____ (be) revived.

4. What _____ (happen) if woolly mammoths _____ (live) in Siberia now?

5. _____ it _____ (improve) the land if woolly mammoths _____ (be) alive today?

6. If my government _____ (spend) money on reviving extinct species, I _____ (be) unhappy.

7. If I _____ (be) a scientist, I _____ (be) interested in researching extinct species.

8. I _____ (major) in biology if I _____ (get) into a good program.

9. _____ fewer species _____ (go) extinct if people

_____ (take) better care of the environment?

10. It _____ (be) better for the environment if scientists _____ (spend) their energy on living species, not extinct species.

13.4 *Wish* + Simple Past/*Would*

1. Use the simple past or past progressive after *wish* to talk about present or future situations that you would like to be different.	We wish we **lived** in a nicer place. I wish I **didn't have to work** tomorrow. I wish I **were sitting** on a beach right now.
2. Use *were* for all subjects after *wish*. *Was* is often used in informal conversation.	**I wish it were** warmer. Then, I could go swimming. I can't pay my bills. I **wish I were** rich.
3. *Could* (not *can*) can be used after *wish*.	I wish I **could go** to the party next week.
4. Use *would* + the base form of the verb when you are dissatisfied or unhappy with something or someone.	I **wish** it **would stop** raining. I **wish** you **wouldn't leave** your dishes in the sink.
5. **Be careful!** Do not confuse *wish* with *hope*. *Wish* expresses a regret for something that will not happen. *Hope* expresses a desire for something that might happen. The simple past is used with *wish*, while the simple present is used with *hope*.	I **wish** I **did** better on tests, but I never do. I **hope** I **do** better on this test. I've studied a lot.

5 Complete the exercises.

A Circle the correct word(s) to complete each statement.

1. I wish I **am** / (**were**) a scientist.

2. I hope I **am helping** / **were helping** the environment.

3. I wish I **do** / **did** more interesting work every day.

4. I hope I **can find** / **could find** a better job.

5. I wish I **can work** / **could work** on a team.

6. I wish I **am sitting** / **were sitting** outside right now.

7. I wish I **live** / **lived** someplace else.

8. I wish my parents **called** / **calls** me more often.

9. I wish I **have** / **had** a fancy car.

10. I wish our teacher wouldn't **gave** / **give** us a lot of tests.

B **SPEAK.** Work with a partner. Say which of the statements in exercise **A** are true for you. Change the other statements to make them true for you.

Number 1 isn't true for me. I wish I were a musician, not a scientist.

PRACTICE

6 Complete the text about keeping wild animals as pets. Use present and future unreal conditionals and *wish* + the simple past or *would*. More than one answer is sometimes correct.

Wild Pets

Sometimes people find animals in the wild that are injured or orphaned and want to bring them home and keep them as pets. However, if they (1) ____understood____ (understand) some of the issues involved with keeping wild animals as pets, they (2) _____ (change) their minds. One issue is cost. Keeping certain kinds of animals can be very expensive. For example, some people want pet tigers, but if these people (3) _____ (realize) that tigers need about 5000 pounds (2 metric tons) of meat a year, they (4) _____ (think) again. Safety is another issue. Even if such people (5) _____ (know) a lot about wild animals, they (6) _____ (not be) able to keep the animals safe and healthy. They and other people might also be in danger, since attacks by wild animals are common. This can be a problem for both the pet and the owner.

Different countries have different laws about keeping wild animals as pets. For example, in England people are sometimes permitted to keep owls as pets. However, some people wish this (7) _____ (change). Animal rights groups wish the laws (8) _____ (be) stricter. Many people argue that if people (9) _____ (stop) buying and selling wild animals, it (10) _____ (help) more endangered species survive.

▼ A trainer with Ada the owl in Aragon, Spain. In some countries such as England, some people are permitted to keep owls as pets.

7 Read the sentences. What does each person wish for? Write a sentence about each person. Use *wish* + the simple past or *wish* + *would*.

1. Kate really wants a pet owl and is sad because she doesn't have one.

    Kate wishes she had a pet owl.

2. Len sees an injured deer in the road and doesn't know how to help it.

    _____

3. Josh's car broke down, and he doesn't have his cell phone with him.

    _____

4. Cars drive fast down Molly's street. She thinks it's very dangerous.

    _____

5. Jen wants to go to Australia, but her parents won't let her.

    _____

6. Meg can't sleep because her neighbors play loud music every night.

    _____

7. Anna's sister borrows her clothes without asking first. This bothers Anna very much.

    _____

8. It bothers Roland that his roommate never cleans their apartment.

    _____

8 WRITE & SPEAK.

A Complete the sentences to make them true about yourself.

1. I wish I _____.

2. I wish people _____.

3. I wish my family _____.

4. I wish my neighbors _____.

5. My family wishes I _____.

6. My family hopes I _____.

B Work with a partner. Share your sentences from exercise **A**. Ask your partner follow-up questions.

A: *I wish I could play the guitar really well.*

B: *Really? Do you want to be in a band?*

9 WRITE & SPEAK.

A Read the situations. Then give advice for each. Use *If I were you . . . .*

> **REAL ENGLISH**
>
> *If I were you* is a common way to give advice.
>
> **If I were you,** *I'd go to the doctor.*
> *I'd do some more research **if I were you**.*

1. I don't feel well, but I have two final exams tomorrow.

   <u>If I were you, I'd try to take the exams on another day.</u>

2. I really want to get a cat, but my roommate is allergic to them.

3. My parents want me to go to college next year, but I want to get a job so that I can make money.

4. My neighbor keeps parking his car in my parking space. I've already spoken to him once about it.

5. I'm very tired, but I haven't finished my assignment for tomorrow yet.

6. I have a friend who is always late. Sometimes I have to spend a long time waiting for her. It's very annoying!

7. I'm supposed to turn in an important assignment tomorrow for one of my classes, but I don't think I can finish it on time.

8. One of my coworkers is always interrupting me to tell me about his problems. I want to help him, but I can't get any work done!

B Think of three problems that you have. Write sentences about them.

   <u>My roommate stays up late every night watching movies. This is a</u>

   <u>problem for me because I have to get up early every morning.</u>

C Work with a partner. Share your problems from exercise **B**. Take turns giving each other advice. Use *If I were you . . . .*

A: *My roommate stays up late every night listening to music. This is a problem for me because I have to get up early every morning.*

B: *If I were you, I would talk to him first. If he doesn't stop, I would move out.*

10 PRONUNCIATION. Read the chart and listen to the examples. Then complete the exercises.

CD4-05

PRONUNCIATION	Contractions of *Would* and *Would Not*

Would and *would not* are often contracted after pronouns in conversation.

Examples:	Full Pronunciation	Contraction
	I **would** get a dog if I could.	I**'d** get a dog if I could.
	You **would** like him if you knew him.	You**'d** like him if you knew him.
	I **would not** open the door if I were you.	I **wouldn't** open the door if I were you.
	I **would not** read it even if I had the time.	I **wouldn't** read it even if I had the time.

The pronunciation of *it'd* sounds like /itəd/.

	It **would** be nice if you came.	It**'d** be nice if you came.

CD4-06

A Listen to the the statements. Write the full form of the missing words you hear.

1. If scientists could revive extinct animals, _____it would_____ be interesting to see them.

2. _____ help the environment if all species were preserved.

3. If extinct animals were brought back to life, _____ be happy.

4. _____ want to put more creatures on the planet if it were possible.

5. _____ be selfish if I wanted to see all the extinct animals revived.

6. If someone asked me to support a de-extinction project, _____ do it.

7. _____ help the environment more if we used fewer natural resources.

8. _____ be good for society if people shared more.

B Work with a partner. Take turns reading the sentences from exercise **A** aloud. Use the contracted forms of *would* and *would not*.

11 WRITE & SPEAK.

A Complete each sentence according to your own opinion and ideas. Use *would* or *would not* and an appropriate verb.

1. If scientists could revive extinct species, it __would be / wouldn't be__ useful.

2. If we released captive animals from zoos, they _____ in the wild.

3. If someone gave me a fur coat, I _____ it.

4. If I knew that a company harmed animals, I _____ their products.

5. If people were vegetarians, they _____ healthier lives.

6. If I found an injured bird, I _____ it as a pet.

7. There _____ less pollution if we used fewer natural resources.

8. If people shared more resources, it _____ the environment.

B Work with a partner. Compare your sentences from exercise **A**. Explain your ideas and opinions. Practice using the contracted forms of *would* and *would not*.

If scientists could revive extinct species, it'd be useful. They might learn things that could help endangered species.

12 WRITE & SPEAK.

A Read the sentences. Then rewrite each sentence with a present or future unreal conditional. Add commas where necessary. Sometimes there is more than one correct way to rewrite the sentence.

1. People want to keep wild animals as pets because they don't understand the consequences.

   If people understood the consequences, they would not want to keep

   wild animals as pets. OR People wouldn't want to keep wild animals as

   pets if they understood the consequences.

2. My sister is allergic to dogs, so we can't get one.

   _____

3. I can't go to the movies tonight because I have to work late.

   _____

4. Nick wants to take guitar lessons, but he doesn't have the time.

   _____

5. I'd like to walk to work every day, but I don't live near my office.

   _____

6. Lila isn't going to run in the race because she isn't in shape.

   _____

7. Tom and Sarah don't need a new car, so they aren't going to buy one.

   _____

8. I don't feel well, so I'm not going to go to the gym this afternoon.

   _____

B In your notebook, write three sentences about yourself. Use present or future unreal conditionals.

If my sister lived closer, I could see her more often.

C Work with a partner. Share your sentences from exercise **B**. Ask follow-up questions.

A: *If my sister lived closer, I could see her more often.*

B: *Where does she live?*

A: *In San Diego. I wish she didn't live so far away. I really miss her.*

13 EDIT. Read the conversation. Find and correct five more errors with conditionals and *wish*.

A: If someone on the street offered you money, ~~you would~~ *would you* take it?

B: No, I don't.

A: Why not? I often wish a stranger would give me money.

B: I guess I don't trust strangers. If a stranger tries to give me money, I'd think it was a trick. Nobody just gives money away without a reason.

A: What would you do if money would fall out of a window?

B: That would never happen either.

A: I guess you're right. I wish things like that happen, but they never do.

B: I know. I wish making money is that easy, but it's not.

14 READ & LISTEN.

A Read the text about sharing money. If a friend had to share $100 with you, how much do you think you would probably get?

What would *you* do?

What would you do if a stranger on the street offered you some money to share with a friend? Would you accept it? Would you give your friend half the money even if you wanted to keep more? Do you think your friend would accept less than half?

According to some economists, if people were being completely rational, they would offer as little money as possible. Researchers wanted to test that idea, so they did an experiment. Surprisingly, they found that when most people were given money to share, they offered their partners between 40 and 50 percent of it. Other studies showed that when people offered their partners less than 30 percent, their partners refused to take it. The results of the experiment clearly show that fairness plays an important role in people's decisions about sharing.

CD4-07

B Listen to the conversation. Do Mike and Jack get to keep the money?

CD4-07

C Listen again. Write the missing words that you hear.

Jack: Only five? Why not ten, Mike? That's what I (1) _____ you if I (2) _____ the money with you.

Mike: That's crazy. The woman gave me the money, not you. If I (3) _____ in your shoes, I (4) _____ happy with five dollars.

Jack: No, you (5) _____ . You (6) _____ upset if I (7) _____ it in half.

Mike: I wish you (8) _____ arguing with me.

15 WRITE & SPEAK.

A Use the words to write questions with conditional clauses. Add commas where necessary. Sometimes there is more than one correct way to write the question.

1. you / talk / to a stranger / if / he or she / stop / you on the street

   Would you talk to a stranger if he or she stopped you on the street?

2. if / a stranger / offer / you / money / take / it

   _____

3. if / you / get / some money / from a stranger / you / share / it

   _____

4. it / be / fair / if / you / keep / all the money / for yourself

   _____

5. if / your friend / not share / the money / you / get / angry

   _____

6. you / be / annoyed / if / the stranger / take / the money back

   _____

B Work in a group. Ask and answer the questions from exercise **A**.

A: *Would you talk to a stranger if he or she stopped you on the street?*

B: *Probably. But if the person seemed unfriendly, I don't think I would. I'd be afraid.*

16 APPLY.

A Work in groups. Discuss the answers to these situations.

1. Sometimes people buy wild animals to keep as pets. What would you do if one of your friends wanted to buy a baby tiger to keep as a pet?

2. Many people try to smuggle[1] exotic animals into or out of countries through airports. One man had a python[2] tied to him. Others have had snakes and spiders in their luggage and socks. One man even had a crocodile in his bag! What would you do if you saw this kind of activity?

   [1] **smuggle:** to bring things into or out of another country or area illegally
   [2] **python:** a large snake that wraps itself around its victims

B Choose one of the situations from exercise **A** and role-play it for the class.

EXPLORE

CD4-08

1 **READ** the article about Paul Salopek and his seven-year walk around the world. How does he stay in touch with the world?

21,000 miles, 3 miles per hour

Paul Salopek wants to slow down. He wants to learn more about our planet at a human pace . . . three miles per hour. That's why he's walking. Salopek is on a seven-year, 21,000-mile (33,796-kilometer) walk to follow the path of human migration[1] out of Africa, which occurred about 60,000 years ago. **If he had continued his work as a newspaper journalist, he would never have begun this incredible journey.**

Salopek's travels began in Ethiopia, across the Afar Triangle, one of the hottest deserts in the world. Water there is very scarce,[2] and the heat is overpowering.[3] Without his guides, Salopek knew he couldn't survive in such a harsh environment. In addition, **if the guides hadn't been so knowledgeable, Salopek could never have learned as much as he did about the land and its people.**

Thanks to modern technology, Salopek has been able to share the things he has learned so far through regular Internet postings. **This wouldn't have been possible if he hadn't taken along a laptop, satellite phone, camera, and digital recorder.**

Even with these devices that connect him with people thousands of miles away, Salopek knows that there will be times of loneliness. There might even be days when he **wishes he had never left home.** However, he also knows that there will be moments of great excitement and discovery, which will strengthen his deep commitment[4] to this journey of a lifetime.

[1] **migration:** movement from one place to another   [3] **overpowering:** too strong
[2] **scarce:** If something is scarce, there is not enough of it.   [4] **commitment:** a strong belief in an idea

► Journalist Paul Salopek leads a pair of camels across Ethiopia's Afar desert (Afar, Ethiopia).

For more information on Pulitzer Prize-winner Paul Salopek's trek, go to learn.outofedenwalk. com; pz.harvard.edu, an initiative of Project Zero, Harvard Graduate School of Education; or pulitzercenter.org/projects/out-of-eden, an initiative of the Pulitzer Center on Crisis Reporting.

2 **CHECK.** Correct the error in each statement to make it true according to the article.

1. Salopek is walking to follow the path of animal migration out of Africa.

2. Salopek walked across Ethiopia alone.

3. People can follow Salopek's journey by reading his newspaper articles.

4. Salopek sometimes feels lonely during his journey, and this may stop his future travels.

3 **DISCOVER.** Complete the exercises to learn about the grammar in this lesson.

A Read each sentence. Then choose the sentence that is closest in meaning.

1. If Salopek had kept his newspaper job, he would never have begun this incredible journey.

   a. He was able to begin the journey because he didn't keep his newspaper job.

   b. He didn't begin the journey because he had to continue working for the newspaper.

2. If the guides hadn't been so knowledgeable, he could never have learned as much as he did.

   a. Because the guides weren't very knowledgeable, he had to learn everything on his own.

   b. Because the guides were very knowledgeable, he could learn a lot from them.

3. Posting messages wouldn't have been possible without modern technology.

   a. Posting messages wasn't possible because Salopek didn't take along electronic devices.

   b. Electronic devices made it possible for Salopek to post messages.

4. There might be days when Salopek wishes he had never left home.

   a. There might be days when Salopek regrets that he left home.

   b. There might be days when Salopek feels he couldn't have left home.

B Look at sentences 1–4 in exercise **A** again. Then choose the correct answer for each question.

1. What time period do the sentences 1–3 refer to?

   a. the past   b. the present   c. the future

2. What verb form is used in the *if* clause in sentences 1 and 2?

   a. the simple past   b. the simple present   c. the past perfect

3. What verb form is used in the main clause in sentences 1 and 2?

   a. *would/could* + verb   b. *would/could have* + past participle   c. the past perfect

4. What verb form is used after *wish* in sentence 4?

   a. the simple past   b. the simple present   c. the past perfect

LEARN

13.5 Past Unreal Conditionals

1. Past unreal conditionals describe past conditions and results that did not happen. The conditions and results are impossible, not true, or imaginary.	**If he had gone to class, he would have seen her.** (He didn't go. He didn't see her.) **I wouldn't have gotten lost if I had used the GPS.** (I got lost. I didn't use the GPS.)
2. The *if* clause gives the condition, and the main clause gives the result. Use *if* + the past perfect in the *if* clause. Use *would have* + the past participle in the main clause.	If you had seen the movie, you would have liked it. *If Clause (Condition)* *Main Clause (Result)* She **would have come** if you **had invited** her. Would he **have taken** the job if they **had offered** it to him? If the weather **had been** nice, **would** you **have gone** to the beach?
3. Other modals such as *could* and *might* can also be used in the main clause.	If I had read the book, we **could have discussed** it. If he had stayed, he **might have enjoyed** himself.
4. **Remember:** Do not use the simple past after *if* to refer to the past. Use the past perfect.	✓ If he **had come** last week, I would have known. ✗ If he <u>came</u> last week, I would have known.
5. **Remember:** Use a comma when the *if* clause comes first in a sentence.	I would have graduated **if I had passed the test.** **If I had passed the test**, I would have graduated.

4 Complete the exercises.

A Circle the correct form of the verb to complete each sentence.

1. Would you have joined Salopek if he **invited /(had invited)** you on his journey?

2. If Salopek **had asked / asked** me to go on his journey, I might have said yes.

3. My family **hadn't been / wouldn't have been** happy if I had gone on such a trip.

4. If I had crossed the Afar Triangle, I **would have kept / had kept** a journal.

5. If I had stayed in the desert for a long time, I **had gotten / might have gotten** sick.

6. If I **had gone / went** to Ethiopia with Salopek, I would have brought a good camera with me.

7. If I **was / had been** in Ethiopia with Salopek, I would have wanted to try some Ethiopian coffee.

8. If you had traveled across the desert with Salopek, what would you **had worn / have worn**?

B **SPEAK.** Work with a partner. Take turns asking and answering questions 1 and 8 from exercise **A**.

A: *Would you have joined Salopek if he had invited you on his journey?*

B: *Yes, I would have.* OR *No, I wouldn't have.*

> **REAL ENGLISH**
>
> We do not repeat the verb in short answers with *would have.*
>
> A: *Would you have come?*
>
> B: *No, I **wouldn't have**.*

5 Complete the sentences about a walk in Kenya. Use the correct form of the verbs in parentheses and *would*.

1. If people _____hadn't chosen_____ (not choose) to participate in the walk, the Makindu Children's Program ____wouldn't have raised____ (not raise) so much money.

2. The trek through Kenya's Rift Valley _____ (be) easier if it _____ (not rain) so much.

3. The participants _____ (not be able) to walk for 10 days if they _____ (not be) in good shape.

4. If they _____ (not have) so much energy, the trekkers _____ (have) a lot of difficulty covering all 150 miles.

5. They _____ (get) sick if they _____ (not drink) a lot of water every day.

6. If they _____ (not use) camels to carry supplies, the trip _____ (not be) a success.

13.6 *Wish* + Past Perfect

1. Use the past perfect after *wish* to express regrets about events or situations that happened (or did not happen) in the past.	I wish I **had studied** harder for last week's test. I'm sorry now. I wish I **hadn't eaten** so much cake. Now I feel sick.
2. **Be careful!** Even though you are referring to a past time, do not use the simple past after *wish* to express regrets.	✓ I wish I **had gone** home yesterday. ✗ I wish I <u>went</u> home yesterday.
3. In short answers, do not include the past participle of the verb after *had*.	A: Do you wish you **had grown up** in California? B: Yes, I wish I **had**.
The past participle can also be omitted in follow-up statements.	A: Did you grow up in California? B: No, I didn't, but I wish I **had**.

6 WRITE & SPEAK.

A Complete the sentences. Use the correct form of the verb in parentheses.

1. I wish I _____had walked_____ (walk) to class today.

2. I wish I _____ (do) something different last weekend.

3. I wish I _____ (go) to bed earlier last night.

4. I wish I _____ (bring) a cup of coffee to class.

5. I wish our teacher _____ (not give) us any homework last night.

6. I wish I _____ (spend) more time on the last homework assignment.

7. I wish I _____ (not move) to this city.

8. I wish I _____ (wear) a different pair of shoes today.

B SPEAK. Work with a partner. Change the statements in exercise **A** to questions, and take turns asking and answering them. Add follow-up statements to your answers.

A: *Do you wish you had walked to class today?*

B: *Yes, I wish I had. I could have gotten my exercise!*

PRACTICE

7 READ & WRITE.

A Read the story from the movie *All Is Lost*.

> A man is on a sailboat in the Indian Ocean. When he wakes up one morning, he sees water in the bottom of the boat. He realizes that his boat has hit a large container that fell off a ship, and the crash has resulted in a hole in his boat. The man is very skillful, so he is able to repair the hole. Soon after, there is a bad storm, and his boat gets badly damaged. Before it sinks, the man takes some supplies and gets into a life raft. When two ships pass near his raft, he tries to signal them. Neither of the ships notices him. He is running out of food and water, so he is very worried. On the eighth night he sees a light in the distance and thinks it might be another boat. He lights a fire in the life raft, but the fire gets out of control, and the raft catches fire. The man falls off the raft into the ocean.

B Rewrite each sentence about the movie as a past unreal conditional. Add commas where necessary. Sometimes there is more than one correct way to rewrite the sentence.

1. There was water in his boat because it hit a large container.

   If his boat hadn't hit the large container, water wouldn't have gotten into

   the boat. OR Water wouldn't have been in his boat if it had not hit the

   large container.

2. The man was able to fix the hole because he was skillful.

   _____

   _____

3. He survived because he got into the life raft.

   _____

   _____

4. The people on the other ships didn't see him, so they didn't rescue him.

   _____

   _____

5. The man fell into the ocean because his life raft caught on fire.

_____

_____

6. The man had this terrible experience because he went out on his boat.

_____

_____

C Read the sentences. Then write sentences about what the man probably wishes. Begin each sentence with *He wishes . . . .*

1. The shipping container hit his boat.

   He wishes the shipping container hadn't hit his boat.

2. The weather wasn't good.

   _____

3. The people on the other ships did not notice him.

   _____

4. He didn't take a lot of food and water from his boat.

   _____

5. He couldn't put out the fire on the life raft.

   _____

6. He didn't stay home.

   _____

▶ A rough sea

8 PRONUNCIATION. Read the chart and listen to the examples. Then complete the exercises.

CD4-09

> **PRONUNCIATION**   **Reduced Forms of *Would Have***
>
> *Would have* and *would not have* are often reduced in conversation. *Have* is often pronounced like the word *of*.
>
> Examples: Full Pronunciation
> If Meg had known, she **would have** called.
> If I had seen her, I **would have** told you.
> If you had stayed, Ray **would not have** left.
> If it had been cold, we **would not have** gone.
>
> Reduced Pronunciation
> If Meg had known, she ***would of*** called.
> If I'd seen her, I ***would of*** told you.
> If you'd stayed, Ray ***wouldn't of*** left.
> If it'd been cold, we ***wouldn't of*** gone.
>
> In informal conversation, *woulda* is common.
>
> If you had asked me, I **would have** helped.   If you'd asked me, I **woulda** helped.

CD4-10

A Listen to the sentences. Write the full forms of the missing words you hear.

1. If the weather hadn't gotten so bad, the ship _____ stuck in ice.

2. The ship _____ its destination if it hadn't gotten stuck.

3. If a helicopter hadn't rescued the people, they _____ in danger.

4. The people _____ if the ship hadn't had plenty of food.

5. If there hadn't been Internet connection, the people _____ able to communicate with the outside world.

6. If they had stayed much longer, many people _____ to worry.

B Work with a partner. Take turns saying the sentences from exercise **A**. Practice the reduced pronunciation of *would have* and *would not have*.

9 WRITE & SPEAK.

A Complete the sentences to make them true about yourself.

1. I wish my parents _had encouraged me to take risks_ when I was a child.

2. If I hadn't heard about _change of status, I wouldn't have the students english_

3. I wouldn't have met _my nice friends if_ _____.

4. I wouldn't have tried _____.

5. I wish I _____ last weekend.

6. I would have gone _____.

7. I wish I _____ when I was in school.

8. I wish I _____ before class.

9. If I had known _____.

10. My _____ wishes _____.

B Work with a partner. Share your sentences from exercise **A**. Ask each other questions for more information.

A: *I wish my parents had encouraged me to take risks when I was growing up.*

B: *What kind of risks?*

A: *Well, I wanted to start my own business, but they thought it would be too expensive to start.*

10 APPLY.

A Think about a decision you made that has affected your life. In your notebook, write a short paragraph about this decision that answers the following questions. Use past unreal conditionals and *wish* + the past perfect.

What do you wish you had done differently?

What might have made you change your mind about your decision?

How would the consequences have been different if you had made a different decision?

How did the decision affect your life?

I once had the chance to take a long trip by myself, but I decided not to. Now I wish I had. I might have gone if my parents had encouraged me, but they were nervous about the idea. If I had traveled alone for six months, I would have learned to make decisions on my own.

B Work in a group. Take turns reading your paragraphs from exercise **A**. Ask each other questions for more information.

1 Match the beginning of each sentence in Column A with the correct ending in Column B.

Column A

1. If I had more time, __f__ .

2. If I drink coffee in the afternoon, _____ .

3. If I hadn't wasted time on the weekend, _____ .

4. Unless it rains on Saturday _____ .

5. Will you be able to finish our project _____ ?

6. You would save time _____ .

7. Even if I had studied more, _____ .

8. I wouldn't have finished the report _____ .

Column B

a. I can't fall asleep at night.

b. if I leave early today

c. if you took the subway instead of driving

d. if you hadn't helped me with it

e. I wouldn't have passed the test

f. I'd go to the movies more often

g. I'm going to go hiking

h. I would've finished all my work

2 WRITE.

A Read each sentence about the future. Is the situation likely or unlikely for you? Write **L** (*likely*) or **N** (*not likely*) next to each sentence.

_____ 1. I will get a very well-paying job.

_____ 2. I will have my own business.

_____ 3. I will go to graduate school.

_____ 4. I will live to be 100.

_____ 5. I will become famous.

_____ 6. I will buy a house next year.

_____ 7. I will work abroad in 10 years.

_____ 8. I will move this year.

B In your notebook, write real and unreal conditionals according to your answers in exercise **A**.

__L__   If I get a very well-paying job, I'll retire at the age of 50.

__N__   If I got a very well-paying job, I'd retire at the age of 50.

3 Complete each conversation with the correct form of the verb in parentheses.

1. **Jesse:** Are you happy to be living in the twenty-first century?

   Carla: Well, sometimes I wish things _____ *moved* _____ (move) more slowly.

2. **Elena:** Why didn't you mention the new book about time travel in your report?

   Eric: I wish someone _____ (tell) me about it. I didn't realize it had been published.

3. **Dan:** I decided to change my topic. I couldn't find information about time machines.

   Kate: I wish I _____ (know). I could've helped you do research.

4. **Deema:** I miss working with you and your team on physics projects.

   Antonio: We miss you, too. We wish you _____ (be) here.

5. **Matt:** I wish Craig _____ (arrive) on time for our meetings.

   Lily: I know. He's always late.

6. **Bill:** We missed you in the lab today. We made a lot of progress.

   Rosa: I wish I _____ (be able) to come, but I had to go to a meeting.

7. **Kitty:** What's the matter? Didn't you like the movie?

   Paul: I wish I _____ (not see) it. It was terrible!

8. **Chris:** Are you reading *The Time Machine* by H. G. Wells?

   Zahra: Yes. We have to read it for class. Some of my classmates wish we _____ (not have to) read it. I love science fiction, though, so I'm enjoying it.

4 EDIT & SPEAK.

Charts 13.1–13.6

A Read the text. Find and correct eight more errors with conditionals and *wish*.

Would you travel in time?

                                              were
Some people wish it ~~is~~ possible to travel back into the past. If it were possible, they can go back to any time they wanted. At least, that's what they think. Actually, this isn't true, but it's easy to get the wrong idea. When you will see movies about time travel, you don't always get the full story. In fact, you can only go back to the time when your time machine was created. For example, if your time machine was created on January 1st, and you traveled in it six months later, then you can't travel back in time any earlier than January 1st.

Why is time travel such an attractive idea? We all have done things in the past that we wish we hadn't done. We wish things happened differently. For example, if I didn't go to the store the day of my car accident, the accident wouldn't have happened. I wouldn't have gotten hurt if it didn't happen. If time travel allowed us to go back in time, it will be possible to prevent bad experiences. Wouldn't we all want to do that if we could? It's too bad we can't.

Future time travel, however, is possible. If scientists figure out how to do it, people will be able to see their lives 20 or 30 years into the future. If you could travel 20 or 30 years into the future, will you want to do it?

B Work in a group. Discuss these questions.

If you could go back in time, what year or time period would you want to visit?

Why would you want to go back to that year or time period?

What do you think you would see?

What would you want to change about that year or time period?

Chart
13.1, 13.3,
13.5

5 LISTEN & SPEAK.

CD4-11

A Read the questions in the chart. Then listen to the podcast about a physicist and take notes on the answers.

1. Why did young Mallett want to go back in time?	His father died.
2. What did he read that made him think about making a time machine?	
3. What could Mallett do if he had a time machine?	
4. Why did Mallett keep his work a secret?	
5. What does Mallet believe will happen if he keeps making progress?	
6. How could time machines be helpful?	

B In your notebook, write sentences using the information from the chart in exercise **A**. Use conditionals.

If his father hadn't died, Mallett wouldn't have wanted to go back in time.

Charts
13.1–13.6

6 WRITE & SPEAK.

A Work with a partner. Your teacher will assign you one of the opinions below. In your notebook, write a list of reasons to support this opinion.

1. Governments should fund research on time machines.

2. Governments should not fund research on time machines.

B Get together with another pair of students who discussed the opposite opinion. Have a debate about this question: Do you think governments should fund research on time machines? Use conditionals when giving your reasons.

Governments should fund work on time machines. If researchers were able to do more work in this area, they might make other important discoveries about our world.

C Decide which team had the better argument. Then discuss your real opinion about this topic.

1 READ & NOTICE THE GRAMMAR.

A When you think about choosing a career, what is most important to you? The salary? The hours? Helping others? Tell a partner your ideas. Then read the essay.

Choosing the Right Career

Parents always ask what we want to be when we grow up. Very often, they wish that we would choose a career that makes a lot of money. They might think this is in our best interest. After all, if you have money, you have fewer financial worries. However, this doesn't mean that a high-paying career will make you happy. For me, having a meaningful, family-oriented job is more important.

I would make this choice for a couple of reasons. First, people who choose a high-paying career just for the money might find they really don't like it. For example, I knew a woman who was a successful attorney, but she was very unhappy. She didn't find any meaning in the work at all. She spent all day doing legal paperwork and preparing tax documents for corporations. You spend most of your life at work, so it is terrible to dislike your job. I think that people who dislike their jobs are not truly happy even if they are wealthy. Unless I made enough money to retire early, I would not choose a job that I disliked. I want to enjoy my work even if it means I will make less money.

In addition, spending time with my family and friends is very important to me. High-paying careers, such as those in finance, law, or medicine, require very long hours. I know a man in finance who is gone about 12 hours a day. He comes home at 7 or 8 p.m. Sometimes he also works at night from home. His wife raises the kids. He really only spends time with them on the weekends. If I had no time for my kids, I would be very unhappy. I know several retired people who wish that they had spent more time with their families. They can't change that now. I don't want to have the same regrets.

Some people value wealth and their careers more than anything else. They may not care if the work they do is interesting, as long as it pays very well. Some people never have children, and their job is their life. But for me, I want a job that I enjoy—one that will give me enough time to spend with family and friends.

GRAMMAR FOCUS

In the essay in exercise **A**, the writer uses the following conditionals to describe conditions and results.

Present real conditionals	• are used to describe facts, general truths, habits, or routines. *. . . if you have money, you have fewer financial worries.*
Present unreal conditionals	• are used to describe situations that are untrue, impossible, or imaginary. *If I had no time with my kids, I would be very unhappy.*

B Read the essay in exercise **A** again. Underline the conditionals. Decide if each conditional is real or unreal. Write **R** (*real*) or **U** (*unreal*) above each conditional. Then work with a partner and compare your answers.

C Complete the chart with information from the essay in exercise **A**. Then work with a partner and compare your answers.

> **Introduction (Background Information):**
> I don't want a job that I don't like even if it pays well.

> **Main Idea:** I want a meaningful job that lets me spend time with my family.

> **Reason #1:** _____

> **Reason #2:** _____

2 BEFORE YOU WRITE.

A Work with a partner. Discuss these questions: What careers would you enjoy or not enjoy? Do these careers pay well? How important is money to you when choosing a career?

B In your notebook, make a chart like the one in exercise **1C** and complete it in response to this question: What is the most important factor for you when choosing a job or career? Write notes about your ideas and reasons in your chart.

3 WRITE about your response to the question in exercise **2B**. Write three or four paragraphs. Use your chart from exercise **2B** and the text in exercise **1A** to help you.

> **WRITING FOCUS   Avoiding Sentence Fragments**
>
> An *if* clause must be attached to a main clause to be a complete sentence. An *if* clause by itself is a sentence fragment. To correct a fragment, connect the *if* clause to the main clause.
>
> ✗ *I want to enjoy my work. Even if it means I will make less money.*
> ✓ *I want to enjoy my work even if it means I will make less money.*

4 SELF ASSESS. Underline the verb forms in your essay. Then use the checklist to assess your work.

- ☐ I used a comma in conditional sentences when the *if* clause came first. [13.1]
- ☐ I used real conditionals correctly. [13.2]
- ☐ I used unreal conditionals and *wish* correctly. [13.3, 13.4]
- ☐ I avoided sentence fragments. [WRITING FOCUS]

Noun Clauses and Reported Speech

▶ An ice cream vendor in Istanbul, Turkey; *Dondurma*, as the treat is known there, is thicker and chewier than traditional ice cream.

EXPLORE

CD4-12

1 **READ** the article about the relationship between food and the brain. According to some scientists, what made the brain of early humans grow fast?

The Power of a Hot Meal

The human brain is considerably larger than the brain of most animals. In fact, our brains have about three times as many neurons[1] as those of gorillas and chimpanzees. Scientists believe **that the human brain grew faster than the brains of other animals**. Research shows **that our brains grew most rapidly about 1.8 million years ago**. Researchers are trying to explain **why this happened**.

Biological anthropologist[2] Dr. Richard Wrangham thinks **that the brain began to grow rapidly when humans first learned to cook**. Cooking made it easier and faster for humans to digest food and gain energy for the brain and the body. By contrast, gorillas, chimps, and other apes continued to eat raw food, which took longer to eat and was harder to process. It also provided less energy.

Neuroscientist[3] Suzana Herculano-Houzel supports the cooking theory. One of her studies looked at the effect of raw food on the body. Her findings showed **that a raw-food diet doesn't provide enough energy for significant brain growth**.

Other scientists wonder **if the cooking theory is right**. Some of them aren't sure **whether or not people were cooking over one million years ago**. That's because there is no evidence of fire being used for food preparation until much later. Scientists also point out the importance of the greater variety of foods that early humans began to eat, which included more protein and fat.

Perhaps we will never know exactly **what caused the rapid growth of the brain**. However, continuing scientific research brings us closer to the truth all the time.

[1] **neuron:** a cell that sends messages to and from the brain
[2] **biological anthropologist:** a scientist who studies the physical and social development of humans and animals
[3] **neuroscientist:** a scientist who studies the brain

2 CHECK. Work with a partner. Discuss answers to the questions according to the information in the article. Then discuss your answers as a class.

1. What is one advantage of cooking food?
2. Why doesn't a raw-food diet support brain growth?
3. Why do some scientists doubt the cooking theory?

3 DISCOVER. Complete the exercises to learn about the grammar in this lesson.

A Find these sentences in the article from exercise **1**. Write the missing words.

1. Research shows _____*that*_____ our brains grew most rapidly about 1.8 millions years ago.

2. Researchers are trying to explain _____ this happened.

3. Other scientists wonder _____ the cooking theory is right.

4. Some of them aren't sure _____ people were cooking over one million years ago.

B What follows each word or phrase that you wrote in exercise **A**?

a. an adjective + verb   b. a verb + object   c. a subject + verb

◀ Replica of a Stone Age house. People have been cooking with fire since prehistoric times. (Senales, Bolzano, Italy)

LEARN

14.1 Noun Clauses with *That*

Noun/Noun Phrase	Noun Clause
Gina discovered **the problem**. The problem is **her food**.	Gina discovered **that her refrigerator is broken**. The problem is **that her food will go bad**.

1. A noun clause can replace a noun or a noun phrase in a sentence. *That* can introduce a noun clause. **Remember:** A clause always has a subject + a verb.	Gina knows **that** <u>her food</u> <u>will go</u> **bad**. Subject Verb
2. Certain verbs that involve thinking or mental activity are often followed by noun clauses.* agree feel hope realize believe find out know show discover forget notice think	I **thought** that you knew the answer. Do you **feel** that you're working too hard?
3. A noun clause can follow *be* + certain adjectives. afraid glad sorry true certain interesting sure upset concerned lucky surprised worried	He **was surprised** that the door isn't locked. It **is interesting** that the door is open.
4. A noun clause can be used after the verb *be*.	The problem is **that I don't have my keys**.
5. In speaking and informal writing, *that* is often omitted.	I realized **that I needed some help.** I realized **I needed some help.**

*See page **A9** for a list of verbs followed by noun clauses.

4 Read the paragraph about raw-food diets. Underline eight more noun clauses.

Is a raw-food diet better for us?

Some people feel <u>that we should eat the way our ancestors did</u>. In other words, they believe that raw food is healthier for human beings. People that think like this eat only raw food, including some meats. Often they believe that a raw-food diet is better for the environment. Some hope they will lose weight by eating only raw food. But not everyone agrees.

"If you're healthy, this is a terrible idea," said neuroscientist Suzana Herculano-Houzel. The problem is that humans have to eat lots of raw food to get all the necessary nutrients. That takes a lot of time. Also, people forget that our bodies have changed over time. Thus, we may not be able to eat exactly as our ancestors did. However, it is true that many diets of the past were healthier. We probably should try to eat more simply as our ancestors did. For example, we can avoid food that is processed. Most people agree that we should eat more vegetables. Some people are also certain that a diet of different-colored foods (red radishes, green spinach, blueberries) is especially beneficial.

5 WRITE & SPEAK.

A Write sentences in your notebook. Combine words from the first column with a noun clause in the second. Express your own opinions.

I (don't) agree	our ancestors had a better diet
I (don't) believe	eating raw food is healthier
I (don't) feel	cooked food tastes better than raw food
I'm (not) surprised	a raw-food diet is a good way to lose weight

I agree that cooked food tastes better than raw food.

B Work with a partner. Discuss your sentences. Give reasons for your opinions.

I don't agree that cooked food always tastes better than raw food. For example, cooked carrots are OK, but I prefer raw ones.

14.2 Noun Clauses with *If* and *Whether*

Yes/No Question	Noun Clause with *If/Whether*
Is dinner ready?	I'm not sure. I'll ask **if dinner is ready.**
Does he eat meat?	I don't know **whether he eats meat.**
Have you had food poisoning?	I'm not sure **if I've had food poisoning.**

1. Use *if* or *whether* to express a *Yes/No* question as a noun clause. A noun clause with *if* or *whether* can be part of a statement or a question.	*Yes/No* Question: Does he have my number? I'm not sure **if he has my number.** Do you know **whether he has my number?**
2. Use statement word order after *if* or *whether*. Do not use question word order.	✓ Do you know whether **he is** coming? ✗ Do you know whether <u>is he</u> coming?
3. Use *whether*, not *if*, after a verb + preposition.	✓ She **talked about whether** she should move. ✗ She talked about <u>if</u> she should move.
4. When *if* or *whether* begins a noun clause, *or not* is sometimes added to the end of the clause. It is possible to add *or not* directly after *whether*, but not after *if*.	I didn't notice **if** the car was locked **or not.** I didn't notice **whether** the car was locked **or not.** ✓ I don't know **whether or not** I passed the test. ✗ I don't know <u>if or not</u> I passed the test.

6 Complete the exercises.

A Complete the sentences. Change each *Yes/No* question to a noun clause. Add a period (.) or question mark (?) to each sentence.

1. Is it a good idea to eat different colored foods?

   Can you tell me whether <u>it's a good idea to eat different colored foods?</u>

2. Should people drink more water?

   I'm not sure if _____

3. Does a salt-free diet benefit everyone?

   Do you know if _____

4. Do most people eat a lot of carbs?

   I'm not sure whether _____

5. Is coffee good for your health?

   Is there research about whether _____

6. Do most people follow a specific diet?

   I'm not sure whether or not _____

7. Have you had an allergic reaction to a food?

   I can't remember if _____

8. Are artificial colors in foods harmful?

   Do you know whether _____

B SPEAK. Work with a partner. Compare your answers to exercise **A**. Then read and respond to each sentence you completed using your own knowledge.

A: *Can you tell me whether it's a good idea to eat different colored foods?*

B: *I think it is a good idea. My mother always said, "A colorful plate is a healthy plate!"*

14.3 Noun Clauses with *Wh-* Words

Wh- Question	Noun Clause with *Wh-* Words
Why did you miss the deadline? When did the teacher arrive? What time do you want to leave?	Please explain **why you missed the deadline**. I wonder **when the teacher arrived**. Can you tell me **what time you want to leave**?

1. A noun clause can begin with a *wh-* word such as *when, where, why, who, what, how, whose, how many, how much,* and *how old*.	I wonder **when the cooking class is starting**. Do you remember **how the oven works**? Did you write down **what the instructor said**? Can you tell me **how much the ring costs**?
2. A noun clause with a *wh-* word can be part of a statement or a question. Use statement word order (subject + verb) in noun clauses with *wh-* words.	✓ I'm not sure **where the park is**. ✗ I'm not sure where <u>is the park</u>. ✓ Can you tell me **how far the park is**? ✗ Can you tell me how far <u>is the park</u>?
3. Do not use *do, does, did* in noun clauses with *wh-* words.	*Wh-* Question: Where do the Smiths live? ✓ I have no idea **where the Smiths live**. ✓ Do you know **where the Smiths live**? ✗ I have no idea where <u>do the Smiths live</u>.

7 Circle the correct answers.

1. I don't understand this recipe. I'm not sure what
   should I do /(I should do) next.

2. Can you tell me how **is this lasagna made / this lasagna is made**?

3. I can't remember when **I've ever eaten / have I ever eaten** such good lasagna.

4. Could you tell me what spices **you have added / have you added** to the lasagna?

5. Do you remember when **were you given / you were given** this recipe?

6. I'm not sure what **foods do I prefer / foods I prefer** the most. I like everything!

7. I don't understand why **some people don't like / don't some people like** cooking?

8. My mother doesn't understand why **cooking is / is cooking** my favorite hobby. She hates being in the kitchen.

REAL ENGLISH

Use words such as *Could you tell me. . .*, or *Can I ask. . .* before a noun clause with a *wh-* word to make a question sound more polite.

Could you tell me what time it is?
Can I ask where the restroom is?

---

8 Complete the sentences. Change each question in parentheses to a noun clause. Add a period (.) or question mark (?) to each sentence.

1. We've been waiting a long time for a table. Can I ask <u>how much longer we have to wait?</u>
   (How much longer do we have to wait?)

2. Nobody has taken our order yet. Could you tell me _____
   (Who is our server?)

3. Can you tell me _____ I'd like to make it at home.
   (How is this salad made?)

4. I've never seen the word *stew* before. Could you explain _____
   (What does *stew* mean?)

5. I'm allergic to peppers. I'd like to know _____
   (What vegetables are in the soup?)

6. I need to get some cash. Do you have any idea _____
   (Where is there an ATM?)

7. I'm not that hungry. Could you tell me _____
   (How much does a half order cost?)

8. I reserved a table. I wonder _____
   (Why isn't my table ready?)

PRACTICE

9 Complete the sentences with *if, that,* or *whether.* Write all possible answers.

1. Did you know _____that_____ we are quickly losing many different varieties of food?

2. Experts believe _____ we used to have more than 7000 types of apples. Now we have fewer than 100.

3. The problem is _____ we may lose even more food varieties in the future.

4. Some people wonder _____ the food varieties we depend on might become extinct.

5. Do you know _____ or not anything can be done to prevent the loss of more foods?

6. Many people hope _____ we will be able to protect our future food supply by saving seeds today.

7. Are scientists worried _____ our food sources will be threatened by climate change?

8. I wonder _____ governments around the world are doing anything to help.

10 Complete the exercises.

A Put the words in the correct order to complete the conversations. Add the correct end punctuation. Each sentence has a noun clause.

Conversation 1

Jen: Do you know where potatoes were first grown? _____
　　　　(1) where / were / know / potatoes / you / first grown / do

Dan: _____
　　　　(2) originally came / think / I / from Ireland / that / potatoes

Jen: _____ They came from Peru.
　　　　(3) that / you're / I'm / wrong / afraid

Dan: _____
　　　　(4) potatoes / I / never realized / South America / came from / that

　　　　_____
　　　　(5) I / how many / are grown there / wonder / varieties of potatoes

Jen: Thousands. They are really important to the people of Peru, too.

Dan: Really?

Jen: Yes. _____
　　　　(6) I / heard / hold a special ceremony / they / after the potato harvest / that

　　　　_____

Conversation 2

Leo: I missed class yesterday. _____
(7) you tell me / can / we covered / what

Ann: Yes. We talked about the Great Potato Famine in Ireland in the 1860s. There wasn't enough to eat, and about a million people died.

Leo: Wow. That's terrible. _____
(8) caused the famine / did / learn / you / what

Ann: _____
(9) that / a harmful fungus / believe / I / destroyed the potatoes

Leo: Can you explain? _____
(10) what / is / I'm not / a fungus / sure

Ann: It's the stuff that can grow on plants and animals. It can kill them. It destroyed all of the potatoes in Ireland.

Leo: What happened then? A lot of people must have left because of the famine.

Ann: Yes, they did.

Leo: _____
(11) you / know / do / where / went / they

Ann: _____
(12) that / over one million people / I / think / emigrated to the United States

▼ The ruins of the village of Slievemore on Achill Island, Ireland.
The people left the village during the Great Potato Famine.

B SPEAK. Work with a partner. What other places have experienced a famine? Why? Discuss your answers.

A: *I read about a famine in Ethiopia in the early 1980s.*   B: *Do you know what caused it?*
A: *I'm not sure why it happened.*

11 Complete the exercises.

A Complete the sentences. Change each question in parentheses to a noun clause. Add a period (.) or question mark (?) to each sentence.

1. Is it true _____ *that people cooked over open fires in prehistoric times?*
   (Did people cook over open fires in prehistoric times?)

2. Do you know _____
   (Were the first cast-iron stoves built by the French?)

3. Do you know _____
   (How did people cook in China before cast-iron stoves were invented?)

4. I'm not sure _____
   (Where was the first wood-burning stove invented?)

5. I have no idea _____
   (When were gas stoves invented?)

6. Can you tell me _____
   (What country was the gas stove invented in?)

7. I'm not certain _____
   (Did people in America use ovens shaped like beehives?)

8. I wonder _____
   (Did people cook first with gas or electricity?)

9. Do you have any idea _____
   (When did people start using microwaves in their homes?)

10. Do you know _____
   (Where did people start using solar ovens?)

B **SPEAK.** Work with a partner. Look at the timeline. Take turns asking and responding to the questions or statements in exercise **A**.

A: *Is it true that people cooked over open fires in prehistoric times?*

B: *Yes, the timeline shows that people cooked over open fires in Egypt then.*

Open-fire cooking	Cast-iron stoves	Wood-burning stove	Gas stove	Beehive-shaped ovens	Electric stove	Microwave ovens in homes	Solar ovens in homes
Egypt (prehistoric)	China (220 AD)	France (1490)	England (1826)	Early America (1800s)	Canada (1882)	US (1960s)	California, US (1980s)

◀ Beehive-shaped ovens (Utah, USA)

CD4-13

12 LISTEN & SPEAK.

A Listen to the beginning of a radio show about solar cooking. Check the benefits you hear.

- [ ] convenient
- [ ] easy
- [ ] fast
- [ ] fun
- [ ] healthy
- [ ] inexpensive
- [ ] modern
- [ ] safe

▲ A solar oven made by Stephen Heckeroth. Mendocino, California

CD4-14

B Listen to the rest of the radio show. Complete the noun clauses with information you hear. More than one correct answer may be possible.

1. The host, Jack, wants to know what _Molly is making_ .

2. Molly is not sure whether _____ better with solar cooking or not.

3. Molly knows that _____ a terrific way to save energy.

4. Jack has always wondered if _____ only on a warm day.

5. Jack asks Molly to explain how _____ .

6. Jack can't understand why _____ with solar energy.

7. Molly thinks that _____ more popular.

8. Molly believes that _____ a very healthy way to cook.

C Work with a group. Take turns answering the questions. Begin your answers with phrases such as, *I (don't) think . . ., I (don't) believe . . ., I'm (not)sure . . ., I (don't) know . . .*

1. According to the audio, how does solar cooking work?

2. Are there any possible problems with solar cooking?

3. Would you like to try solar cooking? Why or why not?

A: *I'm sure the sun cooks the food, but I'm not sure how, exactly.*

B: *I think the woman said something about the color of the pan, but I'm not sure, either.*

13 EDIT. Read the text about prehistoric people's use of spices. Find and correct five more errors with noun clauses.

Ancient Foodies?

Researchers have found $\overset{that}{\cancel{if}}$ ancient Europeans were cooking with garlic mustard seeds over 5000 years ago. The findings come from archaeological sites in Denmark and Germany, where the seeds were found inside pieces of pottery. Archaeologists think people used the seeds in their cooking. Because the seeds have no nutritional value, archaeologists are convinced that were used to add flavor to other foods.

The researchers have explained why are their findings important. Although other examples of ancient spices have been found, these seeds are the first to be linked to cooking. In earlier studies, scientists weren't sure if or not these spices had been used in cooking. Experts believed that prehistoric people simply ate food for energy without caring about its taste. Until the garlic mustard seed discovery, they had no idea how much did early humans think about their food preparation. Now scientists realize that flavor was important to people long ago. In the future, researchers would like to find out what other spices did early humans use, but it won't be an easy task.

14 APPLY.

A Write in your notebooks. Use noun clauses with the phrases in the box to answer the questions. Use your own ideas.

I think (that) . . .	I'm (not) concerned (that) . . .	I don't know if / whether . . .
I believe (that) . . .	I'm (not) sure (that) . . .	I wonder if/whether . . .

1. Is solar cooking a good idea?

   I believe solar cooking is a good idea because it saves energy.

2. Why do you believe that some people choose to become vegetarians?

3. Are you worried about our food varieties disappearing?

4. Are you concerned about eating food that has chemicals in it?

5. A lot of food is wasted. Do you think this is a big problem? Why, or why not?

B Work with a partner. Share your answers to exercise **A**.

A: *I believe solar cooking is a good idea because it saves energy.*

B: *I agree. I think it's healthier, too.*

EXPLORE

CD4-15

1 **READ** the web page about Charles Spence's research on food and the senses. According to Spence, what senses besides taste and smell play a role in our eating experiences?

Flavor and the Senses: Can we taste with our ears and eyes?

Not all scientific research takes place in labs. Just consider the work of Oxford University psychologist, Charles Spence. Spence does some of his work in restaurants because he studies people's perceptions[1] of flavor.

In one of Spence's experiments, guests were served a chocolate-covered sweet and given some printed instructions to follow. The instructions said **the guests should press number 1 or number 2 on their cell phones**. The people who pressed 1 heard the high notes of fast, upbeat music. These people thought the dessert was sweet. Those who pressed 2 heard low, slow, serious music. For this group, the dessert seemed bitter.[2] Spence said **the results show the role of the brain**. It uses information from one sense, such as hearing, to inform another sense—taste.

Comment   Posted 2 hours ago by Chef Charles

I'm sure that music can affect taste. Last night, one of our regular guests at the café asked **who had chosen the music**. He told his server **that the songs made everything taste better**.

Comment   Posted 50 minutes ago by Haley

In an interview I read, Spence said, "We cannot ever eat or drink without being influenced by the environment." He explained how the brain processes all the information around us—sound, color, and even the weight of the dishes.

Comment   Posted 10 minutes ago by Noah

Spence has said, "In many ways, we really do taste with our eyes." He showed that a dessert on a white plate will taste sweeter than one on a black plate. I tried that at home. It's true!

[1]**perception:** the way you notice or understand something using one or more of the five senses
[2]**bitter:** not sweet and slightly unpleasant

2 CHECK. Answer the questions. Write complete sentences.

1. Where does Charles Spence do some of his research?

   Charles Spence does some of his research in restaurants.

2. Which two senses (seeing, hearing, smelling, tasting, touching) play a big part in the chocolate-covered sweet experiment?

   _____

3. What does the brain do when we eat?

   _____

4. How does Spence think a chef could make a dessert taste sweeter?

   _____

3 DISCOVER. Complete the exercises to learn about the grammar in this lesson.

A Complete the sentences with words from the web page. Add commas where necessary.

1. Spence _____ the results show the role of the brain.

2. He _____ that the songs made everything taste better.

3. Spence _____ "We cannot ever eat or drink without being influenced by the environment."

4. Spence _____ "In many ways, we really do taste with our eyes."

B Look at the sentences in exercise **A**. Check the two true statements.

1. _____ *That* is used before quotation marks.

2. _____ *That* is used when there are no words in quotation marks.

3. _____ A comma is used before words in quotation marks.

4. _____ A comma is used when there are no words in quotation marks.

LEARN

14.4 Reported Speech: Statements

Quote	Reported Speech
Troy: "I'm not cooking."	Troy **told me (that) he wasn't cooking**. Noun Clause
Carla: "It's going to rain."	Carla **said (that) it was going to rain**. Noun Clause

1. In reported speech,* you report what someone said using a reporting verb** + a noun clause. No quotation marks (" ") or commas are used. *That* can be omitted.	Anna: "I have to leave the party." Anna **said that she had to leave** the party. Anna **said she had to leave** the party.
2. In reported speech, pronouns must be changed to keep the speaker's original meaning.	Jim: "I need to rest because **my** back hurts." Jim said **he** needed to rest because **his** back hurt.
3. If the reporting verb is in the past (*said, told*), the verb form in the noun clause usually changes.***	
a. Simple present changes to simple past.	a. Sam: "I **don't want** to go." Sam **said** that he **didn't want** to go.
b. Present progressive changes to past progressive.	b. Mary: "I'm **taking** cooking lessons." Mary **said** she **was taking** cooking lessons.
c. Present perfect and simple past both change to past perfect.	c. Tod: "I've **made** a cake." / "I **made** a cake." Tod **said he had** made a cake.

4. It is not necessary to change the verb form in the noun clause from present to past when it is about:
  a. a general truth
  b. something still true
	a. I told him that I **love** to cook.
	b. Mary said Jack **is** in the kitchen.

*Reported speech is sometimes called indirect speech.
See page **A9 for a list of reporting verbs in addition to *say* and *tell*.
***See page **A9** for a list of verb tense changes in reported speech.

4 Read each quote. Then circle the correct answer to complete each sentence in reported speech.

1. Jake: "I'm applying to a culinary art school in New York.

    Jake said he **was applying / has applied** to a culinary art school in New York.

2. Fay: "I want to take a class in restaurant management."

    Fay said she **wanted / had wanted** to take a class in restaurant management.

3. Ray: "We were studying with one of the finest baking instructors."

    Ray: He said that they **are studying / had been studying** with one of the finest baking instructors.

4. Igor: "We gained hands-on experience in the cooking labs."

   Igor said that **he gains / they had gained** hands-on experience in the cooking labs.

5. Nida: "A famous French chef teaches at our school."

   Nida said that a famous French chef **taught / had taught** at their school."

6. Marcel: "I am taking a nutrition class."

   Marcel said he **had taken / was taking** a nutrition class.

7. Antonia: "The college has offered me financial assistance."

   Antonia said the college **was offering / had offered** her financial assistance."

8. Miguel: "Some of the students are having trouble with the nutrition class because it has a lot of information about the science of cooking."

   Miguel said some of the students **had been having / were having** trouble with the nutrition class because it **had / had had** a lot of information about the science of cooking.

5 Jane and Peter graduated from a cooking school and are at a party. Read the conversation. Then complete the sentences with reported speech.

Jane:	I need to leave the party. I feel sick.
Peter:	I'm sorry you're feeling bad. This is such a good party. I want to stay, if that's all right with you.
Jane:	I don't mind. I have my car. I don't need a ride.
Peter:	All right. I hope you feel better. Be safe. I want you to call me when you get home.

1. Jane said that _____ to leave the party.

2. She told Peter that _____ sick.

3. Peter said _____ sorry that _____ bad.

4. He told Jane _____ to stay.

5. Jane told him that _____. She said that _____ car so _____ a ride home.

6. Peter wanted to make sure she was safe. He told her that _____ to call him when _____ home.

14.5 Reported Speech: Modals

Quote	Reported Speech
Students: "We'll be late for class." Lisa: "We can't leave early."	They **mentioned (that) they would be** late for class. She **said (that) they couldn't leave** early.

1. These modals often change as follows in reported speech. a. *will* → *would* b. *can* → *could* c. *must* → *had to* d. *may* → *might*	a. Joe: "I'll see you later." Joe said he **would see** us later. b. Lucy: "I can't see." Lucy said she **couldn't see**. c. Jen: "You must leave by noon." Jen said that we **had to leave** by noon. d. Tim: "I may come later." Tim said that he **might come** later.
2. The modals *should*, *ought to*, *could*, and *might* do not change in reported speech.	Oscar: "You **should be** a chef." Oscar told Jane that she **should be** a chef.

6 Complete the conversations. Use an appropriate modal in each sentence. Sometimes more than one answer is possible.

1. **A:** We should go to the party on Saturday after dinner.

   B: I thought you said we _____ should go _____ early. You said they would have dinner.

2. **A:** I may bake a loaf of bread for the party.

   B: You didn't tell me you _____ a loaf of bread! I love your bread.

3. **A:** I'll bring some beverages, too.

   B: OK, but yesterday you said you _____ a dessert.

4. **A:** We can't drive there. The highways will be busy.

   B: Really? Yesterday you said that we _____ there easily, with no traffic.

5. **A:** We may need to leave early to get to the party on time.

   B: Did you say that we _____ to leave early? I'm not sure I can leave before 4:00.

6. **A:** The party will be fun.

   B: I thought you said the party _____ boring and that you didn't want to go.

7. **A:** We can go swimming at the party.

   B: Swimming? You never told me we _____ swimming. Is there a pool?

8. **A:** Alex may bring his drums.

   B: I don't think so. Last night Alex mentioned that he _____ his guitar.

14.6 Reported Speech: Questions

Quote	Reported Speech
Ben: "Is the cake going to be ready?" Olive: "Did the café open?" Celia: "Who has been taking notes?"	Ben **asked if the cake was going to be ready.** Olive **wanted to know whether the café had opened.** Celia **wanted to know who had been taking notes.**

1. Use statement word order when reporting *Yes/No* questions and *wh-* questions. Do not use question word order.	Omar: "How long has she been talking?" ✓ Omar asked **how long she had been talking.** ✗ Omar asked how long <u>had she been</u> talking.
2. Use *if* or *whether* to report *Yes/No* questions.	Carol: "Did the reporter take photos?" Carol asked **if the reporter had taken photos.** Carol asked **whether the reporter had taken photos.**
3. If the reporting verb is in the past (*asked, wanted to know*), the verb form in the noun clause usually changes.	Ed: "**Will Li be able to attend** the concert?" Ed **asked if Li would be able to attend** the concert.
4. **Remember:** Pronouns are often changed to keep the speaker's original meaning.	Ms. Lee: Do **you** smell the pie in the oven? Ms. Lee asked if **we** smelled the pie in the oven.

7 Read the chef's interview questions in parentheses. Complete the sentences with reported speech.

1. The interviewer asked me _____ *if there was a food I hated* _____ .
   (Is there a food that you hate?)

2. He asked me _____ .
   (Can anyone learn to be a great chef?)

3. He wanted to know _____ .
   (Will you be opening your restaurant soon?)

4. The interviewer asked _____ .
   (How do you think people's eating habits have changed?)

5. The interviewer wanted to know _____ .
   (How big is your garden?)

6. He asked _____ .
   (Is there anything people should eat for their health?)

7. He asked _____ .
   (Do you cook for your family, too?)

8. He asked _____ .
   (Could you share one of your favorite recipes?)

9. I asked _____ .
   (Are you going to post our interview on your blog?)

10. I asked _____ .
   (What time is the photo shoot?)

PRACTICE

8 Read the conversation. Then complete the paragraphs below. Change the speakers' exact words to reported speech.

Dim Sum, Anyone?

Vendor:	The dumplings are delicious!
Man:	I don't know. They've made me sick before.
Vendor:	They won't make you feel bad. Everyone loves the dumplings.
Woman:	Can I try the shrimp dumplings?
Vendor:	Absolutely. You're going to love them. Do you want spicy sauce?
Woman:	I don't think so.
Vendor:	What do you think?
Woman:	I think they're great!

▼ Har Gow, or shrimp dumplings, one of the most popular dishes in Chinese dim sum

The street vendor said that the dumplings (1) __were__ delicious. The man said

(2) _____ because they'd made him sick before. The street vendor

told the man the dumplings (3) _____ feel bad. He also said

(4) _____ them.

The man's wife asked (5) _____ the shrimp dumplings.

The vendor said (6) _____ them. Next he asked her

(7) _____ spicy sauce. She said (8) _____ so.

Then he asked her (9) _____ and she said (10) _____ great.

9 Complete the exercises.

A Match the questions with the answers about street food in Nepal.

_e_ 1. **Kate:** Are you going to have the dumplings?　　a. **Jenny:** All of them are.

___ 2. **Rudy:** How's the rice?　　b. **Dena:** I had some on Sunday.

___ 3. **Luke:** Have you tried the spicy sauce yet?　　c. **Yuri:** They grow wild in the Himalayas.

___ 4. **Rosa:** Where do the spices come from?　　d. **Elsie:** It tastes delicious.

___ 5. **Dave:** How many of the dishes are Nepalese?　　e. **Tony:** I might try one or two.

B **WRITE.** Report what the speakers said in exercise **A**. Write in your notebook.

1. Kate asked Tony if he was going to have the dumplings.
   Tony told her he might try one or two.

10 **EDIT.** Read the story about a foreign student in France. Find and correct seven more errors with reported speech.

she was

Last week, I called Catherine and asked her what ~~was she~~ doing. She said that she and some

friends are going out. I asked her whether I can go with them. She said that I was welcome to come

along. We met at a bakery. Catherine ordered a cake I had never seen before. She asked me if had

I ever tried that kind of cake. I hadn't, so she ordered me a piece. I took a bite and bit something

hard. She laughed and said that there is a toy inside. She told me that I am eating a special cake for

French holidays. I told her that you should have told me before. I thought maybe I had broken my

tooth. She apologized and asked me that I forgave her. I said that I did.

11 **READ, WRITE & SPEAK.**

A Work with a partner. Look at the pie chart showing the results of a survey. What does it show?

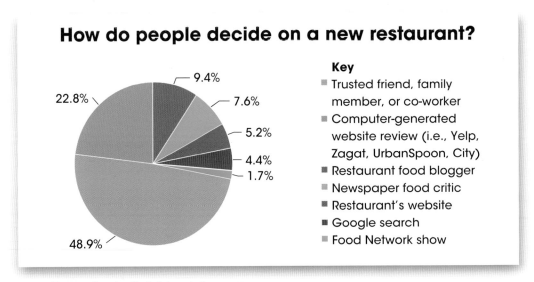

How do people decide on a new restaurant?

9.4%

22.8%

7.6%

5.2%

4.4%

1.7%

48.9%

Key
- Trusted friend, family member, or co-worker
- Computer-generated website review (i.e., Yelp, Zagat, UrbanSpoon, City)
- Restaurant food blogger
- Newspaper food critic
- Restaurant's website
- Google search
- Food Network show

Source: Angelsmith digital marketing agency.

B Look at the results in the chart in exercise **A**. Use the phrases in the box to report what the survey respondents said. Write in your notebook.

check out a restaurant's website	look at recommendations in food blogs
do a Google search	read reviews in newspapers
watch TV shows	pay attention to consumer reviews online

Nearly 49 percent said they followed the recommendations of relatives, friends, and coworkers.

C Work in groups. Discuss how you choose a new restaurant. Then work with a student from another group. Report the results of students from your group. Use reported speech.

12 APPLY.

A Read the restaurant reviews. Write what the food critic said when talking about the restaurants. Write four sentences using reported speech.

FOOD NEWS: ★★★★ Restaurants

Molly's Place:	Great bread, tasty soups and salads, popular and busy but worth the wait
	Sally Smith, *Food News*
Oishi Ramen:	Best noodles in town; cheap, friendly staff. Don't miss the Won Ton soup!
	Juanita Gomez, *About Town*
The Casbah:	Delicious Middle Eastern food, romantic atmosphere, piano bar
	Ravi Gupta, *Dining Out*
Dee's Desserts:	Homemade ice cream and cupcakes; great place to eat after the movies!
	Hector Vega, *Where To Eat*

The food critic of Food News said that the food was tasty at Molly's Place and that it was worth the wait.

B Work with another student. Compare the sentences you wrote in exercise **A**. Then tell each other your opinion of a restaurant that you have tried. Take notes in your notebook about what your partner says.

I loved the Mongolian Hot Pot. Cooking at the table was a lot of fun. I've never been to a place like it before, but I'm sure I'll go back there again.

C Use your notes to report to the class what your partner told you.

Sally said she loved the Mongolian Hot Pot. She said she'd never been to a place like it before, but she was sure she'd go back there again.

EXPLORE

CD4-16

1 READ the blog post about a cooking class. What did the writer learn how to do?

Baking in Ravello

October 15, Ravello, Italy

As we came to the door, Francesco smiled and offered us fresh tomatoes and cheese. We were there for our first cooking class in Ravello, Italy. Francesco was going to teach us how to make pizza.

First, he **told us to knead the dough.**[1] He explained that this makes it easier to work with the dough. He **told us not to stop until it was smooth and slightly sticky**. After that, we left the dough for a while. It needed time to rise, so we toured Francesco's fabulous vegetable garden. He also introduced us to Mamma Lena, a local cheese maker. We **asked her to explain why she was adding lemon juice to the hot milk**. She said it turns hot milk into ricotta, a soft cheese. Apparently, it is easy to make ricotta at home, so I'm looking forward to trying to make it.

Back in Francesco's kitchen, we rolled out the balls of dough into flat round shapes and chose the toppings—sauce, cheese, tomatoes, herbs. Then we used wooden paddles[2] to slide the pizzas into the huge brick oven. Francesco **told us not to get too close to the fire**. He said people cook at high temperatures in order to get the toppings and the crust[3] to cook at the same rate.

When the pizzas were done, we took them out of the oven and waited for them to cool. They made a terrific snack after a very satisfying day.

[1] **knead the dough:** to press a mixture of flour, liquid, and other ingredients with the hands to prepare it for baking
[2] **paddle:** a tool with a handle attached to a broad, flat surface
[3] **crust:** the hard, bread-like layer of a pizza or pie

2 CHECK. Read each statement about the article. Circle **T** for *true* or **F** for *false*.

1. First, the class worked on the sauce for the pizza.   **T**   **F**

2. Francesco explained how to work with the dough.   **T**   **F**

3. The students met Mamma Lena, a baker.   **T**   **F**

4. The writer of the blog wants to make ricotta in her own kitchen.   **T**   **F**

5. According to Francesco, you should bake pizza at a low temperature.   **T**   **F**

3 DISCOVER. Complete the exercises to learn about the grammar in this lesson.

A Find these sentences in the blog post from exercise **1**. Write the missing words.

1. First he told us _____ _____ the dough.

2. He told us _____ until it was smooth and slightly sticky.

3. We asked her _____ why she was adding lemon juice to the hot milk.

4. Francesco told us _____ too close to the fire.

B Look at the sentences in exercise **A**. What form follows the reporting verb + object in each sentence? Choose the correct answer.

a. a noun clause with *that*   b. an infinitive (+ object)

◄ The beautiful hillsides of the town of Ravello on the Amalfi Coast, Italy

LEARN

14.7 Reported Speech: Commands, Advice, and Requests

Quote	Reported Speech
Chef: "Stir the soup." Friend: "You shouldn't add sugar." Manager: "Can you help me?"	The chef **told me to stir the soup**. Her friend **advised her not to add sugar**. The manager **asked me to help her**.

1. Use an infinitive phrase* to report commands.	Teacher: "Turn off your phones." The teacher told us **to turn off our phones**.
2. Often an infinitive phrase is used to report advice or requests with modals.	Jim: You should bake a chocolate cake. Jim told me **to bake a chocolate cake**. Ann: "Could you turn off the oven?' Ann asked me **to turn off the oven**.
3. For negative commands, advice, or requests, *not* comes before the infinitive phrase.	Joe: "Don't cut the cake yet." Joe told me **not to cut** the cake yet.
4. Do not include *please* when reporting a command or request.	Receptionist: "Please wait in the hallway." The receptionist **told us to wait in the hallway**.

*infinitive phrase: *to* + the base form of a verb (+ an object)

4 Complete each sentence with the correct statement from the box. Use reported speech.

"Move it to a cooler spot."	"Don't continue until you wash your hands."
"Weigh the sugar on the scale first."	~~"Stand away from the oven."~~
~~"Could you show me how to do it?"~~	"You should stop mixing the dough."
"Would you explain step 3, please?"	"Can you please tell me how to prepare it?"

1. Chef McClellan said I wasn't stirring properly. I asked _her to show me how to do it_ .

2. I didn't want Jack to burn himself, so I told _him to stand away from the oven_

3. Lisa set the dough on the hot stovetop, so I told _____

   _____ .

4. Jay often mixed the dough too long. I advised _____

   _____ .

5. I didn't understand one step in the recipe, so I spoke to Chef McClellan. I asked _____

   _____ .

6. Jack didn't put the right amount of sugar in the bowl, so I told _____

   _____ .

7. His hands were covered with flour, so I told _____

_____ .

8. Chef (Jane) Grubart hadn't taught us how to make a white sauce, so I asked _____

_____ .

14.8 Reported Speech: Time and Place Changes

1. Words that describe the time and place often change in reported speech. This is done to preserve the speaker's original meaning.	Bob: "I'll be out of the office <u>this afternoon</u>." When I talked to Bob last week, he said he'd be out of the office **that afternoon**.
2. Time words change as follows when reporting speech at a later date (e.g., the next week, year, etc.). now → then this afternoon → that afternoon tomorrow → the next day yesterday → the day before next week → the following week last year → the year before	Jim: "I tried sushi <u>yesterday</u>." I saw Jim last month. He said he'd tried sushi **the day before**.
3. Sometimes *here* changes to *there* when our location is farther from the reference point.	The chef: "Put the plates **here**." The chef said to put the plates **there**.
4. Sometimes *this* changes to *that* and *these* to *those*.	Valerie: "**This recipe** is easy to follow." Valerie said **that recipe** was easy to follow.

5 Circle the correct answers.

1. Ana said, "I took a baking class last week."

   When I saw Ana, she said that she had taken a baking class **last week** / (**the week before**.)

2. Karim said, "I'm going to be on TV next week."

   I just saw Karim. He said he was going to be on TV **next week** / **the following week**.

3. Nick asked, "Can I sign up for courses here?"

   When Nick was at the school, he asked if he could sign up for courses **here** / **there**.

4. Dahlia opened the oven and said, "These cupcakes are perfect!"

   Dahlia said **these** / **those** cupcakes were perfect.

5. We were at a party. Samantha said, "I think this is the best party I've ever been to."

   The next day, Samantha said she thought **that** / **this** was the best party she'd ever been to.

6. Alex said, "I start my new job tomorrow."

   Alex was excited when I saw him. He said he was starting his new job **tomorrow** / **the next day**.

7. Yuri said, "I'm planning to open a business next year."

   When I saw Yuri two years ago, he said he was planning to open a business **next year /
   the following year**.

8. At noon I asked Rob, "Are you leaving now?"

   At noon yesterday I asked Rob if he was leaving **then / now**.

PRACTICE

6 Read what a health inspector and restaurant owner said to each other during a health
inspection last month. Rewrite the quotations in reported speech.

1. "Get the freezer fixed."

   The health inspector told the owner _to get the freezer fixed_ .

2. "Could I have ten days to get the freezer fixed?"

   The owner asked _____ .

3. "Give all employees a food safety training tomorrow."

   The inspector told the owner to _____

   _____ .

4. "Put labels on the food before closing time this evening."

   The inspector told the owner _____

   _____ .

5. "Don't leave any boxes on the floor anymore."

   The inspector told the owner _____

   _____ .

6. "Could you come back later this afternoon?"

   The owner asked the inspector _____

   _____ .

7. "You should get the door fixed by next week."

   The inspector told the owner _____

   _____ .

8. "Can you show me the inspection report tomorrow?"

   The owner asked the inspector _____

   _____ .

7 LISTEN.

CD4-17

A Listen to a conversation between a hotel restaurant manager and a new employee. Check (✓) the things the manager talks about.

_____✓__ a. coffee   _____ e. hotel check-in

_____ b. continental breakfast   _____ f. orange juice

_____ c. delivery   _____ g. purchase order

_____ d. garbage   _____ h. room keys

CD4-17

B Listen again. Then complete the sentences with the manager's requests and instructions.

1. The manager asked Jimmy _____*to come over*_____ so she could explain his tasks.

2. First, she told him _____ to every floor of the hotel.

3. She also told him _____ any garbage or newspapers.

4. After she talked about the continental breakfast, she told him _____ to the side entrance at 5:00 a.m. to pick up the donuts and rolls.

5. She advised him _____ the donuts and _____ there was a variety.

6. Finally, she advised him _____ the night auditor at the hotel front desk if he had any questions.

8 READ, WRITE & SPEAK.

A Read an airline attendant's description of a stressful day at the airport. Underline the commands, advice, or requests.

> It was another stressful day at LaGuardia Airport. Everyone was in a hurry. The lines were extremely slow because there weren't enough security guards on duty that day. Passengers were furious that the lines were slow. They yelled, "<u>Hurry!</u> We're going to miss our flight." One airline attendant was saying to passengers, "Calm down! Don't panic!" Another attendant ran to the gate. He yelled, "Wait!" at the crew. An announcer said, "Everyone flying to Brazil should get in the express line." The passengers lined up. We began taking their food orders. Some customers were worried that the food wouldn't come. We said, "Don't worry about the food."

B Complete the sentences using information from exercise **A**.

1. The passengers told airport security employees ____*to hurry*____.

2. The airline attendant told passengers _____.

3. An attendant told the crew _____.

4. An announcer told passengers flying to Brazil _____.

5. The airline attendant told the passengers _____.

C Write three more commands or instructions from an airline attendant to a passenger or a passenger to an attendant. Then report them to your partner.

The attendant told the passenger to turn off his phone.

9 APPLY.

A Complete the chart. Write statements or things people have told or advised you to do at some time in your life.

Person	Quote
my mother	"Don't be an art major. Study engineering."

B Work with a partner. Take turns reporting what each person in exercise **A** said. When your partner reports to you, write the exact words (quote) in the chart.

My mother told me not to be an art major. She told me to study engineering.

Person	Quote
my mother	"Don't be an art major. Study engineering."

C Look at the chart in exercise **B** in your partner's book. Do your partner's sentences match the sentences you wrote in exercise **A**?

Charts
14.1–14.8

1 Circle the correct answers.

1. Sally asked the server who **the chef is / was the chef**.

2. Do you know **whether / if** or not the café is open on Sundays?

3. Do you know what time it **is. / is?**

4. When a friend needed money to pay for cooking school, I advised her
   don't borrow / not to borrow it from the bank.

5. I met an old friend for coffee last week. She said she **saw / had seen** our high school teacher
   the day before / yesterday.

6. I told you **don't / not to** overcook the beans.

7. I wonder what **she was / was she** doing in the kitchen.

8. After Jen dropped the cake dough on the floor, Joe told her that **she / you** shouldn't worry.

9. When I was young, my grandfather told me that I **can / could** one day have his secret recipes.

10. Do you know who **did make / made** the dessert last night?

11. The customer asked the server when the meal **will / would** be ready**. / ?**

12. After cutting my finger last month, my boss said that I **must / had to** take a few days off.

Charts
14.1–14.8

CD4-18

2 LISTEN & WRITE.

A Read each statement. Then listen. Circle **T** for *true* of **F** for *false*.

1. The woman said the fireworks had smelled like different kinds of   **T**   **F**
   fruit.

2. The woman said she never wanted to experience anything like that   **T**   **F**
   again.

3. The woman said the inventors of the firework display were   **T**   **F**
   experienced chefs in a famous restaurant.

4. The man mentioned that he had read an article about an exhibit   **T**   **F**
   which featured a chocolate waterfall.

5. The woman said she had visited the chocolate waterfall exhibit and   **T**   **F**
   had thought it was a cool idea.

6. The woman said she didn't know what the inventors' next project   **T**   **F**
   would be.

B Listen again. Write the missing words.

1. **Dennis:** How _____was your trip_____ to London?

2. **Dennis:** Tell me _____ like.

3. **Nedra:** I've never _____ like it.

4. **Dennis:** I'd like to know _____ this crazy idea.

5. **Dennis:** Do you have any idea _____ their next project _____?

6. **Nedra:** No, but whatever it is, I'm sure _____ pretty outrageous.

C Now report what the speakers in exercise **A** said. Write in your notebooks.

He asked her how her trip to London was.

▼ At midnight on January 1, 2013, fruit-flavored
fireworks went off over London, England.

3 **EDIT.** Read the story about a child's first cooking experience. Find and correct eight more errors with noun clauses and reported speech.

My First Kitchen Blunder

                                                          whether

I can't remember if or not I've had any extraordinary experiences with food, but I'm certain that have had some unusual cooking experiences. The funniest was when I was about 12 years old. Before then, I had asked my mother many times when would I be allowed to cook dinner. Finally, one Thursday night, she told me I could make roast chicken tomorrow. She told me to wash the chicken first. I asked if I was supposed to wash only the skin of the chicken. She said that I should wash the inside, too. She also told me don't forget to put salt and pepper on the chicken before putting it in the oven. I wrote down exactly what my mother did tell me to do. The next day, I took the chicken out of the fridge and went over to the sink. I turned on the water and put soap all over the inside and the outside of the chicken. When my brother came in, he asked what was I doing. I told him that Mom had said I could make chicken for dinner. He asked where the chicken is. He said all he saw was soap. I said that Mom had told me to wash the chicken. He told me he would never eat it. Then, he called my mother to tell her I had done. I was so embarrassed. It was years before I ever cooked chicken again.

4 **SPEAK & WRITE.**

A Walk around the class. Take turns asking your classmates whether they have had the experiences in the chart. If they say *yes*, write their names and ask for details.

Who has . . . ?	Name
made a big mistake when cooking	
cooked a gourmet meal	
eaten food at a street fair	
eaten something strange	
used food to create art	
seen a celebrity in a restaurant	

A: *Have you ever made a big mistake when cooking?*

B: *Oh, lots of times. The worst was when I put hot peppers in Hungarian goulash. I wasn't sure whether or not the peppers I had were hot peppers . . . I thought they were just regular ones . . .*

B Write the most interesting story you heard. Then report to the class what the person said.

1 READ & NOTICE THE GRAMMAR.

A What are some of the best places to eat in town? Tell a partner your ideas. Then read the text.

Finding Food to *Die* For

Everyone knows how useful online restaurant reviews are, but you can also get great suggestions from your friends. You trust them, and they know what you like and dislike. I surveyed three of my classmates—Nayma, Esra, and Oscar—because I wanted to know where I could go to get some really delicious food.

They each had different opinions. First of all, Nayma is crazy about desserts, so she told me to go to a place called the Chocolate Room. She said that a dessert called "Death by Chocolate" would change my life. Unlike Nayma, Esra is very health conscious. She asked me if I liked salads. When I said that I pretty much liked everything, she told me to try a place called Omer's Garden. According to her, no one else in the world makes such delicious salad. Finally, Oscar likes to eat meat. He asked me if I had ever eaten Brazilian barbecue. When I told him that I had not, he said that I absolutely had to try the Brasilia Grill. I asked him why it was so great. He described how the waiters walk around with freshly grilled meats and slice them directly onto your plate.

All my friends' suggestions sounded terrific. Which place will I try first? Like Nayma, I really love desserts, so I think I will try the Chocolate Room first. I hope that I get a chance to try the other places soon, too. I can't wait to tell my classmates what I think of their recommendations!

GRAMMAR FOCUS

In this essay, the writer used:

Noun Clauses	• to act as the object in a sentence. . . . they know **what you like and dislike**.
Reported Speech	• to report statements and questions. She **said that a dessert called "Death by Chocolate" would change my life**.

B Read the text in exercise **A** again. Underline all examples of noun clauses and reported speech. Then work with a partner and identify whether the reported speech examples are statements, questions, or commands.

The first one—"told me to go to a place called the Chocolate Room"—is a reported command.

C Complete the chart with information from the text in exercise **A**. Discuss your answers with a partner.

Restaurant	Recommended Food & Why
Omer's Garden	
	grilled meat; very fresh

2 **BEFORE YOU WRITE.** Survey three classmates about restaurants that they like. What are their favorite places to eat? Are there any dishes in particular that they recommend? Why? Complete the chart with their answers.

Restaurant	Recommended Food & Why

3 **WRITE** two or three paragraphs discussing the results of your survey. Use your chart from exercise **2** and the text in exercise **1A** to guide you.

WRITING FOCUS   Using *According To* to Report an Opinion

To state someone's opinion, you can use *according to* followed by the person's name or *him/her*.

According to her, *no one else in the world makes such delicious salad.*

Put a comma after *according to* + (name/pronoun).

---

4 **SELF ASSESS.** Underline the noun clauses and the reported speech in your survey results. Then use the checklist to assess your work.

☐   I used noun clauses with statements and questions correctly. [14.1–14.3]

☐   I used reported speech for statements correctly. [14.4]

☐   I used reported speech for questions correctly. [14.5]

☐   I used reported speech with commands, advice, and requests correctly. [14.6]

☐   I used *according to* correctly to report an opinion. [WRITING FOCUS]

Combining Ideas

▲ The third-class cabin of the ship
Titanic is re-created in a traveling
exhibit (Denver, Colorado).

EXPLORE

CD4-19

1   READ the article about how Brendan Mullan motivates people to learn about astronomy. What are some of the ways that Mullan communicates information?

Where are the aliens?

"Hey Aliens, Earth for Sale." With this advertisement written on a large sign, Brendan Mullan began his science presentation. Mullan, an astrobiologist,[1] asks difficult questions about the universe. The biggest question is why aliens have never visited our planet. As Mullan explains, conditions on Earth are perfect to support life. **As a result,** it should be an excellent place for aliens to live. Not only could they live here, Mullan explains, but they could travel here easily. After all, we have sent astronauts into space for years. **Nevertheless,** no aliens have ever appeared. For Mullan, **however,** this does not mean that there is no life on other planets. In fact, he is convinced that in other parts of the universe, there must be life.

Mullan's presentations captivate[2] audiences. They are just one way he shares his passion for astrobiology. **In addition,** he uses social media, with podcasts about the universe for scientists, students, and ordinary people. Mullan directs the planetarium[3] and observatory at the Carnegie Science Center. The center allows people to see stars and planets in the dome[4] or through telescopes. Mullan is an expert scientist and talented teacher with a unique sense of humor. **As a result,** he makes astronomy fascinating to learn about.

[1] **astrobiologist:** a scientist who studies life on Earth and in space
[2] **captivate:** hold the attention of
[3] **planetarium:** a building where lights on the ceiling show the planets, moons, and stars
[4] **dome:** a rounded roof (in this case, of an observatory)

2 **CHECK.** Read the statements. Circle **T** for *true* or **F** for *false*.

1. Brendan Mullan is an astronaut.   **T**   **F**

2. Mullan believes that Earth is the only planet with living things.   **T**   **F**

3. The Internet plays an important part in Mullan's teaching strategy.   **T**   **F**

4. At the Carnegie Science Center, people study clouds.   **T**   **F**

5. Mullan makes studying the universe exciting.   **T**   **F**

3 **DISCOVER.** Complete the exercises to learn about the grammar in this lesson.

A Find these sentences in the article from exercise **1**. Write the missing words and punctuation.

1. _____ no aliens have ever appeared.

2. For Mullan _____ this does not mean that there is no life on other planets.

3. _____ he uses social media, with podcasts about the universe for scientists, students, and ordinary people.

4. _____ he makes astronomy fascinating to learn about.

B Look at the article in exercise **1** again. Find the sentence that comes just before each sentence in exercise **A**. Then complete the statements below with the words you wrote in exercise **A**.

1. __Nevertheless__ and _____ are similar in meaning to *but*.

2. _____ is similar in meaning to *so*.

3. _____ is similar in meaning to *and*.

LEARN

15.1 Contrast: *However, Nevertheless, On the Other Hand*

1. Transition words connect ideas between or within sentences. They are commonly used in formal writing and speaking. Transition words of contrast are similar in meaning to *but*.	The professor knew his subject well, but his lectures were hard to understand. The professor knew his subject well. **However**, his lectures were hard to understand.

2. Transition words often come at the beginning of a sentence. Some can also occur within or at the end of a sentence.
  a. When a transition occurs at the beginning, put a comma after it.
  b. When it occurs within the sentence, put a comma before and after it.
  c. When it occurs at the end, put a comma before it and a period after it.
	a. It can be cold in April in New York. **However,** it doesn't snow very often.
	b. It can be cold in April in New York. It does not**, however,** snow very often.
	c. It can be cold in April in New York. It doesn't snow very often**, however.**

3. Use *however* and *nevertheless* to introduce information that is surprising or that contrasts with what has just been said.	The exam was difficult. **However**, everyone in the class got a good grade. Jan got very good grades. **Nevertheless**, she didn't get into graduate school.
4. Use *on the other hand* to introduce the second of two ways of looking at something.	The job is not interesting. **On the other hand**, it pays well.

4 Read each statement. Then choose the statement that logically follows it.

1. In my city, it's hard to see the stars because there are too many lights.

    ⓐ On the other hand, the lights from the buildings and bridges are beautiful.

    b. On the other hand, it's hard to see the stars from my apartment.

2. I never liked studying science in high school.

    a. However, in college I developed an interest in astronomy.

    b. However, I studied history in college.

3. At first, I thought astronomy would be boring.

    a. Nevertheless, I decided to sign up for a course in it.

    b. Nevertheless, I didn't sign up for a course in it.

4. When I began to study astronomy, finding individual stars was hard.

    a. On the other hand, I couldn't find one.

    b. On the other hand, finding them was very rewarding.

5. The class lectures were not always interesting.

   a. The video presentations, however, were boring.

   b. The video presentations, however, were fascinating.

6. By my sophomore year, I loved to study the planets and stars.

   a. Nevertheless, I didn't choose astronomy as my major.

   b. Nevertheless, I decided to major in astronomy.

7. I took several more courses in astronomy.

   a. However, none of them were as captivating as the first course I took.

   b. However, they were all as captivating as the first course I took.

8. I'm still fascinated by the nighttime sky.

   a. However, I regret not having majored in astronomy.

   b. However, I don't regret my decision not to major in astronomy.

5 Read each statement below and notice the word in parentheses. Find the sentence in the box that logically follows it. Rewrite the sentence from the box using the word in parentheses. Add commas where necessary.

They must work alone during the exam.	They shouldn't ask questions that are too personal.
Many students still prefer traditional classes.	Reading is better for visual learners.
They must not to hurt anyone's feelings.	~~They need to make their expectations clear.~~

1. It is fine for teachers to have high expectations for their students. (however)

   However, they need to make their expectations clear.

2. Students should feel free to ask about their classmates' interests. (on the other hand)

   _____

3. It it is fine for students to study together for exams. (however)

   _____

4. It can be helpful for students to comment on their classmates' writing. (however)

   _____

5. Listening to lectures is the best way for some students to learn new information. (on the other hand)

   _____

6. Online classes are becoming more popular. (nevertheless)

   _____

15.2 Result: *As a Result, Therefore, Thus*

1. Transition words of result are similar in meaning to *so*. Notice the difference in punctuation.	The exam was long, so it was tiring.
	The exam was long. **Therefore,** it was tiring.
2. *Therefore* can come at the beginning or within a sentence. It is similar in meaning to "for that reason."	Pat missed the lecture. **Therefore,** he's going to ask Rina for her notes.
	Pat missed the lecture. He is, **therefore,** going to ask Rina for her notes.
3. *Thus* can come at the beginning or within a sentence. It is similar in meaning to *therefore*.	Mars has a rocky surface. **Thus,** it is the same type of planet as Mercury, Venus, and Earth.
4. *As a result* is usually used at the beginning of a sentence.	She has a good telescope. **As a result,** she was able to see the rings around Saturn.

See chart 15.1 on page **428** for rules on comma usage with transition words.

6 Rewrite each sentence as one or two sentences. Replace *so* with the words in parentheses. Add commas where necessary.

1. Digital learning is becoming more popular, so teachers' roles are changing. (as a result)

    Digital learning is increasing. As a result, teachers' roles are changing.

2. Digital learning gives students more control, so they become more active learners. (thus)

    _____

    _____

3. Digital learning gives students more responsibility, so they become more independent. (as a result)

    _____

    _____

4. We can often both see and hear content online, so it is more interactive. (therefore)

    _____

    _____

5. That course is very popular, so it fills up quickly. (therefore)

    _____

    _____

6. Our university has an excellent biology department, so many students major in biology. (thus)

    _____

    _____

7. The final exam was very difficult, so many students didn't pass. (as a result)

_____

_____

8. Professor Chen is well known in her field, so a lot of students want to take her classes. (therefore)

_____

_____

15.3 Addition: *In Addition, Moreover*

1. Transition words of addition are similar in meaning to *and*. Notice the difference in punctuation.	Lisa recommended me for the job, and she introduced me to the head of the company.
	Lisa recommended me for the job. **In addition,** she introduced me to the head of the company.
2. *In addition* and *moreover* usually come at the beginning of a sentence.	An essay should be clear and well organized. **In addition,** it should be interesting.
	He had enough money to build a new lab. **Moreover,** he received funding to do more research.

7 Read the sentences about learning with video chat applications (apps). Then rewrite the sentences using the words in parentheses. Add commas where necessary.

1. With video chat apps, you can talk online for free. They're easy to use. (in addition)

   With video chat apps, you can talk online for free. In addition, they're

   easy to use.

2. Video chat apps allow you to make phone calls. They let you have group chats. (in addition)

   _____

   _____

3. These apps make it easy for you to talk to your classmates. They connect you to other students. (moreover)

   _____

   _____

4. Teachers can give feedback with these apps. Students can comment on each other's work. (in addition)

   _____

   _____

5. During video chats, students can watch artists at work. They can learn about the artists' techniques. (moreover)

_____

_____

6. You can learn about foreign countries through video chats. You can find a language partner. (moreover)

_____

_____

7. With video chatting, students can listen to authors read their work. They can talk to the authors. (in addition)

_____

_____

8. Students can use these apps to go on virtual field trips. They can give presentations. (in addition)

_____

_____

▲ Co-stars and co-filmmakers Jemaine Clement and Taika Watiti
in a Skype chat at the 2014 Music, Film + Interactive Festival

PRACTICE

8 Circle the correct words to complete the article.

Social Media: Good or Bad?

Social media is changing the way we learn and communicate with each other, and there are both advantages and disadvantages to using it. Social media allows us to connect with people from all parts of the world and learn from them. (1) **In addition, / Nevertheless,** we can communicate with those who share our interests. Age, gender, and nationality become less important online. (2) **However, / As a result,** we can make friends that we would not otherwise make. Thanks to social media, we are able to discuss important political, social, and environmental issues with a wide variety of people. (3) **Moreover, / However,** it helps us connect with other professionals in our field.

(4) **On the other hand, / Moreover,** social media has some drawbacks.[1] For example, more online communication means less face-to-face communication. (5) **However, / As a result,** people can start to forget how to communicate in person. (6) **In addition, / Nevertheless,** online communication can make us less sensitive to other people's feelings. We can't see people's facial expressions on social media. (7) **Therefore, / Nevertheless,** it's more difficult to know how someone feels about a comment we've made. We may be less polite when communicating online, or we might post comments that are hurtful without realizing it. Social media has made learning and communication easier in many ways. (8) **However, / Thus,** we need to think carefully about how we use it.

[1] **drawback:** a disadvantage

9 Complete the sentences with the words in the boxes. Add commas where necessary.

however	in addition	therefore

1. Social media sites are a great way to communicate with friends. _____However,_____ spending too much time on them can be unhealthy.

2. You can meet new people through social media sites. _____ you can contact old friends.

3. People's posts aren't always honest. _____ you shouldn't believe everything you read.

as a result	moreover	nevertheless

4. Frank joined a social networking site. _____ he has been able to connect with other doctors.

5. It's sometimes necessary to provide personal information online. _____ you should make sure the site is secure.

6. Social media is a great way to keep in touch with family and friends. _____ it allows us to share and broaden our interests.

10 Circle the correct transition words to complete the sentences about Internet research.

1. The Internet is an amazing source of information. **In addition, / Nevertheless,** much of the information is free and easy to use. **Therefore, / However,** it is important to remember that not all websites are accurate and up to date.

2. Anyone can post content on the Internet, both experts and non-experts alike. **Therefore, / Moreover,** student researchers may find it difficult to tell whether or not the information on a particular site is reliable.

3. Online encyclopedias are popular and often excellent sources of information. **Nevertheless, / Thus,** the information in them is not always up to date. Students, **therefore, / however,** need to be careful and cross-check the information they find with other sources.

4. Even articles on the websites of major newspapers can contain errors. **As a result, / However,** these errors are often corrected within minutes. **Moreover, / Therefore,** many professors encourage students to use newspaper websites for their research.

5. Online professional journals are also good sources of information. In **addition, / Thus,** student researchers may find reliable information on the websites of university libraries.

11 **SPEAK & WRITE.** Work with a partner. Write a sentence that logically follows each sentence below. Use six of the transition words in the box and your own ideas. Add commas where necessary.

however	nevertheless	on the other hand	therefore
~~as a result~~	in addition	moreover	thus

1. Some students have been using video chatting to practice their English.
   As a result, their English is getting better and better.

2. The Internet helps students find and check information quickly.
   _____

3. Tablets are easy to carry from place to place.
   _____

4. The Internet has a lot of useful information.
   _____

5. Many educational apps are free.
   _____

6. Some students like to use apps to study for exams.
   _____

7. Other students prefer to use textbooks.
   _____

8. Others form study groups.

12 LISTEN & WRITE.

CD4-20 **A** Listen to the conversation about MOOCs. Circle **T** for *true* or **F** for *false*.

1. Sarah explains what the letters M-O-O-C stand for.   **T** **F**

2. Sarah tells her friend the subject of the course she is taking. **T** **F**

3. Sarah says there are a lot of requirements for the course. **T** **F**

4. Sarah will never sign up for another MOOC.   **T** **F**

CD4-20 **B** Listen again. Match each sentence in Column A with the correct sentence in Column B according to the conversation.

Column A

1. Students comment on each other's essays. __b__

2. Sarah didn't get college credit. _____

3. There were lectures, readings, and discussion questions. _____

4. The subject of the course was interesting. _____

5. Sarah enjoyed the course. _____

6. Students do not have to take a test before signing up. _____

Column B

a. Anyone can register for a MOOC.

b. They get a lot of feedback on their writing.

c. She plans to sign up for another MOOC.

d. She got a certificate of completion.

e. The lectures were great.

f. There were no final exams.

C In your notebook, write six sentences to connect the information in exercise **B**. Use *as a result, however, in addition, moreover, nevertheless,* and *therefore.*

13 APPLY.

A Check (✓) the things you have used as learning tools.

_____ Apps _____ MOOCs _____ Tablets _____ Digital textbooks _____ Social media _____ Other

B Work in a group. Discuss these questions about the learning tools in exercise **A**.

What is the most effective learning tool you have ever used?
How did it help you? How could it have worked better?
What new learning tool would you like to try?
How would you use it?
How do you think it could help you?

C In your notebook, write five sentences about two or more of the questions you discussed in exercise **B**. Connect your ideas with transition words where appropriate.

The most effective learning tool I've ever used is YouTube. There are a lot of free lectures on it. As a result, I've learned about some very interesting topics . . .

EXPLORE

CD4-21

1 READ the article about a learning experiment. What did the students learn how to do?

Let Learning Happen

Professor Sugata Mitra wanted to do an experiment. He went to a part of New Delhi, India, where children rarely attended school and had never seen a computer. Mitra set a computer into one of the walls on the street and connected it to the Internet. Then he turned on the computer and left.

Surprisingly, the children learned to use the computer in a few hours. **Despite** their lack of formal education, they figured out how to browse and download information, and they helped each other learn. When Mitra repeated the experiment in India and other countries, the same thing happened. **As a result of** these findings, Mitra became convinced that students will learn what they want to learn.

Mitra did more experiments to see what else groups of students could learn. He found that some figured out how to play music and send e-mails; others learned complex subjects such as biotechnology.[1] All of the students improved their English. They were **so** successful **that** Mitra wanted to provide them with even more opportunities to teach themselves.

The benefit of group learning was an important discovery for Mitra. He realized that students learn more in groups **due to** their constant communication with each other. They do **such** a good job in groups **that** Mitra decided to build SOLEs (self-organized learning environments). These allow groups of students to do Internet research on a wide range of subjects. There is no teacher in the traditional sense. SOLEs reflect Mitra's strongly held view: "It's not about making learning happen. It's about *letting* learning happen."

[1] **biotechnology:** the use of living things, such as cells or bacteria, for industrial purposes

▲ Boys exploring the Internet at one of Sugata Mitra's SOLEs

2 **CHECK.** Read each statement about the article. Circle **T** for *true* or **F** for *false*.

1. Sugata Mitra began his learning experiments with wealthy children.   **T**   **F**

2. It took the children a few days to learn to use the computer.   **T**   **F**

3. Mitra's research shows that students learn best in groups.   **T**   **F**

4. Mitra discovered that children learned complex subjects when they wanted to.   **T**   **F**

3 **DISCOVER.** Complete the exercises to learn about the grammar in this lesson.

A Find these sentences in the article from exercise **1**. Write the missing words.

1. _____ their lack of formal education, they figured out how to browse . . .

2. _____ these findings, Mitra became convinced that students will learn what they want to learn.

3. They were _____ successful _____ Mitra wanted to provide them with even more opportunities to teach themselves.

4. He realized that students learn more in groups _____ their constant communication with each other.

5. They do _____ a good job in groups _____ Mitra decided to build SOLEs.

B Choose the correct answers based on the sentences you completed in exercise **A**.

1. *Despite* introduces _____.   a. a result   b. a contrast

2. *Due to* and *as a result of* introduce _____.   a. a cause   b. a contrast

3. *Despite, due to,* and *as a result of* are followed by _____.   a. a noun phrase   b. a noun clause

◀ Kolkata, India (formerly Calcutta)

LEARN

15.4 Cause and Effect: *As a Result of, Because of, Due to*

Effect	Cause
	Prepositional Phrase
She will get good grades	**as a result of** her hard work.
We didn't take the field trip	**because of** the weather.
The class was canceled	**due to** a lack of interest.

1. *As a result of, because of,* and *due to* are multi-word prepositions. They begin a prepositional phrase that gives the cause of or reason for the event in the rest of the sentence.	The tree fell **as a result of the storm.** Driving was difficult **because of the snow.** Class was cancelled **due to the bad weather.**
2. **Remember:** A prepositional phrase is a preposition + a noun or noun phrase. When a prepositional phrase is first in a sentence, put a comma after it.	**Because of the traffic,** we were late. We were late **because of the traffic.**
3. **Be careful!** *Because of* and *because* are similar in meaning, but they are used with different structures: a. *because of* + noun/noun phrase b. *because* + subject + verb	a. We stayed home **because of** the rain. b. We stayed home **because** it was raining.
4. In formal writing, *due to the fact that* + subject + verb is sometimes used instead of *due to* + noun phrase.	They left town **due to** the hurricane. They left town **due to the fact that** a hurricane was approaching.
5. **Be careful!** *As a result of* is used to introduce the cause of an event. *As a result* introduces the effect or result of the cause mentioned in the previous sentence.	**As a result of** poor sales, the company closed. Cause Effect Sales were poor. **As a result,** the company closed. Cause Effect

4 Circle all correct words. Sometimes more than one answer may be correct.

1. Children learned to use Mitra's computer **because / because of** their curiosity and intelligence.

2. **Because / Due to the fact that** children organized their own learning, Mitra thinks they can learn without a teacher.

3. Mitra wants learning to change **because / because of** he thinks schools are not effective.

4. **As a result, / Due to** recent research, the teachers have changed their methods.

5. Children learn differently **because / because of** different learning styles.

6. **As a result of / Because,** computers, students do not practice writing as much as before.

7. Computers are common in schools today. **As a result, / As a result of** students do not practice writing as much as before.

8. The test scores went up this year, perhaps **due to / because** the tutoring program.

9. Some students are good at group work **due to / due to the fact that** they enjoy interacting with others.

10. Teachers pay attention to different learning styles **due to / due to the fact that** their influence on learning.

5 Complete each sentence with the correct prepositional phrase from the box. Add a comma where necessary.

because of the noise	~~because of the teachers' strike~~
as a result of their low test scores	as a result of the fire
due to the class website	due to the spread of the flu

1. _____ Because of the teachers' strike, _____ classes were cancelled.

2. The students had to sign up for tutoring _____.

3. Some students dislike working in groups _____.

4. _____ more shy students were participating in discussions.

5. _____ the school nurse was working long hours.

6. The school received insurance money _____.

▶ Educators around the world now use a variety of methods to teach their students. Here, a Chinese astronaut speaks to students from space.

15.5 Cause and Effect: *So/Such . . . That, So Many/Much . . . That*

Cause	Effect
So . . . / Such . . .	*That* Clause
Jonathan was **so** funny	**that** people were crying.
He ran **so many** miles	**that** he needed new shoes.
There was **so little** time	**that** we had to run.
It was **such** a nice day	**that** we ate outside.

1. Use *so* + an adjective/adverb to give a cause or reason; the effect or result follows in a *that* clause.	The exam was **so easy that** we finished it early. He drove **so quickly that** he crashed the car.
2. *Many, much, few,* or *little* + a noun can also go between *so* and a *that* clause.	He had **so much homework that** he didn't go out. She had **so few friends that** she often felt lonely.
3. You can also use *such* + an adjective + a noun to give a cause or reason for an effect or result in a *that* clause.	It was **such an easy exam that** I finished it early.
4. **Remember:** *That* is often omitted in conversation.	It was such an easy exam **that I finished early.** It was such an easy exam **I finished early.**

6 Circle the correct answers to complete the text.

Learn Anything in Just 20 Hours!

Has this happened to you? You try to learn a new skill, but you are (1) **so / such** bad at it that you give up. Practicing the skill becomes (2) **so / such** boring that you stop after an hour or two. Or you might think it will take (3) **so many / so much** hours to learn, you will never learn it. But Josh Kaufman, writer and entrepreneur, says you can learn any skill. First, realize you don't have to become an expert. Second, don't spend (4) **so many / so much** time worrying about failing that you never try to learn anything new. Third, give yourself 20 hours to learn the skill. The first few hours can be (5) **so much / such** a frustrating time that you will want to give up. However, Kaufman says, you will soon get better at it. When you do, you will feel (6) **so / so much** good that you will keep practicing. Kaufman taught himself (7) **so many / so much** new skills in one year that he wrote a book about it. It is (8) **so much / such a** good book that you'll want to read it twice!

7 Complete the sentences with the correct missing words. Use *so, so much, so many, so little,* or *such.*

1. There are _____ so many _____ ways to teach yourself that you can learn just about anything.

2. The Internet offers _____ a wide range of information that you can learn about anything.

3. There is _____ art on museum websites that you can see famous paintings without leaving home.

4. Speakers on podcasts are _____ interesting that it's easy to listen and learn.

5. YouTube has _____ how-to videos that it makes learning by watching easy.

6. E-books are _____ easy to download that you can read them in minutes.

7. It takes _____ time to look up new words on smartphones that learning words is easier.

8. I have _____ a good time learning new things that I spend hours online.

15.6 Contrast: *Despite, In Spite of*

	Despite/In Spite of + Noun/Noun Phrase
Some people did well on the test Others didn't do very well	despite the pressure. in spite of their hard work.

1. *Despite* and *in spite of* introduce information that is surprising or unexpected or that contrasts with information in the rest of the sentence.	She got the job **despite her lack of experience.** She got the job **in spite of her lack of experience.**
2. *Despite* and *in spite of* are followed by a noun or noun phrase.	We went on a picnic **despite the storm.** We went on the picnic **in spite of the storm.**
3. *Despite of* and *in spite of* can come at the beginning or end of a sentence. Use a comma when they come at the beginning of the sentence.	**Despite the cold water,** I went swimming. I went swimming **despite the cold water.**
4. In formal writing, *the fact that* + subject + verb is sometimes added to *despite* and *in spite of*.	We went on a picnic **in spite of the fact that there might be a storm.**

8 Use the choices in the box to complete the sentences. Add a comma where necessary.

my inexperience singing on stage	I didn't know anything about music
I don't play the guitar well now	~~I took lessons as a child~~
my dreams of being a musician	my fear of failure
my parents' threats of punishment	my lack of singing talent

1. Despite the fact that _____ I took lessons as a child, _____ I never learned to play the piano well.

2. In spite of the fact that _____
   I taught myself the guitar.

3. I didn't practice the piano often despite _____.

4. I won a piano competition in spite of _____.

5. Despite the fact that _____
   I played it a lot when I was young.

6. Despite _____
   I will probably have to work a regular job.

7. In spite of _____
   I got to sing in the school play.

8. Despite _____ _____ I was very relaxed on stage.

PRACTICE

9 Complete the text. Circle the correct words.

A Self-Taught Painter: Paul Gauguin

He was a famous artist from the nineteenth century. (1) (Despite) / As a result of his fame and talent, Paul Gauguin was never formerly trained as a painter. (2) **Despite / Despite the fact that** he was never trained in art, he excelled at it. Gauguin first saw art when he was a child. His family went to Peru, where his father was from. (3) **As a result, / Despite** Gaugin experienced the art of Indian cultures. Gauguin always wanted to be an artist (4) **despite the fact that / in spite of** he worked in business.

▲ Oil painting (1892) by Paul Gauguin

Finally, (5) **despite / as a result of** his success as a businessman, Gauguin made enough money to quit his job and start painting. He spent his free time in the cafés of Paris. (6) **As a result of / In spite of** this, he made friends with other artists. Gauguin painted and traveled. He especially liked islands. He liked them (7) **so much / such** that he left Europe for Tahiti and never came back. Tahiti was a spiritual place for Gauguin. It inspired him (8) **such / so much** that he painted his best works there. (9) **Because of / In spite of** Gauguin's interest in other cultures, he used painting styles from Africa and Japan. Gauguin died at age 54. He had completed over 228 paintings. (10) **Despite / Due to** his early death, Gauguin was an important influence on modern art.

10 Use the words in parentheses to combine the sentences. Add a comma where necessary.

1. Kate had a fear of heights. She learned to ski. (in spite of)

   In spite of Kate's fear of heights, she learned to ski.

   OR Kate learned to ski in spite of her fear of heights.

2. Margaret is an excellent dancer. She was not chosen by the dance company. (despite the fact)

   _____

   _____

3. Josh has a passion for winter sports. He learned to snowboard. (due to)

   _____

   _____

4. Maya worked on a farm. She never learned how to grow vegetables. (in spite of the fact)

   _____

   _____

5. Mark has natural musical talent. He learned to play the violin by himself. (as a result of)

   _____

   _____

6. Ben is a very impatient person. He stopped taking art lessons after just one month. (so)

   _____

   _____

7. Henry has good computer skills. He was able to build his own website without any help. (because of)

   _____

   _____

8. Tomas is a wonderful pianist. His friends love to hear him play. (such)

   _____

   _____

11 WRITE & SPEAK.

A Use the words in parentheses to write sentences about your own experiences. Use the present or past.

1. (so difficult) <u>Learning English was so difficult at first that I thought I would</u>

   <u>never speak.</u>

2. (so easy) _____

   _____

3. (so fascinating) _____

   _____

4. (such an interesting place) _____

   _____

5. (so much fun) _____

   _____

6. (so many mistakes) _____

   _____

B Work with a partner. Share your sentences.

A: *Learning English was so difficult at first that I thought I would never speak.*

B: *Really? It wasn't hard for me to speak, but writing is still hard.*

12 EDIT. Read the text about learning how to dance. Find and correct six more errors with phrases of cause and effect, contrast, and result. There is more than one way to correct some errors.

Shall we dance?

    Watching a friend compete in a dance contest was ~~so~~ ^{such} a great experience that I decided
to learn how to dance. Despite my lack of rhythm, I wanted to learn. I watched such many
YouTube videos that I started to dream about dancing. However, I got very frustrated. It was
so hard for me to learn from the videos that I almost gave up. Then, my friend told me about a
dance class. I signed up, but the first time I went I was shy that I couldn't move. In spite of my
fear, I kept going. I had so few free time that I couldn't practice a lot. But a half hour before
dinner every night, I put on music and practiced the steps I had learned in class. Because the
teacher's patience, I eventually learned to dance. I'm such good dancer now that I'm going to be
my friend's partner in a dance contest. As a result my experience, I am convinced that a person
can learn just about anything. All you need is the desire and an effective way to learn.

13 APPLY.

A Work with a partner. Look at the picture and imagine that you are one of the dancers. Write three or four sentences about learning to dance. Use the phrases in the box. Then read your sentences to the class.

| as a result of | because of | due to | despite | in spite of | so . . . that | such . . . that |

My legs hurt so much at the end of every class that I had to sit down!

B Work in groups. Think of something you have learned to do or would like to learn to do. Speak for one minute about the experience or what you think it would be like. Use some of the phrases in the box in exercise **A**.

Last summer I took a folk dance class in my country. My dancing was so bad at first that I stepped on my partner's feet. But soon I was having so much fun that I didn't want to stop.

▼ Chinese national dancers perform a traditional dance in Chengdu, China.

1 Circle the correct words to complete the article.

Science for Non-Scientists

We can learn about many things, even the stars, with social media. In the past, to learn about the stars, we used books and maps. (1) **However, / Moreover,** today, we use different sources such as astronomy websites. (2) **As a result of / On the other hand,** sites like Twitter, we can post new scientific information. (3) **Due to / Despite** all of these sources, there are now more opportunities for everyday people to get involved with science. (4) **Despite the fact that / Due to the fact that** we need scientists to lead experiments, non-scientists can also play a part in scientific research. (5) **Because of / In spite of** the need for a lot of data, non-scientists can help. They can collect data for scientists. When a lot of people collect data, scientists are able to get information more quickly. Today, more scientists are encouraging non-scientists to get involved. (6) **In spite of / Due to** social media sites, it is now possible for scientists and non-scientists to work together on many projects. For many non-scientists, these projects are (7) **so / such** interesting that they want to help out as volunteers.

2 WRITE. Read the sentences. Then rewrite them using the words in parentheses. Add commas where necessary.

1. Zooniverse is a web portal. It is a citizen science project. (In addition)

   _____

   _____

2. Non-scientists are welcome in many science projects. They can't always be included. (Despite the fact that)

   _____

   _____

3. Some sciences require specific advanced knowledge. Other sciences are more accessible. (However)

   _____

   _____

4. Most scientists of the past were professionally trained. Isaac Newton was a citizen scientist. (On the other hand)

   _____

   _____

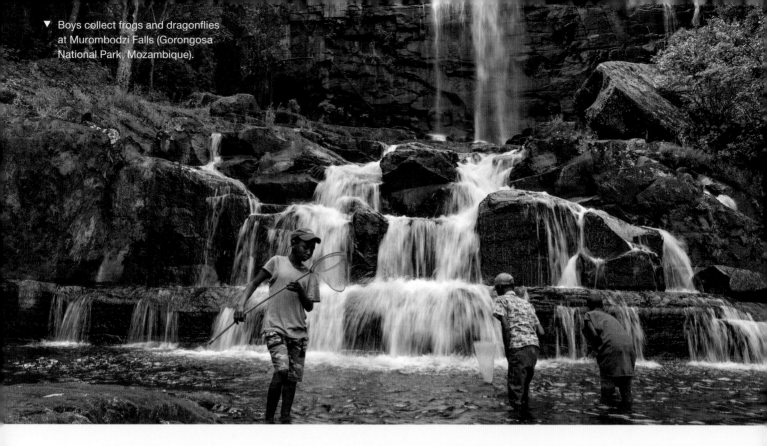

Charts
15.1–15.6

3 READ & WRITE. Read the information about a kind of nature project called a bioblitz. Then complete the sentences using information from the text. Add commas where necessary.

Bioblitz

We often don't notice the biodiversity—the variety of plants and animals—right in our own backyards. Participating in a bioblitz can change that. A bioblitz lasts 24 hours. During that time, both scientists and non-scientists look around in one area carefully. They try to locate and identify as many different species of living things as possible. Hundreds of people look for species of plants, mammals, fish, birds, and insects. Large groups can cover a lot of ground. Although they usually find known species, sometimes new ones are discovered. Everyone gets very tired and dirty, but the work can be fun, and it's a great learning experience. In fact, most people want to do it again.

If you'd like to participate in a bioblitz, here are some important reminders:

- You have to register by a certain date in order to participate, so check the schedule.

- No experience is necessary.

- Weather conditions may change during the day, so wear layers of clothing.

- You will need sunglasses, sunscreen, and a hat.

- The event will take place rain or shine.

1. We don't often consider the biodiversity around us. However _____

   _____ .

2. In a bioblitz, people look for different species of plants. In addition _____

   _____ .

3. Despite the fact that _____ sometimes new species are discovered.

4. People who participate in bioblitzes usually get very dirty. Nevertheless, _____

_____ .

5. It's such _____ most people want to do it again.

6. The weather may change. Therefore _____

7. If it's hot and sunny, you need to protect yourself. Thus _____ .

8. Bioblitzes are hardly ever canceled because of _____

Charts
15.1–15.6

4 LISTEN.

CD4-22

A Listen to the report about a bioblitz in New York City's Central Park. Check (✓) the names of the creatures mentioned.

_____ ants   _____ bears   _____ catfish   _____ spiders
_____ bats   _____ birds   _____ frogs   _____ turtles

CD4-22

B Listen again. Write the missing words you hear. Add commas where necessary.

1. _____ the people had only 24 hours to work, they were able to find a great variety of wildlife.

2. _____ insect experts were pleased to find 44 beetle species and 31 types of spiders.

3. _____ during a bioblitz, nighttime is especially important. Participants were able to identify many different species of animals in the dark, such as owls and bats.

4. There is _____ a variety of species in Central Park _____ scientists are trying to find out why.

5. Many believe that it is _____ the conservation work that has been going on for years.

6. _____ the improvements in the land and water, a large number of living things are now living happily there.

7. _____ their bioblitz work, they now realize that there's a lot of natural beauty as well.

8. In fact, they saw _____ new things _____ they will never think of New York City in quite the same way again.

5 **EDIT.** Read the blog post about an expedition in Mongolia. Find and correct eight more errors with transition words and phrases of cause and effect, result, and contrast. There is more than one way to correct some errors.

Trekking Tina

OCTOBER 6

On our first day in Mongolia, we saw ~~such~~ ^{so} many amazing mountains that I didn't know what to photograph first. We came for the Eagle Festival. Later, our guide gave a talk about eagles and life in Mongolia. We learned that because Western influences, many young people in Mongolia move to the cities. Despite this, traditional life in Mongolia is threatened.

We saw Kazakhs training their eagles. They do so a good job that the eagles will hunt for them. We spent time on horseback with the Kazakhs. In fact, we spent such time on the horses that I was in a lot of pain later. After the Eagle Festival, we visited with a Kazakh family. Despite of the fact that I was very tired, I was very interested in learning about their lives. However, I stayed up very late talking to them.

We have been such busy that I have hardly had time to think about home, though I do miss my family. Therefore, I'm having a wonderful time.

Charts
15.1–15.6

6 **WRITE & SPEAK.**

A Read the statements. Write the number that best describes your opinion:

1 = strongly agree   3 = neither agree nor disagree   5 = strongly disagree
2 = agree somewhat   4 = disagree somewhat

_____ 1. Some things can never be learned in a classroom.

_____ 2. We learn more useful things from experience than from classroom learning.

_____ 3. Learning is only possible when we're interested in what we're trying to learn.

_____ 4. We learn better if we have someone to guide us.

_____ 5. We learn from our mistakes.

B In your notebook, write sentences that explain your opinions from exercise **A**. Use words and phrases that show cause and effect, result, and contrast.

We can learn a lot from our mistakes. Therefore, we should try to keep a positive attitude when we make one.

C Work in a group. Share your sentences from exercise **B** and discuss your opinions.

Connect the Grammar to Writing

1 READ & NOTICE THE GRAMMAR.

A Have you ever taken an online class? Do you know anyone who has? How was the experience? Share your thoughts with a partner. Then read the essay.

Online Learning: Here to Stay

One of the most exciting new developments in higher education in the past few years has been the growth of online learning, especially MOOCs, massive open online courses. Despite some of the disadvantages, I believe that online classes are better than traditional college classes for a number of reasons.

To begin with, they are free. College tuition rates have been increasing for many years. As a result of these high rates, many people can't afford a traditional college education. Moreover, people all around the world can access MOOCs as long as they have a computer and an Internet connection. Thus, the student body is much more diverse than in a traditional classroom.

It is true that MOOCs provide fewer opportunities for direct contact with the professor. On the other hand, you learn from experts from all over the world. It is also true that you don't meet with your classmates face to face; however, you can interact with them online.

Due to the exciting opportunities that MOOCs offer, I think that the traditional college classroom will have a difficult time competing. Who wants to pay for a traditional class when you can be taught by the best in the world for free?

GRAMMAR FOCUS

In this essay, the writer uses transition words and prepositional phrases to indicate contrast, cause, effect or result, and addition.

Transition word	• *Moreover, people all over the world can access . . .*
Prepositional phrase	• *Despite some of the disadvantages, I believe that online classes . . .*

B Read the essay in exercise **A** again. Find examples of sentences that use transition words and prepositional phrases. Then work with a partner and indicate what each of your examples indicates: contrast, cause, effect or result, or addition.

Transition words

1. _____

2. _____

Prepositional Phrases

1. _____

2. _____

C Complete the charts below with information from the text in exercise **A**. Write in your notebook if you need more room. Then work with a partner and compare your answers.

Traditional College Classroom		Online Learning or MOOC	
Advantages	**Disadvantages**	**Advantages**	**Disadvantages**
direct contact with professor (+)	expensive	diverse student body (+)	

2 BEFORE YOU WRITE.

A Work with a partner. Brainstorm more advantages and disadvantages of both traditional college classes and online classes. List your ideas in your notebook.

B Make a chart like the ones in exercise **1C**. Decide which has more benefits: traditional classes or online classes.

3 WRITE to convince your reader that either traditional college classes or online classes are better. Write three or four paragraphs. Use your chart from exercise **2B** and the text in exercise **1A** to help you.

> **WRITING FOCUS Using Semicolons**
>
> Writers use semicolons when they want to connect two sentences that have closely related ideas. They are commonly used when the second sentence begins with a transition word. See the examples below:
>
> *College tuition rates have been increasing for many years**; as a result, many people are not able to afford a traditional college education**.*
>
> *It is also true that you don't meet with your classmates face to face**; however, you can interact with them online**.*
>
> Remember to put a comma after a transition word.

4 SELF ASSESS. Read your essay. Underline the transition words and prepositonal phrases that indicate contrast, cause, effect or result, or addition. Then use the checklist to assess your work.

- ☐ I used transition words indicating contrast, result, and addition correctly. [15.1–15.3]
- ☐ I used prepositional phrases indicating cause and contrast correctly. [15.4–15.6]
- ☐ I used semicolons correctly. [WRITING FOCUS]

1 Common Irregular Verb Forms

Base Form	Simple Past	Past Participle
be	was, were	been
beat	beat	beaten
become	became	become
begin	began	begun
bend	bent	bent
bite	bit	bitten
blow	blew	blown
break	broke	broken
bring	brought	brought
build	built	built
buy	bought	bought
catch	caught	caught
choose	chose	chosen
come	came	come
cost	cost	cost
cut	cut	cut
dig	dug	dug
dive	dived/dove	dived
do	did	done
draw	drew	drawn
drink	drank	drunk
drive	drove	driven
eat	ate	eaten
fall	fell	fallen
feed	fed	fed
feel	felt	felt
fight	fought	fought
find	found	found
fit	fit	fit/fitted
fly	flew	flown
forget	forgot	forgotten
forgive	forgave	forgiven
freeze	froze	frozen
get	got	got/gotten
give	gave	given
go	went	gone
grow	grew	grown
hang	hung	hung
have	had	had
hear	heard	heard
hide	hid	hidden

Base Form	Simple Past	Past Participle
lay	laid	laid
lead	led	led
leave	left	left
lend	lent	lent
let	let	let
lie	lay	lain
light	lit/lighted	lit/lighted
lose	lost	lost
make	made	made
mean	meant	meant
meet	met	met
pay	paid	paid
prove	proved	proved/proven
put	put	put
quit	quit	quit
read	read	read
ride	rode	ridden
ring	rang	rung
rise	rose	risen
run	ran	run
say	said	said
sit	sat	sat
sleep	slept	slept
slide	slid	slid
speak	spoke	spoken
spend	spent	spent
spread	spread	spread
stand	stood	stood
steal	stole	stolen
stick	stuck	stuck
strike	struck	struck
swear	swore	sworn
sweep	swept	swept
swim	swam	swum
take	took	taken
teach	taught	taught
tear	tore	torn
tell	told	told
think	thought	thought
throw	threw	thrown
understand	understood	understood

1 Common Irregular Verb Forms

Base Form	Simple Past	Past Participle
hit	hit	hit
hold	held	held
hurt	hurt	hurt
keep	kept	kept
know	knew	known

Base Form	Simple Past	Past Participle
upset	upset	upset
wake	woke	woken
wear	wore	worn
win	won	won
write	wrote	written

2 Patterns with Gerunds

Verb + Gerund

They **enjoy dancing**.
She **delayed going** to the doctor.

admit	detest	miss	resent
advise	discuss	permit	resist
anticipate	dislike	postpone	risk
appreciate	enjoy	practice	stop
avoid	finish	put off	suggest
can't help	forbid	quit	tolerate
complete	imagine	recall	understand
consider	keep	recommend	
delay	mention	regret	
deny	mind	remember	

Verb + Preposition + Gerund

He **succeeded in winning** the prize.
Are you **thinking about taking** another course?

apologize for	concentrate on	object to	thank (someone) for
argue about	dream about/of	plan on/for	think about
believe in	insist on	succeed in	warn (someone) about
complain about	keep on	talk about	worry about

Noun + Preposition + Gerund

What's the **purpose of doing** this exercise?
I don't know his **reason for being** late.

benefit of	interest in	purpose of
cause of	problem with	reason for

Adjective + Preposition + Gerund

I'm **excited about studying** abroad.
Are you **interested in going**?

accustomed to	excited about	nervous about	tired of
afraid of	famous for	responsible for	upset about/with
bad/good at	(in)capable of	sick of	used to
concerned about	interested in	sorry about/for	worried about

3 Patterns with Infinitives

Verb + Infinitive			
*They **need to leave**.* *I **am learning to speak** English.*			
agree	claim	know how	seem
appear	consent	learn	swear
arrange	decide	manage	tend
ask	demand	need	threaten
attempt	deserve	offer	try
be able	expect	plan	volunteer
beg	fail	prepare	want
can afford	forget	pretend	wish
care	hope	promise	would like
choose	intend	refuse	

Verb + Object + Infinitive			
*I **want you to leave**.* *He **expects me to call** him.*			
advise	convince	hire	require
allow	dare	instruct	select
appoint	enable	invite	teach
ask*	encourage	need*	tell
beg*	expect*	order	urge
cause	forbid	pay*	want*
challenge	force	permit	warn
choose*	get	persuade	would like*
command	help**	remind	

*These verbs can be either with or without an object. (*I **want [you] to go**.*)

After *help*, *to* is often omitted. (*He **helped me move.*)

4 Adjectives Followed by Infinitives

afraid	embarrassed	lucky	sad
ashamed	excited	necessary	shocked
careful	glad	pleased	sorry
certain	good	proud	stupid
challenging	happy	ready	surprised
determined	hard	relieved	upset
difficult	important	reluctant	useful
disappointed	impossible	rewarding	willing
easy	likely	right	wrong

5 Transitive Verbs

arrest	control	found	observe	refuse	steal
avoid	cost	generate	offer	regard	take
attract	create	get	order	release	threaten
bother	damage	give	owe	remove	throw
bring	destroy	harm	pass	repair	train
buy	discover	hurt	plant	report	trap
call	disturb	identify	pollute	rescue	use
catch	do	kill	post	save	want
chase	estimate	lend	prepare	say	wash
complete	expect	limit	produce	see	tell
conserve	feed	locate	propose	send	surround
consider	find	lock	protect	shape	
consume	follow	make	provide	show	
contact	force	name	put	solve	

Intransitive Verbs

appear	exist	occur	stay
arrive	fall	rain	survive
be	fly	rise	take place
come	go	run	talk
cough	happen	sit	wait
cry	laugh	sleep	walk
die	live	smile	
disappear	look	snow	
dry (up)	matter	stand	

Verbs That Are Transitive and Intransitive

answer	increase	promise	teach
bite	know	read	think
clean (up)	leave	sell	try
eat	lose	serve	visit
finish	move	sign	walk
flood	pay	sing	write
hunt	play	start	

6   Phrasal Verbs and Their Meanings

Transitive Phrasal Verbs (Separable)

(s.o. = someone   s.t. = something)

Phrasal Verb	Meaning	Example Sentence
blow (s.t.)* up	cause something to explode	The workers **blew** the bridge **up**.
bring (s.t.) back	return	She **brought** the shirt **back** to the store.
bring (s.t.) up	1. raise from childhood 2. introduce a topic to discuss	1. My grandmother **brought** me **up**. 2. Don't **bring up** that subject.
call (s.o.)** back	return a telephone call	I **called** Rajil **back** but there was no answer.
call (s.t.) off	cancel	They **called** the wedding **off** after their fight.
call (s.t.) out	say something loudly	He stood up when someone **called** his name **out**.
check (s.t.) out	find out information	I **checked** several places **out** before making a decision.
cheer (s.o.) up	make someone feel happier	Her visit to the hospital **cheered** the patients **up**.
clear (s.o.) up	clarify, explain	She **cleared** the problem **up**.
cut (s.t.) down	cut through the trunk of a tree so that it falls down	The town **cut** many trees **down** to make room for new roads.
do (s.t.) over	do again	His teacher asked him to **do** the essay **over**.
figure (s.t.) out	solve, understand	The student **figured** the problem **out**.
fill (s.t.) in	complete information on a form	I **filled** the blanks **in** on a hob application.
fill (s.t.) out	complete an application or form	I had to **fill** many forms **out** at the doctor's office.
find (s.t.) out	learn, uncover	Did you **find** anything **out** about the new plans?
get (s.t.) across	succeed in making people understand an idea	Leo **gets** his ideas **across** with pictures.
give (s.t.) away	offer something freely	They are **giving** prizes **away** at the store.
give (s.t.) back	return	The boy **gave** the pen **back** to the teacher.
give (s.t.) up	stop doing	I **gave up** sugar last year. Will you **give** it **up**?
help (s.o.) out	aid, support someone	I often **help** my older neighbors **out**.
lay (s.o.) off	dismiss workers from their jobs	My company **laid** 200 workers **off** last year.
leave (s.t.) on	allow a machine to continue working	I **left** the lights **on** all night.
let (s.o./s.t.) in	allow someone or something to enter	She opened a window to **let** some fresh air **in**.
look (s.t.) over	examine	We **looked** the contract **over** before signing it.
look (s.t.) up	find information by looking in something like a reference book or list	I **looked** the word **up** in the dictionary.
make (s.o./s.t.) into	change someone or something to become someone or something else	They **made** the book **into** a movie.
make (s.t.) out of	produce something from a material or existing object	Lily **made** the costume **out of** old clothes.
make (s.t.) up	say something untrue or fictional (a story, a lie)	The child **made** the story **up**. It wasn't true at all.
pay (s.o./s.t.) back	return money, repay a loan	I **paid** my friend **back**. I owed him $10.
pick (s.o./s.t.) up	1. get someone or something 2. lift 3. acquire a skill over time without a lot of effort	1. He **picked up** his date at her house. 2. I **picked** the ball **up** and threw it. 3. Joe **picked** the language **up** just by talking to people
point (s.t.) out	tell someone about a fact or mistake	I **pointed** the problem **out** right away.
put (s.t.) aside	keep something to be dealt with or used at a later time	Let's **put** the list of names **aside** until we need them.
put (s.t) away	put something in the place where it is normally kept when it is not used	Please **put** your books **away** before we start the test.

Transitive Phrasal Verbs (Separable) *(Continued)*

put (s.t.) off	delay, postpone	*Don't **put** your homework **off** until tomorrow.*
put (s.t.) on	place clothing or makeup on your body in order to wear it	*Emma **put** her coat **on** and left.*
put (s.t.) out	1. take outside 2. extinguish	1. *He **put** the trash **out**.* 2. *Firefighters **put out** the fire.*
set (s.t.) up	1. arrange 2. start something	1. *She **set** the tables **up** for the party.* 2. *They **set up** the project.*
show (s.t) off	make something obvious to a lot of people because you are proud of it	*Tom's mother **showed** his award **off** to everyone.*
shut (s.t.) off	1. stop something from working 2. stop the power	1. *Can you **shut** the water **off**?* 2. *I **shut** the oven **off**.*
slip (s.t.) off	remove clothing quickly	*They **slip** their shoes **off** when they enter a room.*
sort (s.t.) out	make sense of something	*We have to **sort** this problem **out**.*
straighten (s.t.) up	make neat and orderly	*I **straightened** the living room **up**. It was a mess.*
take (s.t.) back	own again	*He **took** his tools **back** that he loaned me.*
take (s.t.) out	remove	*I **take** the trash **out** on Mondays.*
talk (s.t.) over	discuss a topic until it is completely understood	*Let's **talk** this plan **over** before we do anything.*
think (s.t.) over	reflect, ponder	*She **thought** the job offer **over** carefully.*
throw (s.t.) away/ throw (s.t.) out	get rid of something, discard	*He **threw** the old newspapers **away**. I **threw out** the old milk in the fridge.*
try (s.t.) on	put on clothing to see if it fits	*He **tried** the shoes **on** but didn't buy them.*
turn (s.o./s.t.) down	refuse	*His manager **turned** his proposal **down**.*
turn (s.o.) off	disgust or offend	*People who brag **turn** me **off**.*
turn (s.t.) off	stop something from working	*Can you **turn** the TV **off**, please?*
turn (s.t.) on	switch on, operate	*I **turned** the lights **on** in the dark room.*
turn (s.t.) up	increase the volume	***Turn** the radio **up** so we can hear the news.*
wake (s.o.) up	stop sleeping	*The noise **woke** the baby **up**.*
write (s.t.) down	write on paper	*I **wrote** the information **down**.*

*s.t. = something   **s.o. = someone

Transitive Phrasal Verbs (Inseparable)

*We'll **look into** the problem.*

Phrasal Verb	Meaning	Example Sentence
account for (s.t.)	explain or give the necessary information about something	*What **accounts for** Ned's problems in school?*
come across (s.t.)	find something accidentally	*I **came across** a very old family photo.*
come from (somewhere)	be a native or resident of	*She **comes from** London.*
come up with (s.t.)	invent	*Let's **come up with** a new game.*
count on (s.o/s.t.)	depend on	*You can always **count on** good friends to help you.*
drop out of (s.t.)	quit	*Jin **dropped out of** the study group.*
fall for (s.o.)	be strongly attracted to someone and to start loving the person	*Chris **fell for** her the moment he saw her.*
follow through with (s.t.)	complete	*You must **follow through with** your promises.*
get off (s.t.)	leave (a bus/a train)	*I forgot to **get off** the bus at my stop.*
get on (s.t.)	board (a car/a train)	*I **got on** the plane last.*

Transitive Phrasal Verbs (Inseparable) (Continued)

get out of (s.t.)	1. leave (a car/a taxi) 2. avoid	1. *I got out of the car.* 2. *She got out of doing her chores.*
get together with (s.o.)	meet	*I got together with Ana on Saturday.*
get over (s.t.)	return to a normal state	*I just got over a bad cold. I feel much better now!*
go over (s.t.)	review	*Let's go over our notes before the exam.*
keep up with (s.o./s.t.)	move at the same speed or progress at the same rate	*Slow down. I can't keep up with you.*
look after (s.o./s.t.)	take care of	*He has to look after his sister. His parents are out.*
look for (s.o./s.t.)	try to find someone or something that you want or need	*I'm looking for someone who can help me.*
look into (s.t.)	investigate	*The police looked into the crime and solved it.*
pass by (s.o./s.t.)	go past a person, place, etc., on your way to another place	*If you pass by the house, call first.*
put up with (s.t.)	tolerate or accept something even though you find it unpleasant	*We have to put up with a lot of noise in this building.*
run into (s.o.)	meet accidentally	*She ran into Mai on campus.*
turn into (s.t.)	become something different	*The trip turned into a nightmare.*
turn to (s.o.)	ask someone for help or advice	*I turn to my parents when I need advice.*
take up (s.t.)	use an amount of time, space, or effort	*The table takes up too much space.*

Intransitive Phrasal Verbs (Inseparable)

My car broke down again!

Phrasal Verb	Meaning	Example Sentence
add up	make sense	*What he says does not add up.*
break down	stop working	*This machine breaks down all the time.*
break up	separate	*Their marriage broke up after a year.*
catch up	reach the same level as others in a group	*You can catch up with the others in the class, but you have to work hard.*
check out	pay the bill and leave a hotel	*We have to check out by noon.*
come back	return	*I'll come back soon.*
come on	(of a machine) start working	*It takes a few minutes for the copier to come on.*
come out	reach a result	*The meeting came out well. We were all satisfied.*
cry out	make a loud sound because you are frightened, unhappy, or in pain	*When the children saw the bear, they cried out.*
die out	become less and less common and eventually disappear completely	*Many languages have died out.*
dress up	put on more formal clothes	*He dressed up in his best suit to attend the wedding.*
drop in	visit without an appointment	*Drop in when you can.*
drop out	leave or stop	*She dropped out of school very young.*
eat out	eat in a restaurant	*She hates to cook so she eats out frequently.*
end up	come finally to a particular place or position	*We couldn't decide where to eat. We ended up at a pizza place.*
fall down	fall accidentally	*I wasn't looking and fell down.*
fool around	play with	*He fools around with old cars for fun.*
get ahead	succeed, improve oneself	*Now that she has a new job, she is getting ahead.*
get along	have a friendly relationship	*My coworkers and I get along well together.*

get around	go from one place to another in a certain way	I *get around* by bike.
get up	awaken, arise	I *got up* late this morning.
give up	stop trying	I played the piano for seven years but then *gave up*.
go ahead	begin or continue to do	You can *go ahead*. We'll wait for Jane.
go away	leave, depart	The rabbits in the garden finally *went away*.
go down	decrease	Prices of cars have *gone down* recently.
go on	continue	How long do you think this speech will *go on*?
go out	1. leave one's home 2. have a romantic relationship with someone	1. Jon has *gone out*. He should return soon. 2. Lee and Sam have been *going out* for a year.
go up	rise, go higher	The price of gasoline has *gone up*.
grow up	become and adult	Our daughter has *grown up* now.
hang on	wait	*Hang on* while I change my shoes.
hang out	spend time with others informally	My friends and I like to *hang out* on Friday nights.
hold on	1. struggle against difficulty 2. keep your hand on or around something	1. *Hold on* just a little longer. It's almost over. 2. *Hold on* so that you don't fall.
look around	examine an area	We *looked around* before choosing a place to camp.
look out	be careful	*Look out!* You'll fall!
loosen up	become more relaxed	My boss used to be very tense, but she has *loosened up* over the years.
make up	agree to be friends again	They had a fight, but soon *made up*.
move in	start to live in	We *moved in* last week. We love the area!
move out	leave a place permanently	When is your roommate *moving out*?
pass away	die	My father *passed away* last year.
run out	use all of something	Is there more of paper for the printer? We *ran out*.
set out	start a journey	We're going to *set out* at 6 a.m.
show up	arrive (sometimes unexpectedly or late)	They *showed up* after the train left.
sign up	join, agree to do something	The course looked interesting, so I *signed up*.
sit down	seat oneself	I *sat down* on a bench in the park.
speak up	talk louder	Will you *speak up*? I can't hear you?
stand out	be very noticeable	Can you make his face *stand out* more so that everyone can see him?
stand up	get on one's feet	The teacher asked the students to *stand up*.
stay on	remain somewhere after other people have left or after when you were going to leave	We haven't seen everything, so we'll *stay on* another day.
stay up	keep awake	The student *stayed up* all night to study.
take off	1. leave the ground and start flying 2. increase quickly	1. After a long wait, the airplane finally *took off*. 2. Sales of the new product have *taken off*.
turn out	happen in a particular way or have a particular result	I hope everything *turns out* well.
watch out	be careful	*Watch out!* There's a lot of ice on this road.
work out	exercise	The football player *works out* three times a week.

7 Verbs Followed by Noun Clauses

Learning & Noticing Verbs	Predicting Verbs	Reporting Verbs	Showing Verbs	Suggesting Verbs	Thinking & Feeling Verbs
learn	anticipate	answer	demonstrate	advise	agree
discover	expect	add	indicate	propose	assume
find (out)	hope	claim	reveal	recommend	believe
hear	predict	explain	show	suggest	consider
notice		inform			dream
read		mention			fear
realize		notify			feel
		promise			forget
		remind			know
		reply			remember
		respond			think
		say			understand
		scream			worry
		shout			
		state			
		tell			
		warn			

8 Reported Speech Verb and Modal Changes

Tense Changes

Tense	Quote	Reported Speech		
Simple present	"I **eat** lunch."		ate	
Present progressive	"I'm **eating** lunch"		was eating	
Simple past	"I **ate** lunch."	Sue said she	ate *or* had eaten	lunch.
Present perfect	"I **have eaten** lunch."		had eaten	
Past perfect	"I **had eaten** lunch."		had eaten	
Be going to	"I'm **going to eat** lunch."		was going to eat	

Modal Changes

Modal	Quote	Reported Speech		
Can	"We **can** come."		could	
May	"We **may** come."	They said they	might	come.
Must	"We **must** come."		had to	
Will	"We **will** come."		would	

No Modal Changes

Modal	Quote	Reported Speech		
could	"I **could** help."		could	
might	"I **might** help."	Bill said he	might	help.
ought to	"I **ought to** help."		ought to	
should	"I **should** help."		should	

9 Guide to Pronunciation Symbols

	Vowels	
Symbol	Key Word	Pronunciation
/a/	hot	/hat/
	far	/far/
/æ/	cat	/kæt/
/aɪ/	fine	/faɪn/
/aʊ/	house	/haʊs/
/ɛ/	bed	/bɛd/
/eɪ/	name	/neɪm/
/i/	need	/nid/
/ɪ/	sit	/sɪt/
/oʊ/	go	/goʊ/
/ʊ/	book	/bʊk/
/u/	boot	/but/
/ɔ/	dog	/dɔg/
	four	/fɔr/
/ɔɪ/	toy	/tɔɪ/
/ʌ/	cup	/kʌp/
/ɛr/	bird	/bɜrd/
/ə/	about	/əˈbaʊt/
	after	/ˈæftər/

	Consonants	
Symbol	Key Word	Pronunciation
/b/	boy	/bɔɪ/
/d/	day	/deɪ/
/dʒ/	just	/dʒʌst/
/f/	face	/feɪs/
/g/	get	/gɛt/
/h/	hat	/hæt/
/k/	car	/kar/
/l/	light	/laɪt/
/m/	my	/maɪ/
/n/	nine	/naɪn/
/ŋ/	sing	/sɪŋ/
/p/	pen	/pɛn/
/r/	right	/raɪt/
/s/	see	/si/
/t/	tea	/ti/
/tʃ/	cheap	/tʃip/
/v/	vote	/voʊt/
/w/	west	/wɛst/
/y/	yes	/yɛs/
/z/	zoo	/zu/
/ð/	they	/ðeɪ/
/θ/	think	/θɪŋk/
/ʃ/	shoe	/ʃu/
/ʒ/	vision	/ˈvɪʒən/

Source: The *Newbury House Dictionary plus Grammar Reference, Fifth Edition*, National Geographic Learning/Cengage Learning, 2014

Unit 9, Lesson 1, Exercise 8B, Page 242

1. Researchers say that at least 60 million sharks are killed each year. Many estimate that the number is much higher, possibly well over 200 million sharks per year.
2. Fewer than 100 people are attacked by sharks each year.
3. The megamouth shark was discovered in 1976.
4. More than 100 shark species are threatened by human activity.
5. The fins are sold for food.
6. Shark-fin soup is most popular in Asia.
7. Shark-fin soup is often served at weddings.
8. Sharks can be protected if people stop hunting them.

GLOSSARY OF GRAMMAR TERMS

action verb: a verb that shows an action.
  ➢ He **drives** every day.
  ➢ They **left** yesterday morning.

active voice: a sentence in which the subject performs the action of the verb. **(See** *passive*.)
  ➢ *Michael ate the hamburger.*

adjective: a word that describes or modifies a noun or pronoun.
  ➢ She is **friendly**.
  ➢ Brazil is a **huge** country.

adjective clause: (See *relative clause*.)

adverb: a word that describes or modifies a verb, an adjective, or another adverb.
  ➢ He eats **quickly**.
  ➢ She drives **carefully**.

adverb clause: a kind of dependent clause. Like single adverbs, they can show time, reason, purpose, and condition.
  ➢ **When the party was over**, everyone left.

adverb of frequency: (See *frequency adverb*.)

adverb of manner: an adverb that describes the action of the verb. Many adverbs of manner are formed by adding *-ly* to the adjective.
  ➢ You sing **beautifully**.
  ➢ He speaks **slow**ly.

affirmative statement: a statement that does not have a verb in the negative form.
  ➢ *My uncle lives in Portland.*

article: a word used before a noun; *a, an, the*.
  ➢ I looked up at **the** moon.
  ➢ Lucy had **a** sandwich and **an** apple for lunch.

auxiliary verb: (Also called *helping verb*.) a verb used with the main verb. *Be, do, have*, and *will* are common auxiliary verbs when they are followed by another verb. Modals are also auxiliary verbs.
  ➢ I **am** working.
  ➢ He **won't** be in class tomorrow.
  ➢ She **can** speak Korean.

base form: the form of the verb without *to* or any endings such as *-ing, -s*, or *-ed*.
  ➢ eat, sleep, go, walk

capital letter: an uppercase letter.
  ➢ New York, Mr. Franklin, Japan

clause: a group of words with a subject and a verb. (See *dependent clause* and *main clause*.)
  ➢ We watched the game. (one clause)
  ➢ We watched the game after we ate dinner. (two clauses)

comma: a punctuation mark that separates parts of a sentence.
  ➢ After he left work**,** he went to the gym.
  ➢ I can't speak Russian**,** but my sister can.

common noun: a noun that does not name a specific person, place, thing, or idea.
  ➢ man, country, book, help

comparative: the form of an adjective used to talk about the difference between two people, places, or things.
  ➢ I'm **taller** than my mother.
  ➢ That book is **more interesting** than this one.

conditional: a structure used to express an activity or event that depends on something else.
  ➢ **If the weather is nice on Sunday**, we'll go to the beach.

conjunction: a word used to connect information or ideas. *And, but, or*, and *because* are conjunctions.
  ➢ He put cheese **and** onions on his sandwich.
  ➢ I wanted to go, **but** I had too much homework.
  ➢ We were confused **because** we didn't listen.

consonant: a sound represented by the following letters and combinations of the letters:
  ➢ b, c, d, f, g, h, j, k, l, m, n, p, q, r, s, t, v, w, x, y, z.

contraction: two words combined into a shorter form.
  ➢ did not → **didn't**
  ➢ I am → **I'm**
  ➢ she is → **she's**
  ➢ we will → **we'll**

count noun: a noun that names something you can count. They are singular or plural.
  ➢ I ate an **egg** for breakfast.
  ➢ I have **six apples** in my bag.

definite article: the article *the*. It is used when you are referring to a specific, person, place, or thing.
  ➢ I found it on **the** Internet.
  ➢ **The** children are sleeping.

demonstrative pronoun: a pronoun that identifies a person or thing.
  ➢ **This** is my sister, Kate.
  ➢ **Those** are Jamal's books.

dependent clause: a clause that cannot stand alone as a sentence. It must be used with a main clause.

➢ *I went for a walk **before I ate breakfast**.*

direct object: a noun or pronoun that receives the action of the verb.

➢ *Aldo asked a **question**.*
➢ *Karen helped **me**.*

direct quote: a statement of a speaker's exact words using quotation marks.

➢ *Our teacher said, **"Do exercises 5 and 6 for homework."***

exclamation point: a punctuation mark that shows emotion (anger, surprise, excitement, etc.) or emphasis

➢ *We won the game!*
➢ *It's snowing!*

formal: describes language used in academic writing or speaking, or in polite or official situations rather than in everyday speech or writing.

➢ *Please do not take photographs inside the museum.*
➢ *May I leave early today?*

frequency adverb: an adverb that tells how often something happens. Some common adverbs of frequency are *never, rarely, sometimes, often, usually,* and *always*.

➢ *I **always** drink coffee in the morning.*
➢ *He **usually** leaves work at six.*

frequency expression: an expression that tells how often something happens.

➢ *We go to the grocery store **every Saturday**.*
➢ *He plays tennis **twice a week**.*

future: a form of a verb that expresses an action or situation that has not happened yet. *Will, be going to,* present progressive, and simple present are used to express the future.

➢ *I **will call** you later.*
➢ *We're **going** to the movies tomorrow.*
➢ *I'm **taking** French next semester.*
➢ *The show **starts** after dinner.*

future conditional: expresses something that we believe will happen in the future based on certain conditions; the *if* clause + simple present gives the condition, and *will* or *be going to* + the base form of the verb gives the result.

➢ *If you don't go to practice, the coach will not let you play in the game.*

future perfect: a verb form used to talk about an action or event that will happen before a certain time in the future.

➢ *I'll **have finished** the work by the time you return.*

generic noun: a noun that refers to people, places, and things in general

➢ ***Hospitals** are for sick **people**.*
➢ *I like **music**.*

gerund: an *-ing* verb form that is used as a noun. It can be the subject of a sentence, or the object of a verb or preposition. (See page A4 for lists of common verbs followed by gerunds.)

➢ ***Surfing** is a popular sport.*
➢ *We enjoy **swimming**.*
➢ *The boy is interested in **running**.*

gerund phrase: an *-ing* verb form + an object or a prepositional phrase. It can be the subject of a sentence, or the object of a verb or preposition.

➢ ***Swimming in the ocean** is fun.*
➢ *I love **eating chocolate**.*
➢ *We are thinking about **watching the new TV show**.*

helping verb: (See *auxiliary verb*.)

***if* clause:** a clause that begins with *if* that expresses a condition.

➢ ***If you drive too fast**, you will get a ticket.*

imperative: a sentence that gives an instruction or command.

➢ ***Turn** left at the light.*
➢ ***Don't use** the elevator.*

indefinite article: *a* and *an*, articles used when you are not referring to a specific person, place, or thing. They are used before singular count nouns.

➢ *We have **a** test today.*
➢ *She's **an** engineer.*

indefinite pronoun: a pronoun used to refer to people or things that are not specific or not known. *Someone, something, everyone, everything, no one, nothing,* and *nowhere* are common indefinite pronouns.

➢ ***Everyone** is here today.*
➢ ***No one** is absent.*
➢ *Would you like **something** to eat?*

independent clause: a clause that can stand alone as a complete sentence. It has a subject and a verb.

➢ ***I went for a walk** before breakfast.*

infinitive: *to* + the base form of a verb.

➢ *He wants **to see** the new movie.*

infinitive of purpose: *to* + the base form of the verb used to express purpose or to answer the question *Why?* (also *in order to*)

➢ *Scientists studied the water **in order to learn** about the disease.*
➢ *We went to the store **to buy** milk.*

informal: language used in casual, everyday conversation and writing.

> ➤ *Who are you talking to?*
> ➤ *We'll be there at eight.*

information question: (See *Wh-* question.)

inseparable phrasal verb: a phrasal verb that cannot have an noun or pronoun between its two parts (verb + particle). The verb and the particle always stay together.

> ➤ *I **ran into** a friend in the library.*
> ➤ *Do you and your coworkers **get along**?*

intonation: the rise or fall of a person's voice. For example, rising intonation is often used to ask a question.

intransitive verb: a verb that cannot be followed by a direct object.

> ➤ *We didn't **agree**.*
> ➤ *The students **smiled** and **laughed**.*

irregular adjective: an adjective that does not change form in the usual way.

> ➤ *good → better*
> ➤ *bad → worse*

irregular adverb: an adverb that does not change form in the usual way.

> ➤ *well → better*
> ➤ *badly → worse*

irregular verb: a verb with forms that do not follow the rules for regular verbs.

> ➤ *swim → swam*
> ➤ *have → had*

main clause: a clause that can stand alone as a sentence. It has a subject and a verb. (*See independent clause.*)

> ➤ *I **heard the news** when I was driving home.*

main verb: the verb that is the main clause.

> ➤ *We **drove** home after we had dinner.*

measurement word: a word used to talk about a specific amount or quantity of a non-count noun.

> ➤ *We need to buy a **box** of pasta and a **gallon** of milk.*

modal: an auxiliary verb that adds a degree of certainty, possibility, or time to a verb. *May, might, can, could, will, would,* and *should* are common modals.

> ➤ *You **should** eat more vegetables.*
> ➤ *Julie **can** speak three languages.*

negative statement: a statement that has a verb in the negative form.

> ➤ *I **don't** have any sisters.*
> ➤ *She **doesn't** drink coffee.*

non-count noun: a noun that names something that cannot be counted.

> ➤ *Carlos drinks a lot of **coffee**.*
> ➤ *I need some **salt** for the **recipe**.*

non-identifying relative clause: a relative clause that gives extra information about the noun it is describing. The information is not necessary to understand who or what the noun refers to.

> ➤ *Nelson Mandela, **who was a great leader**, died in 2013.*

noun: a word that names a person, place, or thing.

> ➤ *They're **students**.*
> ➤ *He's a **teacher**.*

noun clause: a kind of dependent clause. A noun clause can be used in place of a noun, a noun phrase or a pronoun.

> ➤ *Could you tell me **where the bank is**?*

object: a noun or pronoun that receives the action of the verb.

> ➤ *Mechanics fix **cars**.*

object pronoun: takes the place of a noun as the object of the sentence; *me, you, him, her, it, us, them.*

> ➤ *Rita is my neighbor. I see **her** every day.*
> ➤ *Can you help **us**?*

passive: a verb form that expresses who or what receives the action of the verb, not who or what performs the action

> ➤ *My wallet **has been stolen**.*

past perfect: a verb form used to talk about an action that happened before another action or time in the past.

> ➤ *They **had met** in school, but then they didn't see each other again for many years.*

past perfect progressive: *a verb form used for an action or event that was happening until or just before another action, event, or time.*

> ➤ *He**'d been driving** for twelve hours when they ran out of gas.*

past progressive: a verb form used to talk about an action that was in progress in the past.

> ➤ *He **was watching** TV when the phone rang.*

period: a punctuation mark used at the end of a statement.

> ➤ *She lives in Moscow**.***

phrasal verb: a two-word or three-word verb. The phrasal verb means something different from the two or three words separately. (See pages A7–A9 for lists of common phrasal verbs.)

> ➤ ***Turn off** the light when you leave.*
> ➤ *She's **come up with** an interesting idea.*

phrase: a group of words that go together; not a complete sentence (i.e., does not have both a subject and a verb).

> ➤ He lives **near the train station**.

plural noun: the form of a noun that indicates more than one person, place, or thing.

> ➤ He put three **boxes** on the table.
> ➤ Argentina and Mexico are **countries**.

possessive adjective: an adjective that shows ownership or a relationship: *my, your, his, her, its, our, their*.

> ➤ **My** car is green.
> ➤ **Your** keys are on the table.

possessive noun: a noun that shows ownership or a relationship. To make most singular nouns possessive, use an apostrophe (') + -s. To make plural nouns possessive, add an apostrophe.

> ➤ **Leo's** apartment is large.
> ➤ The **girls'** books are on the table.

possessive pronoun: a pronoun that shows ownership or a relationship: *mine, yours, his, hers, ours, theirs*. Possessive pronouns are used in place of a possessive adjective + noun.

> ➤ My sister's eyes are blue. **Mine** are brown. What color are **yours**?

preposition: a word that describes the relationships between nouns; prepositions show space, time, direction, cause, and effect. Often they occur together with certain verbs or adjectives.

> ➤ I live **on** Center Street.
> ➤ We left **at** noon.
> ➤ I'm worried **about** the test.

present continuous: (See *present progressive*.)

present perfect: a verb form that connects the past to the present.

> ➤ Julia **has lived** in London for 10 years.
> ➤ Monika **has broken** the world record.
> ➤ Zack and Dan **have never been** to Germany.

present perfect progressive: a verb form used for ongoing actions that began in the past and continue up to the present.

> ➤ You'**ve been working** too hard.

present progressive: (also called *present continuous*) a verb form used to talk about an action or event that is in progress at the moment of speaking; the form can also refer to a planned event in the future.

> ➤ That car **is speeding**.
> ➤ I **am taking** three classes this semester.
> ➤ We **are eating** at that new restaurant Friday night.

pronoun: a word that takes the place of a noun or refers to a noun.

> ➤ <u>The teacher</u> is sick today. **He** has a cold.

proper noun: a noun that names a specific person, place, or thing.

> ➤ **Maggie** lives in a town near **Dallas**.

punctuation: a mark that makes ideas in writing clear. Common punctuation marks include the comma (,), period (.), exclamation point (!), and question mark (?).

> ➤ John plays soccer**,** but I don't.
> ➤ She's from Japan**.**
> ➤ That's amazing**!**
> ➤ Where are you from**?**

quantifier: a word used to describe the amount of a noun.

> ➤ We need **some** potatoes for the recipe.
> ➤ I usually put **a little** milk in my coffee.

question mark: a punctuation mark used at the end of a question.

> ➤ Are you a student**?**

regular: a noun, verb, adjective, or adverb that changes form according to standard rules.

> ➤ apple ⟶ apple**s**
> ➤ talk ⟶ talk**ed**/talk**ing**
> ➤ small ⟶ small**er**
> ➤ slow ⟶ slow**ly**

reported speech: part of a sentence (a noun clause or infinitive phrase) that reports what someone has said.

> ➤ They said **they would be late**.
> ➤ They told **us not to wait**.

sentence: a thought that is expressed in words, usually with a subject and verb. A sentence begins with a capital letter and ends with a period, exclamation point, or question mark.

> ➤ The bell rang loudly.
> ➤ Don't eat that!

separable phrasal verb: a phrasal verb that can have a noun or a pronoun (object) between its two parts (verb + particle).

> ➤ **Turn** the light **off**.
> ➤ **Turn off** the light.

short answer: a common spoken answer to a question that is not always a complete sentence.

> ➤ A: Did you do the homework?
> ➤ B: **Yes, I did./No, I didn't.**
> ➤ A: Where are you going?
> ➤ B: **To the store.**

simple past: a verb form used to talk about completed actions.

> ➤ Last night we **ate** dinner at home.
> ➤ I **visited** my parents last weekend.

simple present: a verb form used to talk about habits or routines, schedules, and facts.

> ➤ He *likes* apples and oranges.
> ➤ Toronto *gets* a lot of snow in the winter.

singular noun: a noun that names only one person, place, or thing.

> ➤ They have *a son* and *a daughter*.

statement: a sentence that gives information.

> ➤ My house has five rooms.
> ➤ He doesn't have a car.

stative verb: a verb that does not describe an action. Non-action verbs indicate states, sense, feelings, or ownership. They are not common in the progressive.

> ➤ I *love* my grandparents.
> ➤ I *see* Marta. She's across the street.
> ➤ They *have* a new car.

stress: to say a syllable or a word with more volume or emphasis.

subject: the noun or pronoun that is the topic of the sentence.

> ➤ *Patricia* is a doctor.
> ➤ *They* are from Iceland.

subject pronoun: a pronoun that is the subject of a sentence: *I, you, he, she, it,* and *they*.

> ➤ *I* have one brother.
> ➤ *He* lives in Miami.

superlative: the form of an adjective or adverb used to compare three or more people, places, or things.

> ➤ Mount Everest is *the highest* mountain in the world.
> ➤ Evgeny is *the youngest* student in our class.

syllable: a part of a word that contains a single vowel sound and is pronounced as a unit.

> ➤ The word *pen* has one syllable.
> ➤ The word *pencil* has two syllables (pen-cil).

tense: the form of the verb that shows the time of the action.

> ➤ They *sell* apples. (simple present)
> ➤ They *sold* cars. (simple past)

third-person singular: in the simple present, the third-person singular ends in –s or –es. Singular nouns and the pronouns *he, she, it,* take the third-person singular form.

> ➤ She *plays* the piano.
> ➤ Mr. Smith *teaches* her.

time clause: a clause that tells when an action or event happened or will happen. Time clauses are introduced by conjunctions, such as *when, after, before, while,* and *since*.

> ➤ I have lived here *since I was a child*.
> ➤ *While I was walking home,* it began to rain.
> ➤ I'm going to call my parents *after I eat dinner*.

time expression: a phrase that tells when something happened or will happen. Time expressions usually go at the end or the beginning of sentence.

> ➤ *Last week* I went hiking.
> ➤ She's moving *next month*.

transitive verb: a verb that is followed by a direct object.

> ➤ We *took* an umbrella.

transition word: a word or phrase that connects ideas between sentences.

> ➤ I'd like to go. *However,* I have too much work to do.

unreal: used to describe situations that are contrary-to-fact, impossible, or unlikely to happen.

> ➤ If I *weren't learning* English, I *would have* more free time.
> ➤ I *wish I had* a million dollars.

verb: a word that shows action, gives a state, or shows possession.

> ➤ Tori **skated** across the ice.
> ➤ She **is** an excellent athlete.
> ➤ She **has** many medals.

voiced: a sound that is spoken with the vibration of the vocal cords. The consonants *b, d, g, j, l, m, n, r, th* (as in *then*), *v, w, z,* and all vowels are typically voiced.

voiceless: a sound that is spoken without the vibration of the vocal cords. The consonants *k, p, s, t,* and *ch,* sh, *th* (as in *thing*) are voiceless.

vowel: a sound represented in English by the letters: *a, e, i, o, u,* and sometimes *y*.

***Wh-* question:** a question that asks for specific information, not "Yes" or "No." (See *Wh- word*.)

> ➤ *Where do they live?*
> ➤ *What do you usually do on weeeknds?*

***Wh-* word:** a word such as *who, what, when, where, why,* or *how* that is used to begin a *Wh-* question.

***Yes/No* question:** a question that can be answered by "Yes" or "No."

> ➤ *Do you live in Dublin?* Yes, I do./No I don't.
> ➤ *Can you ski?* Yes, I can./No, I can't.

INDEX

Note: All page references in blue are in Split Edition B.

Text and Listening

236: Exercise 1. Source: http://www.nationalgeographic.com/explorers/bios/sylvia-earle. **246:** Exercise 1. Source: National Geographic Magazine, March 2013, pp. 60–77. **254:** Exercise 1. Sources: http://environment.nationalgeographic.com/environment/natural-disasters/hurricane-profile; http://www.hurricanehunters.com/mission.html: Geiger, Beth. *Hurricane Hunters*. National Geographic Explorer Collection. **268:** Exercise 1. Source: National Geographic Magazine, August 2009. **274:** Exercise 9. Source: http://blogs.nybg.org/plant-talk/2013/04/science-alex-popovkin-botanist-extraordinaire. **275:** Exercise 1. Source: http://www.sciencedaily.com/releases/2010/01/100111112845.htm. **282:** Exercise 1. Sources: http://www.nationalgeographic.com/explorers/bios/lucy-cooke; http://animal.discovery.com/mammals/sloths-slow.htm; http://www.aviary.org/animals/two-toed-sloth; http://www.worldanimalfoundation.net/f/Sloth.pdf. **286:** Exercise 6. Source: http://www.ted.com/talks/denis_dutton_a_darwinian_theory_of_beauty. **288:** Exercise 9. Source: http://phenomena.nationalgeographic.com/2012/10/02/beauty-in-the-right-eye-of-the-beholder-finch-chooses-better-mates-with-its-right-eye. **290:** Exercise 1. Source: http://animals.nationalgeographic.com/animals/bugs/stick-insect. **296:** Exercise 1. Source: Dipanjan Mitra/National Geographic My Shot. **308:** Exercise 1. Source: www.michaelnicknichols.com. **310:** Exercise 4. Source: www.npr.org/blogs/pictureshow/2009/09/redwoods.html. **314:** Exercise 8. Source: rippleeffectimages.org. **316:** Exercise 10. Source: www.pbs.org/atcloserange/whoisjoel.html. **317:** Exercise 11. Sources: http://www.ted.com/speakers/913; http://www.ted.com/talks/jr_s_ted_prize_wish_use_art_to_turn_the_world_inside_out. **334:** Exercise 1. Source: http://www.nytimes.com/2011/02/13/books/review/Silver-t.html. **345:** Exercise 1. Source: http://www.bostonglobe.com/metro/2013/09/21/bicycling-dutch-way/kFRT0ABSPtUnXMIUj5zONM/story.html. **358:** Exercise 1. Source: www.adsvvy.org/the-power-of-framing-effects-and-other-cognitive-biases. **365:** Exercise 12. Source: http://blog.bufferapp.com/8-things-you-dont-know-are-affecting-your-decisions-every-day. **366:** Exercise 1. Sources: www.nationalgeographic.com/deextinction; news.nationalgeographic.com/news/2013/03/130311-deextinction-reviving-extinct-species-opinion-animals-science; National Geographic Magazine, April 2013. **377:** Exercise 1. Sources: National Geographic Magazine, December 2013; outofedenwalk.nationalgeographic.com **387:** Exercise 5. Source: http://www.decodedscience.com/doc-mallett-the-time-of-his-life/4431. **392:** Exercise 1. Sources: news.nationalgeographic.com/news/2012/10/121026-human-cooking-evolution-raw-food-health-science; Outofedenwalk.nationalgeographic.com/2013/02/08/gona-first-kitchen; scienceblogs.com/purepedantry/2007/06/25/did-cooking-allow-for-the-incr. **394:** Exercise 4. Source: news.nationalgeographic.com/news/2012/10/121026-human-cooking-evolution-raw-food-health-science. **401:** Exercise 12. Source: http://video.nationalgeographic.com/video/solar-cooking. **402:** Exercise 13. Source: http://news.nationalgeographic.com/news/2013/08/130823-prehistoric-hunter-gatherers-garlic-mustard-spices. **403:** Exercise 1. Source: http://www.theglobeandmail.com/life/food-and-wine/food-trends/the-5-senses-of-flavour-how-colour-and-sound-can-make-your-dinner-taste-better/article9957597. **410:** Exercise 11: http://angelsmith.net/inbound-marketing/groundbreaking-survey-reveals-how-diners-choose-restaurants. **426:** Exercise 1. Source: www.nationalgeographic.com/explorers/bios/brendan-mullan; science.psu.edu/news-and-events/Brendan-mullan-selected-as-a-2013-national-geographic-emerging-explorer. **436:** Exercise 1. Sources: www.ted.com/prize/sole_toolkit#intro; newswatch.nationalgeographic/tag/sugata-mitra; huffingtonpost.com/sugata-mitra/2013-ted-prize_b_276598.html. **440:** Exercise 6. Source: http://www.forbes.com/sites/danschawbel/2013/05/30/josh-kaufman-it-takes-20-hours-not-10000-hours-to-learn-a-skill/ **447:** Exercise 1. Source: Nationalgeographic.com/explorers/projects/bioblitz. **449:** Exercise 5. Sources: http://www.nomadicexpeditions.com/trip-finder/golden-eagle-festival; http://www.geoex.com/trips/mongolia-golden-eagle-festival; http://discover-bayanolgii.com/golden-eagle-festival.

Definitions for glossed words: Sources: *The Newbury House Dictionary plus Grammar Reference,* Fifth Edition, National Geographic Learning/Cengage Learning, 2014; *Collins Cobuild Illuminated Basic Dictionary of American English,* Cengage Learning 2010, Collings Cobuild/Harper Collins Publishers, First Edition, 2010; *Collins Cobuild School Dictionary of American English,* Cengage Learning 2009, Collins Cobuild/Harper Collins Publishers, 2008; Collins Cobuild Advanced Learner's Dictionary, 5th Edition, Harper Collins Publishers, 2006.

Photo Credits:

Inside Front Cover, left column: ©Cristina Mittermeier/National Geographic Creative, Courtesy of The Thayer Collection, Reprinted with permission of Barton Seaver, photo by Katie Stoops, ©Calit2, Erik Jepsen, ©Vander Meulen, Rebecca J/National Geographic Creative; right column: ©Cengage/National Geographic Creative, ©Tyrone Turner/National Geographic Creative, ©Cengage/National Geographic Creative, ©Rebecca Hale/National Geographic Creative, ©Jay Ullal/Black Star/Newscom.

234-235: ©Frans Lanting/National Geographic Creative; **236:** ©Bates Littlehales/National Geographic Creative; **237:** ©Wolcott Henry/National Geographic Creative; **241:** ©Brian J. Skerry/National Geographic Creative; **244:** ©Robin Smith/Getty Images; **246-247:** ©Diane Cook and Len Jenshel/National Geographic Creative; **247:** ©FLPA/Alamy; **248:** ©epa european pressphoto agency b.v./Alamy; **250-251:** ©Tino Soriano/National Geographic Creative; **254-255:** ©Ian Cumming/Getty Images;